YOU
AND YOUR BIKE

YOU AND YOUR BIKE

BRIAN CRICHTON

PELHAM BOOKS
London

First published in Great Britain by
Pelham Books Ltd
44 Bedford Square
London WC1B 3DU
1985

British Library Cataloguing in Publication Data

Crichton, Brian
You and your bike
1. Motorcycles
1. Title
629.2'275 TL440

ISBN 0-7207-1628-4

Typeset by Wordsmiths, Street, Somerset
Origination by Gee & Watson Ltd, Sutton, Surrey
Printed and bound in Italy

This book was edited, designed and produced by The
Paul Press Ltd, 22 Bruton Street, London W1X 7DA

Consultant Editor Brian Crichton
Contributing Editors Nick Edwards; Dave Minton; Dave
Walker
Project Director Stephen McCurdy
Art Assistants Sue Brinkhurst, Jacek Depczyk; Pat
Newton; Tony Paine
Illustrators Julian Baker (The Maltings Partnership);
Haywood and Martin; Graham Duckett; Richard
Duckett; Jacek Depczyk; Janos Marffy
Photography Jon Bouchier; Dick Atkins, Bruton
Photography

Art Director Stephen McCurdy
Editorial Director Jeremy Harwood
Publishing Director Nigel Perryman

Contents

Introduction

I hope you will think of *You and Your Bike* as a friend – one which will help you to get the best out of the majority of your activities on two wheels.

I have deliberately aimed *You and Your Bike* at the non-technical reader. Throughout, I have tried to anticipate all the questions you might ask – and the common problems that could arise – whether you ride a motor cycle, a scooter, moped, or sidecar outfit – in a straighforward, readable way. I have also, I hope, avoided the trap of trying to tie you in knots with technical terminology!

I have also tried to make the coverage as broad as possible. This means beginning at the beginning, dealing with buying a machine, both new and second hand and all associated requirements, such as raising finance, insurance and warranties. From this, the book goes on to tell you what is the most suitable riding gear to wear, while, later, it lays out what are the essential riding techniques and what is involved in rider training.

So much for the rider. Now, what about the machine itself? Here, we start our coverage with clear explanations of the various mechanical systems of the motor cycle – the engine (two-stroke and four-stroke), the ignition, the transmission and so on. A basic checklist is included to complement each of these subject areas, so that theory and practice can be clearly related. What you obviously want to ensure is that you can keep your machine on the road in good, safe running order. So, following the essential theory, comes an easy-to-follow problem diagnosis section, plus a detailed listing of the basic repairs and checks you can make to stay on the road.

These pages are essential. They are intended to act as a catalyst – to help you to get to know your bike more thoroughly and quickly than otherwise might be the case and thus reap the rewards of greater motor cycling fulfilment. With *You and Your Bike* at your side, you need never feel that you lack guidance and, I hope, the inspiration to get to know your machine better by working on it.

As well as all of this, *You and Your Bike* will show you not only how best to maintain the value of your investment, but also how to improve it through accessory fittings, painting and other modifications. That's how the motor cycle is viewed in this book – an investment in practicality and pleasure.

Obviously, though, *You and Your Bike* cannot cover *all* aspects of *all* machines. When it comes to checks, fault diagnosis and repairs, it should be used as a supplement to your workshop manual, rather than as a replacement for it. As already outlined, the book is a compendium of the broader aspects and obligations of owning and running a machine.

Obviously, too, the book does have a slant. It caters first and foremost for the novice motor cyclist and scooter rider in search of knowledge. This is a deliberate decision, since the book appears at a time when the needs of this class of rider are being neglected by the specialist press, which, in the main, seems to be adopting a big bike bias. Yet, while it is intended that *You and Your Bike* should stimulate and satisfy that thirst for knowledge, it is also anticipated that experienced motor cyclists will find information, advice and answers that hitherto may have been lacking.

I hope that *You and Your Bike* is interesting and an investment. In fact, I hope that it becomes a friend for life.

Owning a motor cycle

There is very little that compares with the thrill that comes from owning your own motor cycle or scooter, especially if you are a first time buyer.

Each ride is a new adventure, the bond between rider and machine immediately becoming apparent as you crank through corners and take on all weathers. The liveliness, nimbleness, manoeuvrability, throttle response and the general readiness of the machine to react to the slightest rider command all combine to instill a feeling of 'oneness', which no other form of mechanical transport provides.

In fact, using a motor cycle or scooter to get from place to place is just part of the story. Riding a two- or three-wheeler is so exhilarating that it soon becomes a sport, rather than something matter of fact.

Legal requirements

However, while the fun and freedom of being able to ride on the wind counts for much, there is a serious side to owning a three- or two-wheeler. Firstly, there are legal requirements that you must satisfy before you can set off on the public road. You must be old enough to apply for a driving licence and that licence must be valid for the type of machine you want to ride. You must have a valid road fund licence, insurance cover and, if the machine is three years old or more, a current DoT test certificate.

An application form for a driving licence can be obtained from your local post office. The licence itself costs £3. You get your road tax disc from the post office as well. Here, the amount of tax you have to pay varies according to your bike's engine capacity; at the start of 1985, the figures were £8 for a bike up to 125cc, £16 for a machine between 126cc and 250cc and £32 for solo bikes over 251cc and all three-wheelers. Insurance cover can be obtained direct from an insurance company, via your dealer, or through a broker.

The DoT test

Once a machine is three years old, the law requires it to be DoT tested for road worthiness. Many motor cycle dealers are licenced to carry out the test and, if your machine passes it, they will issue you with a certificate, valid for one year, which you must produce the next time you need a road tax disc.

If your machine fails the test, you will be told what needs attention in order to pass. You can either authorize the dealer to carry out the necessary repairs, or, as long as it is safe, you can ride the bike away, carry out the repairs yourself and then submit the machine for retest.

At the start of 1985, the cost of a DoT test was £6.00 (including VAT) for solo machines and £10.00 for sidecars. If your bike fails its test – and it is left with the dealer who tested it for the necessary repairs – there is no extra fee for the retest and no time limit put on the repairs. Thus, if your bike fails the test, it is well worth asking the dealer who tested it to carry out any necessary work, provided you ask for an estimate of how much this will cost in terms of both parts and labour.

If the bike fails the test and you remove it from the test station for repair, a re-test fee of £5.00 is charged if the machine is brought back within 14 days. If you exceed this deadline, the full test fee is charged.

One useful thing to remember is that you are allowed to have your machine tested a month before the expiry date of its current DoT certificate. The date of expiry of the new certificate will be entered as one year after the expiry of the current certificate.

Log books and road tax

The vehicle registration licence

– more popularly termed the log book – lists details of the machine, including engine and frame numbers and the colour of the main cycle parts. Your name and address should be entered in the book as soon as the machine passes into your hands and the document should then be sent off to the appropriate registration authority to record the official change of ownership. The log book will then be returned duly altered.

If your machine does not already have a valid road tax disc, you must fill in the appropriate application form. You can get one from your local post office. In addition, you must have the log book, the appropriate fee for the tax, your certificate of insurance or insurance cover note and an DoT certificate, where applicable.

Most main post offices will issue road tax discs over the counter, provided you produce all the necessary documentation. Alternately, you can apply for road tax by post, sending all the documents to the local road fund licensing authority.

Once you have received the tax disc, you should put it in a waterproof holder – you can buy one of these from any motor cycle dealer – and attach it to the left side of the machine, forward of the seat. This positioning is required by law. The law also requires a current tax disc to be displayed at all times when a machine is on the public road – even when parked outside your home.

If you have any queries about the legalities of riding a bike, ask at your local police station.

On the road

No novice biker should consider riding on the road without first having taken a training course (see p. 134). Once you are ready for the road, bear in mind that the public highways are there for all to share. You should ride with confidence and command your section of the road, but always remember to be polite and considerate to other road users. Some motor cyclists adopt an 'us and them' attitude to drivers of larger vehicles. It is far better to live and let live.

As you ride, you will quickly begin to learn how to read road surfaces for grip, how to corner safely and how much room you need to stop in an emergency. These skills will be enhanced during your training and by practical experience. You must cultivate an instinct for anticipating what other road users will do.

Be alert for people who turn without signalling and suddenly hit their brakes for no apparent reason, for instance. According to the rules, this sort of thing should not happen. But, life being what it is, such behaviour is the rule, rather than the exception. And invariably, when a motor cyclist is involved in an accident with a car, van or truck, it is the motor cyclist who comes off the worst.

As the rider of a powered two- or three-wheeler, you must consider your vulnerability as part of the responsibility of being on the road. Hospital accident wards are often heavily populated with motor cycle and scooter accident victims. Some are innocent of their injuries and others are guilty, but all, without exception, are hurt.

Also, you must be aware that other could be hurt if you relax your riding standards and make an error of judgement. Just as you ought to keep your machine in top condition, so you should keep your riding skills polished. Read the following sections of this book thoroughly and they will help you to achieve both these aims.

Welcome to the ranks of people who know the thrill of bike riding and ownership! With your companions, you will share all the joys of the road.

Buying a bike/1

Choosing and buying a motor cycle or scooter of your own is not as simple and clear cut as it might seem, since the demands the law makes on you, the rider, will play an important part in the final choice.

If you compare a bike rider's legal position with that of a car driver, you will see that the demands are much stricter for first-time riders. So, before deciding on which model to buy, it is only common sense to take into consideration the limitations that may be imposed on you by the law of the land.

Your choice and the law
At present, the legal position is as follows:
*No person under the age of 16 may ride a vehicle powered by an internal combustion engine on public roads. From the age of 14, however, you can ride an electrically-powered two- or three-wheeler.
*At the age of 16, you are legally entitled to ride a moped – but not a motor cycle.

By law, the engine capacity of any moped registered after August 1977 has to be 50cc or under, while the machine's maximum design speed must be no more than 30mph (48k/hr). Such mopeds are popularly termed 'restricted' models.

Mopeds registered before August 1977 must be fitted with pedals, which are capable of propelling the machine. Because such models do not have a maximum speed restriction, they are termed 'pre-restricted' or 'non-restricted' mopeds, though their engine capacity is still limited to a maximum of 50cc.
*At the age of 17, you are legally entitled to ride a motor cycle or scooter as a learner rider under the terms of your provisional driving licence. Again, however, there are legal limitations.

If the motor cycle or solo scooter is a model registered after 1 February 1983, its engine capacity must be no more than 125cc, with a specified maximum power to weight ratio. In nearly all cases, this works out to a nominal 12bhp engine output figure.

The engine output of solo machines registered before 1 February 1983 is not restricted, although they are still limited to a maximum capacity of 125cc.

A 17-year-old learner motor cyclist may also ride a motor cycle and side car combination of any capacity. The term side car is capable of varying definition – at its simplest, it can be nothing more than a third wheel.

Popularly referred to as a 'wheel on a stick', this side car is not designed to carry a passenger, its primary function being to allow a learner rider to bend the rules and ride a machine of any capacity. It is extremely light weight and can be banked around corners. This means that, even with a 'side car' the motor cycle still performs like a solo machine.
*At the age of 17 a provisional licence holder can apply for the motor cycle driving test. If you are riding solo, this involves two examinations – the Part One test and the Part Two test. The first test is designed to determine machine control and basic riding skills and is held off the public road. When you pass it, you may then apply to take the second test. This tests your roadcraft skills – it also requires you to answer questions on the basics of the Highway Code.

If you are learning to ride on a side car combination, however, you do not have to take the Part One test, though you must take the Part Two test. This, too, allows you to carry an unlicenced sidecar passenger; with a provisional licence, you can only carry a passenger who holds a full licence himself.
*Your provisional licence lasts only for two years. If you do not pass the Part Two test within that time – the Part One test, though recommended, is not as yet compulsory – your licence is revoked for a year and you cannot apply for another one during that period.
*If you hold a full car licence, you can ride a moped without L-plates and a solo machine of up to 125cc engine capacity, or a side car machine of any engine capacity, provided that L-plates are displayed. The two-year provisional licence limit also does not apply.

If in doubt about any of these provisions, check with a dealer or the police.

Buying – the golden rules
The cost of buying a motor cycle and its resale value are only two of the factors you must take into account when deciding on any purchase. In addition, you should consider how much the machine will actually cost to run, how much the appropriate clothing will be and the price of any accessories you may require. So, the first golden rule to remember is always to think beyond the initial purchase price.

This advice applies particularly to insurance. It will always pay you to get an insurance quotation in advance. The cost of insurance has risen dramatically in recent years – so much so that many second-hand buyers now find that their insurance is costing them more than the actual bike.

Another golden rule is to be as objective as you can, rather than subjective, when you come to make a choice. Though it can be hard to achieve this goal, try hard to be logical thinking clearly what you want your bike for and what you want it to do. At the same time, show financial common sense – nothing is more burdensome than trying to pay for a bike you cannot really afford to run.

Think about your weekly mileage, how much you will spend on fuel, oil, tyres, chains, parts and servicing costs and how much the machine will make when you come to sell it, or trade it in. Never, ever, take sales claims for granted – investigate them. Does the model you are thinking of buying have a bad reliability record, for instance? Is it so rare that you will find it hard to obtain spares? How will you get to work if it is off the road?

When you work out a rough budget, base calculations on an estimate of annual mileage. For example, 10,000 miles (16,000km) a year at, say, 40 miles (64km) per gallon means that your bike will use 250 gallons (1137l) of fuel – a cost of around £500. But, if the machine is a powerful one, you might also get through three rear tyres – these cost around £50 each – plus a front tyre and perhaps a chain. You must also take into account the cost of things such as oil, spark plugs and other essential spares.

Two-stroke and four-stroke
You should also take the difference between two-stroke and four-stroke engines into account. If you are considering machines of the same engine size and same number of cylinders, a two-stroke version will be more powerful, but use more fuel. As such engines are designed to burn oil in their fuel, they will also require topping up with oil fairly frequently.

Most modern two-strokes are fitted with special oil tanks to minimize inconvenience. On some older models, however, the oil has to be mixed with the fuel in the fuel tank. This means that you have to measure the oil quantity in order to add the correct amount to the fuel.

WHAT IT WILL COST

Purchase price of bike	£ _____
Monthly loan repayments	£ _____
Road tax	£ _____
Insurance	£ _____
Petrol	£ _____
Oil	£ _____
Major service	£ _____
Standard service	£ _____
Tyres	£ _____
Year total	£ _____
Monthly cost	£ _____

The cost of owning a motor cycle is only beginning when you take the bike out of the showroom. There are several other factors to be taken into account. Use this chart as a rough guide to the price of running a bike for a year and work out a monthly cost. Then you can check whether or not the bike you want fits in with what you can afford.

EXTRAS

Helmet	£ _____
Clothing	£ _____
M.O.T. test	£ _____

Buying a bike/2

Check which system applies to the two-stroke you have in mind. Remember, too, that, because a two-stroke is oil-burning, the exhaust will inevitably smoke to some extent. On some machines, this is hardly noticeable; on others, it is hard to miss.

Four-stroke engines run on pure fuel and tend to have a quieter exhaust note than two-strokes. They also run cleaner.

New or second-hand?

The advantages of buying a new motor cycle, rather than a second-hand one, are obvious. They include:
*An extended warranty period. This usually lasts for a year, with unlimited mileage. Depending on the terms of the particular warranty, mechanical faults or failures will be rectified free of charge by your dealer.
*You start from scratch with a machine in showroom condition and so can control the way it is run in and maintained.
*You have no major worries about reliability.
*A new bike or scooter, supposing that it is a fresh model, should have the latest features and be a better machine than the previous year's marque.
*Owning a brand new machine encourages pride of ownership.
*There is no need for an DoT test certificate.

However, second-hand purchase has its advantages as well:
*The price you pay should be much lower than the cost of a new model.
*Because the price is lower, you should find it easier to raise the money to buy the machine, assuming that you cannot pay spot cash.
*A second-hand bike does not loose its resale value as quickly as a new one. New bikes depreciate in value faster than second-hand machines.
*A cheaper bike is generally easier to re-sell. The lower the asking price, the wider the potential market.

Now, take the disadvantages into account. In the case of a new machine, these include:
*The high initial outlay, or high loan repayments.
*The need to pay dealer service costs to remain within the terms of your warranty.
In the case of a second-hand bike, the disadvantages include:
*The likelihood that the machine's past history will be unknown.
*Inevitably, it will be mechanically worn and its reliability may be questionable.
*If any warranty is offered, it will cover only a very limited period.
*If the machine is three years old or more, it must have an DoT certificate.

In broad terms, the deciding factor between buying new or second-hand is usually cost. If you can afford a new machine, it is certainly better to buy one.

Buying second-hand is always something of a gamble – sometimes you will be lucky, but at other times not. To cut down the risk, establish as much of the machine's history as you can before making your decision. If, for instance, a friend is about to sell his bike – and you know that it has been maintained religiously – then you are obviously reducing this risk factor if you decide to buy it.

Know your rights

Whether you buy a second-hand bike from a dealer or privately, you still have legal rights as a purchaser. If you buy second-hand from a dealer, you may be offered a warranty for a limited period. On the other hand, it is more likely that you will be offered a 'sold as seen' agreement, in which case you accept that, should something go wrong with the machine, you bear the cost of repairs.

If you buy privately, the machine must be 'as described'. This means that, if you are deliberately misled by the bike's owner, you can sue under the terms of the 1979 Sale of Goods Act. If, for example, a machine is advertised as being in 'A1 condition, never raced or crashed' and you later find that it has been raced, is badly worn and has suffered crash damage, you can demand your money back. The bike simply is not 'as described'.

The Sale of Goods Act applies to dealers just as much as to private sellers. Any bike on offer must be 'as advertised' and 'of merchantable quality'. This means that the bike must be fit for its normal purpose, bearing in mind the price paid. When you buy, you can protect yourself still further by making the purpose clear to the dealer in advance. If, for instance, you want a machine capable of cruising at 60mph (96k/hr) and make the dealer aware of this, he is breaking his contract if the machine he sells you is capable of only 50mph (80k/hr) flat out.

Making a complaint

If you have cause for complaint, go to the seller first – not the manufacturer – and discuss the problem face to face. Well-established dealers, for instance, have usually built up a reputation for fairness, which is obviously in their interests to maintain. Very often, by discussing the matter in a calm and courteous way, such problems can be amicably resolved. This is naturally far preferable to getting involved in a legal wrangle.

If you have a genuine case and a discussion is fruitless, then you may be forced to take your complaint further. Before deciding to embark on legal proceedings, however, it will pay you to seek professional advice from a solicitor, the Citizens Advice Bureau, or the Consumer Protection department of your local authority.

When you are pursuing a complaint, keep a copy of all correspondence, make notes of the various steps you are taking and ask for the names of the various people who are dealing with the complaint. Once you have established contact with a particular person, always ask for that person when you need to discuss developments.

If you are dealing with a dealer, try to find out if he is a member of a trade association. The main trade body is the Motor Cycle Association of Great Britain Ltd. It will investigate a written complain made against one of its members.

If you have to sue, you do this through the County Court, which deals with claims of up to £5,000. You will need an application form, on which you give brief details of your claim, from your local court office. You will also have to pay a fee – the amount depends on the size of the claim.

Buying tips
Legal dramatics, however, are the exception, rather than the rule. If you use common sense when you buy a bike, you should avoid such problems.

If you are buying from a dealer, try to establish and assess his reputation. If you can, talk to at least two people who have bought machines from him before making any decision.

Buy locally, if possible. If your machine breaks down, or needs servicing, it is much more convenient to discuss problems and arrange the delivery and collection of the bike with a neighbourhood dealer. Though buying a bike from a dealer a long way from home might save you money initially, think of the inconvenience this could cause you if the machine breaks down while it is still covered by its warranty.

If you are a first-time rider, take someone along to the showroom with you who can speak from experience and offer sound advice. The excitement of a first-time purchase can blind an inexperienced owner to inherent faults in the bike, or to faults it is likely to develop. A steadying influence can save you from what might prove to be a costly blunder, particularly when it comes to looking at a second-hand machine.

Before committing yourself, ask to see the warranty. Take this home with you and study the small print, so that you know for how long the machine is covered and what conditions you have to meet to keep the warranty valid. If, for instance, you modify a new bike's engine, or fail to have the machine serviced by the dealer from whom you bought it at the specified intervals, then the dealer may be within his rights if he cancels the warranty.

If you intend to buy a new machine, check on when it will be ready for the road. It is folly just to assume that the bike can be ready the next day – if it is a popular model, there may well be a waiting list. Find out, too, exactly what charges over and above the list purchase price are involved in the transaction.

Some dealers, for example, will quote you an 'on the road' price for a new machine, which includes VAT, the cost of a the rear number plate, the PDI (pre-delivery inspection) charge, the cost of a road fund licence and holder and, where necessary, L-plates. Others quote a price that is usually inclusive of VAT, but charge extra for the PDI, road fund licence and the other legal essentials.

The PDI charge may well make you stop and think. The reason for it is simple – when most machines are delivered to a dealer, they arrive crated, with the front wheel and handlebars separate. Thus, the dealer has to complete the final assembly and check the whole machine over before passing it on to you.

If you would like a test ride before you decide to buy, ask the dealer whether he will agreed to this in advance. Though this facility is normally not made available to learner riders, the dealer may be willing to take the machine to somewhere off the road, so that a potential first time customer can decide whether or not he or she can cope with it.

Some major retailers also stock 'demonstrator' machines, which they will sometimes allow experienced full licence holders to try. In the main, however, dealers are reluctant to do this.

Checking the machine
If you consult a dealer, do the thing thoroughly, especially if you are inexperienced. Your

Buying a bike/3

physical size may well have a bearing on the type of machine best suited to you, for instance. With this in mind, it is worth seeing if you find it easy to put the machine on its mainstand or not. Often, the key to this is technique, rather than brute strength.

It may pay you to have what dealers often term 'convenience facilities' on the machine too, whether as standard fittings or as optional extras. These include such options as electric start, an ignition key operated steering lock and so on. In this case as well, the time spent discussing your needs, queries and uncertainties with your dealer or a knowledgeable friend will be invaluable.

Be especially on the alert if you are buying a second-hand machine, especially if you are a first-time buyer. The first rule here is not to be in a hurry to buy. Make sure that the machine has a log book, with the owner's name and address in it, and that the owner is who he says he is. If the machine is three years old or more, check that it has a current DoT certificate.

Check the machine over as thoroughly as you can. Look for signs of accident damage, such as scraped or broken handlebar levers, scraped footrests, a broken headlight and so on. Make sure that the machine starts readily and ticks over when warm. Pull the clutch lever in and put the machine into gear with the engine running. Though there will be some gearbox noise, this should not be unduly harsh.

Check the tyre treads, the smoothness of the suspension, the brakes, the state of the chain and the oil levels. All these are good indications of how well the machine has been maintained. Check that the lights work. See if the battery is topped up and the standard tool kit is on the machine. Ask yourself if the owner appears honest. Does the machine look well maintained? Does the engine sound in good condition?

Even before making an appointment to view, check the average asking price for a machine of the same type and year. Any of the several trade magazines on the market will give you a clear indication of average value. Make sure that the machine being advertised is the model you are interested in – 'Suzuki 125', for instance, could mean one of many models.

If you like the machine, do not be afraid to barter, especially if the abbreviation 'o.n.o' (or near offer) is included in the advertisement. When you buy, make sure that you are given a receipt, whether you are paying in cash or with a cheque. It helps to have a witness present – this can be invaluable in the event any claim or statement made by the owner turns out to be false and you want to get some – or all – of your money returned.

Use common sense and do not be in too much of a hurry to buy. If you follow these rules, you should be able to decide between an honest seller and someone who is trying to get rid of a problem machine for an unrealistic price.

Above all, do not be fooled by so-called 'bargains'. If, say, a bike of a certain year is being offered for sale for far below its generally accepted second-hand value, it is more likely than not that there is something wrong with it.

Throttle
Check that the twistgrip operates smoothly, with no tight spots. Check the cable for wear or fraying.

Lights
Check that the headlight operates on main and dipped beam and the tail light works. Check indicators flash at the correct rate. Operate the brakes and see whether or not the brake light functions.

Forks
Check fork legs for rust and pitting. Look for signs of oil leaks. Bounce the suspension to check that it is not too spongy and returns to its normal position without bouncing. Check for head bearing wear by trying to rock the forks backwards and forwards.

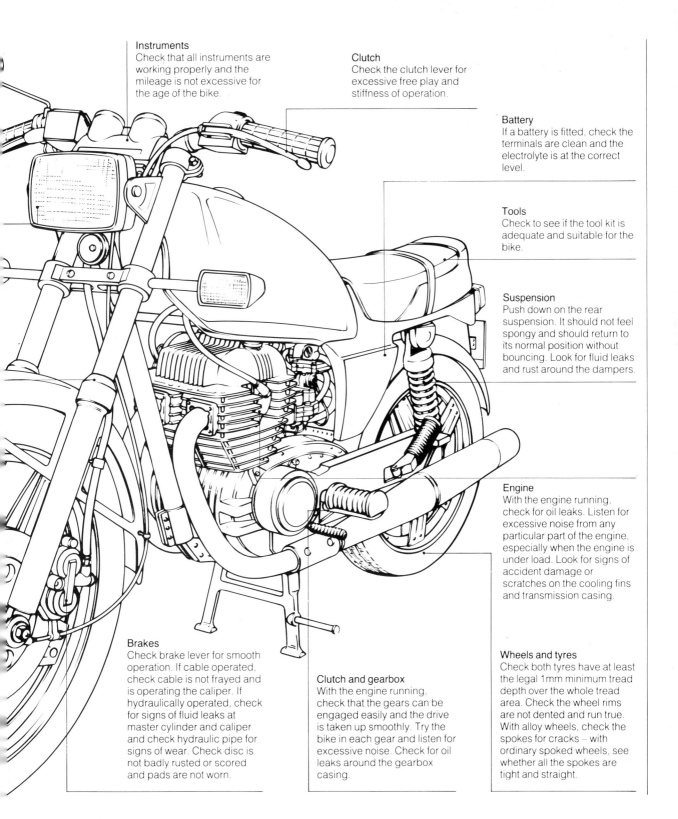

Instruments
Check that all instruments are working properly and the mileage is not excessive for the age of the bike.

Clutch
Check the clutch lever for excessive free play and stiffness of operation.

Battery
If a battery is fitted, check the terminals are clean and the electrolyte is at the correct level.

Tools
Check to see if the tool kit is adequate and suitable for the bike.

Suspension
Push down on the rear suspension. It should not feel spongy and should return to its normal position without bouncing. Look for fluid leaks and rust around the dampers.

Engine
With the engine running, check for oil leaks. Listen for excessive noise from any particular part of the engine, especially when the engine is under load. Look for signs of accident damage or scratches on the cooling fins and transmission casing.

Brakes
Check brake lever for smooth operation. If cable operated, check cable is not frayed and is operating the caliper. If hydraulically operated, check for signs of fluid leaks at master cylinder and caliper and check hydraulic pipe for signs of wear. Check disc is not badly rusted or scored and pads are not worn.

Clutch and gearbox
With the engine running, check that the gears can be engaged easily and the drive is taken up smoothly. Try the bike in each gear and listen for excessive noise. Check for oil leaks around the gearbox casing.

Wheels and tyres
Check both tyres have at least the legal 1mm minimum tread depth over the whole tread area. Check the wheel rims are not dented and run true. With alloy wheels, check the spokes for cracks – with ordinary spoked wheels, see whether all the spokes are tight and straight.

Finance, insurance and warranties/1

Today, raising the money to buy a motor cycle or scooter is easier in general than it was even a few years ago. Many riders simply do not have the ability to pay spot cash for a machine; current trends show that many new bikes are being bought on credit terms of one sort or another.

If you are one of the fortunate few who is prepared – and able – to pay cash on the nail for the bike of your choice, then you will have no problems. If, however, you need credit, it will pay you to look carefully at the various ways in which money can be raised before making a final decision on which is the best route to take.

Credit facilities

There are various ways of arranging a loan. Naturally enough, some are more expensive than others, but one of them will probably suit your particular needs. These include a credit sale arranged by a dealer; a bank loan; a bank overdraft; hire purchase; an arrangement with a credit or insurance firm; paying with a credit card; or an agreement with a credit broker.

Only you can decide which of these methods best suits your individual circumstances, though much depends on prevailing interest rates. One thing worth watching out for is a special offer. For instance, a manufacturer may promote a particular model, or a machine of a certain capacity, by offering interest free credit over a period stretching from one to two years. If you compare this with taking out a conventional type of loan at the prevailing standard interest rates, you can see immediately that a clear saving can be made by taking advantage of such an offer.

Sorting out a loan

It is basic commonsense to look carefully into any scheme offered to you before making a decision. Here, it is well worth asking a friend or relation for advice – particularly if you have no head for figures. Otherwise you could end up committed to a painfully expensive repayment scheme.

If you are acting on your own, you must watch out for yourself. Always ask for a written quotation and take this home to study thoroughly before committing yourself. A little basic arithmetic can save you from costly blunders. Assume, for instance, that the purchase price of a new bike is £1200, that the deposit is £200 and that you want to pay the outstanding £1000 over a two year period. First, ask how much the repayments will be a month and ask for this to be confirmed in writing. If the salesman will not spell out such details, you should be on the alert from the start.

Then, work back from the monthly repayments figure to see how much the loan is actually costing. If, for example, you are quoted 24 monthly payments of £65 each, you can see at once that the true cost is £1565. With this figure in mind, look for a second quotation – obviously you will be on to a better deal if you can find someone who will provide you with £1,000 for 24 monthly repayments of, say, £55.

Understanding interest

You should also establish at what rate loan interest is being charged. Since the 1974 Consumer Credit Act became law, all loan companies and agencies are legally required to quote what is termed the 'annual percentage rate'(APR).

The APR rate allows you to compare the various rates rival finance companies are offering easily. It is the true rate of interest, unlike 'flat rate' interest, which some advertisers display prominently because the flat rate quote is numerically about half the APR equivalent.

If, for example, you borrow £1,000 at a flat rate interest of 10% for a year, you have to pay back £1100 (£91.67 per calendar month). If you took out the same loan at the same rate of interest over two years, it would cost you £1200 (£50 per calendar month). You pay interest annually on the amount you were originally loaned, even though the amount outstanding decreases each time you pay back an instalment. Hence the term flat rate interest.

APR, on the other hand, takes into account the reducing amount of debt. On the same scale of monthly repayments, the APR equivalent to 10% flat rate interest is 19%.

Finance schemes

Arranging the necessary credit through a dealer is a very popular way of financing a bike purchase, largely because it is convenient. So long as you are regarded as creditworthy and can put down at least 15% of the purchase price as a deposit, you can literally walk into a showroom and ride away complete with bike, insurance and motor cycle clothing – all paid for under a credit scheme.

To obtain this credit, you normally have to satisfy several requirements. As already stated, the normal deposit is a minimum of 15%, although in rare cases you may be able to buy your bike without this.

You must be a regular wage

earner and be prepared to disclose your take-home pay – that is, the amount you actually receive after all government and other deductions have been made. If you are not a householder, or do not rent your accomodation, you will need a parent, relation or friend to stand as 'guarantor'. This means that, if you fail to keep up the loan repayments, they then become the responsibility of the guarantor. If you are 21 or under, you are likely to need a guarantor in any case, especially if you do not possess a bank account, or savings account.

If you do not work regularly, the chances of you obtaining a loan are almost nil. And, if you have had a country court action brought against you for debt, you will be refused credit.

Checking your credit rating

The dealer does not provide you with credit himself. He acts as the agent for a credit company. Thus, as soon as he has obtained the necessary information from you, he telephones the company to arrange the details.

The company concerned will run a rapid check on you to see whether you have outstanding credit arrangements elsewhere, or a bad debt record. Having established this, they will 'phone the dealer back with their decision. If you get the go-ahead, the dealer will then advise you to take out an insurance policy to protect your repayments, should you be injured or fall sick and so be unable to work.

Insuring yourself so that your repayments are protected is well worth considering. For an additional fee, you may also be able to obtain cover against the risk of redundancy, though this type of cover is harder to obtain now than it was a few years ago.

Should you find you cannot keep the repayments up for any reason, you should contact the credit company immediately and discuss the problem. If, for instance, you fall seriously behind with your repayments on a hire purchase scheme – and no arrangement has been made – the company has the legal right to regain possession of your bike. If this happens, you lose the benefit of any repayments you may have already made.

If, on the other hand, you want to pay the balance of the loan off before it falls due, the credit company may agree to what is termed an 'early settlement'. In most cases, this means that the total interest charge is reduced.

Credit and hire purchase

When you enter into a credit arrangement, it is important to establish whether you are buying your bike under the terms of a true credit sale, or through hire purchase. Though most people refer to all types of credit buying as hire purchase, or HP, there is a crucial difference between the two schemes.

If you buy a bike on hire purchase, then the company providing the loan actually owns the machine until you have made the final payment. In other words, you only have the bike on hire – you cannot sell it, for instance, unless the HP company agrees that you can do so. The same does not necessarily apply to a credit scheme, when you can sell the bike and then make the necessary repayments.

Personal loans

If you decide to obtain credit from a finance house, or credit broker, you must ensure that you understand the terms of any agreement fully before signing it. The same thing applies to a personal loan from your bank. More and more people are finding such loans attractive because of the extremely competitive interest rate usually being offered.

Normally, you can arrange to pay back such a loan over one, two, or three years – again in monthly instalments. You do not even have to have a bank account, though, naturally enough, such a loan is far easier to arrange if you have one. What you must do is to convince the bank that you are in regular work, are at least 18 years old and can make a 20% deposit on the bike.

Once you have made the agreement, you need to open a repayment account with the bank concerned. As with a credit sale arranged via a dealer, the repayments are made at a fixed rate of interest and so are not subject to fluctuation. Most banks and other institutions offering the same service also ask for a 'setting up' fee. This may be a straight charge, or, in the case of a typical high street bank, 1% of the amount you borrow.

Borrowing by taking out a bank overdraft is even cheaper. To take advantage of this, however, you need a proven track record with the bank concerned. You can also ask your bank for a short term bridging loan – this again very much depends on your banking track record.

Credit cards

Unless all you need is a short term loan, it is not really worth buying via a bank credit card,

Finance, insurance and warranties/2

since the interest involved is extremely high. Usually under a credit card scheme, you have to pay off the balance within four months.

Some bike importers, however, have introduced their own credit cards, which enable their customers to buy goods, have their machines serviced and so on up to their credit limit, which is usually a few hundred pounds. As with a normal credit card, you can pay back what you have borrowed when you get a statement, or pay the loan back month by month.

Life insurance and mortgages
Though you can borrow against a life insurance policy, this route has a severe drawback. In the early years of the policy, the surrender value is usually low and so the amount you can borrow is by definition limited.

If you have a mortgage, you can use this as security to obtain a loan from a building society, bank, or insurance company. Interest rates in such cases are usually very competitive because of the high degree of security a mortgage provides.

Whichever method you opt for, think very carefully before committing yourself in writing and study all the small print. Remember, cash is best – or, at least, as much cash as possible. If you doubt this, ask yourself if in two or three years time, you still want to have to budget for that monthly repayment.

Insurance
If you ride a motor cycle or a scooter on a public road, you must be insured. This is a legal requirement – and for very good reasons. Should anyone be injured, or property damaged,

compensation can be claimed from the company that provides the insurance. Such compensation can be substantial – well beyond the means of the individual.

Types of cover
You will find that you can choose between three main types of insurance cover – third party, third party fire and theft (TPFT) and fully comprehensive. The term 'third party' means exactly what it says – any third party is protected against injury or loss as a result of a riding mistake. For example, if you were to loose control of your machine and slide into the side of a car, the car's owner would claim against you for damages. These would be paid by your insurance company to him or her – the 'third party'. You cannot claim, however, for any damage to your machine.

If the roles were reversed – in other words, the car has knocked into your bike – you would claim against the car's driver. The cost of the claim would be met by the driver's insurance company.

The basic cover provided by a third party fire and theft policy is the same as third party, with the added bonus of protection against fire and theft. Remember, though, in both instances, the insurance company will pay only current values and that these are not necessarily the same as list values.

If you can afford it, fully comprehensive cover is best for several reasons. It provides all the protection detailed above, plus paying for the cost of repairs or replacement parts should you damage the machine accidentally, or should it be damaged by persons unknown.

With all such policies, certain

conditions are often stipulated as part of the cover. For example, with third party fire and theft cover, the policy may require you to keep the machine under lock and key in a garage after dark, when not in use. If you ignore this stipulation and the machine is stolen, your insurance company might say that you were negligent and would be within the rights if it refused to meet your claim.

For this reason, it always pays to read the small print, so that you can establish exactly what cover you are entitled to under the policy's terms. Do not be afraid to ask questions – either general or specific – at your insurance office, of your broker, or of your dealer if there is any uncertainty in your mind.

Obtaining a policy
Before buying a machine, you should decide first which type of cover you require and then obtain a quotation to establish its cost. This can vary considerably, so it is always best to consult at least two companies – preferably more – to find not only the cover that best suits your needs, but also the most competitive price.

If you do not want to deal with an insurance company directly, you can consult an insurance broker, who will act as a middleman. Alternatively, you can ask your dealer if he can arrange cover. Most dealers are now prepared to do this, especially if you are buying a new machine. In this instance, they act on behalf of an insurance company, just as a broker does.

Insurance cost
As you might expect, third party insurance is cheaper than third party fire and theft and this, in

turn, is less expensive than a fully comprehensive policy. What young motor cyclists in particular find is that even third party insurance is usually expensive; in some cases, a year's cover may well cost more than a second-hand machine.

Most owners wrongly think that the cost of repairs is responsible for such high annual fees – these are usually termed 'premiums'. In fact, the main reason is the compulsory pillion passenger insurance that all policies must include. If a pillion passenger is injured severely, damages can run into hundreds of thousands of pounds.

All insurance companies offering cover for motor cyclists and scooter riders split their scale of fees into capacity ratings. One leading company divides these as follows: up to 100cc; 101cc to 225cc; 226cc to 350cc; 351cc to 600cc; 601cc to 900cc; and over 900cc. The bigger the bike's capacity, the more expensive the cover will be. However, you may find that some companies quote a lower premium for sidecar combinations than for a solo of the same engine capacity.

Once you have found a company that can offer you the cover to suit your needs, you have to fill in a proposal form and pay the first year's premium in full. If you deal with a broker, you may find that you can pay the premium in stages. In either case, you will then be given an interim 'cover note', which confirms that you are insured to ride, to tide you over until the full policy can be prepared. Once this is ready, the cover note, which normally is valid for 30 days, can be discarded. The full policy is renewed annually.

'No claims' and special schemes
The 'no claims' bonus scheme, which is a standard feature of car insurance, is not a standard part of motor cycle insurance, though some companies do offer it. Some companies, however, offer what is termed a 'rider policy', which allows the policy holder to ride as many machines as he likes under one policy.

Every so often, a major importer may work out a deal with an insurance company, so that bike and insurance can be offered together. In such a case, the price of the insurance will be highly competitive.

Insurance watchpoints
When looking into cover and quotes, bear in mind that the cheapest is not necessarily the best – or even the most economic in the long run. It may be better to pay a few pounds extra to be covered by a well-known company, rather than by an unknown small concern.

There is also a lot to be said for obtaining your cover locally. If you have to make a claim, it is far easier to call into your local insurance office to seek help in filling in forms and so on than having to deal with a company 200 miles away by letter and telephone.

As with most aspects of motor cycling, seeking advice from other riders is often a quick way of establishing advantages and pitfalls. Do not skimp on the homework. After all, it is in your interest to obtain the exact cover to suit your needs at the best possible price.

Warranties
A warranty is your guarantee against the costs – if not the pitfalls – of mechanical failure. In theory, if your machine breaks down through no fault of your own while covered by warranty, then the company issuing the warranty is legally obliged to have the necessary repairs carried out.

Theory is not necessarily the same as practice, however. For this reason, when you buy a new or second-hand machine from a dealer, you should always establish whether or not a warranty is on offer and, if so, what it covers. Ask for a copy to study before committing yourself, since the small print may contain some conditions you simply may not have anticipated.

Terms and conditions
If you are buying a new machine, the warranty in many cases lasts for one year and is valid no matter how many miles you cover. Some warranties, however, restrict the mileage to, say, one year/12,000 miles (19,000km). This means that if you cover 12,000 miles in eight months, the warranty is invalid from that moment. Or, if you only cover 4,000 miles (6,500km) in the year, the warranty still expires at the end of the year.

If you have a one year warranty, you may be able to extend it for an extra year by paying a further premium – in other words, it is just as if you are taking out an extra insurance policy to protect you against mechanical problems. Often, however, an extended warranty will cover only major engine components, so it is again important to read the terms of such a contract to find out exactly what is being covered and for how long.

When buying a second-hand machine from a dealer, you may

be able to obtain a one month warranty. Frequently, however, most dealers simply promise that, if anything goes wrong with the machine during that month, they will check the bike over if you return it to them.

This 'verbal warranty' is only as good as the dealer's word. If you know the dealer personally – or if he has a good reputation – this form of agreement may be just as good as a formal warranty in writing. But, without a signed warranty, you have no legal rights other than those specified by the Sale of Goods Act. This means that, if you accept a verbal undertaking, you are relying on the dealer's good will to carry out any necessary repairs.

Buying privately

If you buy privately, you should try to persuade the seller to state, in writing, that he or she will make good any defects that appear during the first fortnight, month, or whatever, of ownership. You will need an independent witness to any such agreement, which must be signed by all three parties if it is to be of any legal value.

This is the ideal, but, in practice, it is hard to achieve. In the case of a private sale, the machine is usually bought 'as seen' – though there is the safeguard that the machine must be 'as described' by the seller. If you put yourself in the seller's shoes, you can see why such a person would be reluctant to give a warranty. He or she has no idea how you are going to treat the machine, while, because the sale is private, the asking price is likely to be less than if the bike was coming from a dealer. However, you are still protected by law to a certain extent.

Terms of sale

Many dealers use the same reasoning when selling second-hand machines, particularly worn, high mileage models. It is therefore important to be clear about the terms of sale, while, as the buyer, you must also be aware of your obligations – concerning adequate maintenance, for instance – contained in any warranty. Normally, these obligations include some or all of the following stipulations: *The product must be purchased from and serviced at the recommended intervals by an authorized dealer.
*Any repairs must be carried out by an authorized dealer and, at your own expense, you will arrange the delivery and collection of the machine.
*This assurance does not apply to the routine replacement of parts such as tyres, spark plugs, control cables, transmission chains or any other parts which deteriorate during normal usage, nor to normal service and maintenance adjustments.
*Any part repaired or replaced will be covered for the remainder of the warranty period and the defective part will become the property of the manufacturer.
*This assurance is in addition to, and does not detract from, the contractual rights you have under Statute or at Common Law.

You can see from this that, to keep the warranty valid, the machine must be serviced by an authorized dealer – preferably by the dealer from whom you purchased the machine – at the service intervals specified by its manufacturer. If you break the terms of the warranty, you have no justifiable claim in law.

Warranty documentation

On purchasing your new machine, you should be given a warranty document. This may be in the form of a card, which may be replaced by vouchers from the manufacturer when he receives details of machine and buyer from the dealer. Should your machine need repairing under warranty, the dealer will want to see both card and vouchers, so it is important to keep them safe.

You will also be given a service book, or a similar document, which the dealer should stamp in the appropriate place as proof that the service has been carried out. Keep this safe, too. If you do not observe the recommended service intervals, the dealer is within his rights if he cancels the warranty.

You pay for each service in the normal way. Should you wish to sell your machine during the warranty period, you should be able to transfer the warranty.

If you change address, notify your dealer immediately, together with the manufacturer or importer with whom your warranty is registered. This is important, since a new model may be subject to a 'recall'. This occurs if, for instance, it is discovered that a component is prone to failure.

Having a warranty to rely on is one of the major benefits of buying new, rather than second-hand. But always remember that you will have obligations under its terms as well. Before buying, therefore, acquaint yourself with all relevant warranty details. Be on the alert, too, for sales drives, since an extended warranty period may well be offered as part of them.

Clothing/1

Right from the start of your riding career, you will need to budget for specialist clothing specifically designed to meet the demands of motor cycle and scooter riding. The need for this will quickly become obvious, especially if you try to skimp on essentials.

The first priority is a crash helmet, as it is a legal requirement to wear one. In addition, you need specialist clothing to keep you warm and protect you – both from the weather and from the risk of injury in the event of a fall.

Crash helmets

Since 1 June 1973 it has been a legal requirement for a crash helmet to be worn when riding a powered two- or three-wheeler on a public road. In June 1977, the law was tightened up to stipulate that helmets must meet certain safety requirements. Today, a new helmet must either carry the BSI (British Standards Institution) 'kitemark' – BS5361:1976 or BS2495:1977 (the second being the higher of the two) – or be of equivalent quality. What this means in practice is that you can wear a helmet which does not have a BSI sticker on it, as long as it is the same as the lower of the two BSI standards.

The BSI has played a major part in improving the quality of helmets in other ways. Concern over the deterioration of plastic helmets through possible contact with solvents, such as petrol, led to another BSI test. Helmets which meet this extra standard have the wording 'inc. amend. 5' added to the kitemark.

Choosing a helmet

When choosing a crash helmet, the golden rule is to buy the best you can afford. Look for one up to

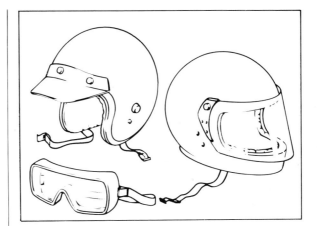

There are two types of helmet – open face (far left) and integral (left). Open face helmets tend to be cheaper, though you will have to buy a separate pair of goggles. Integral helmets, though more expensive, offer a higher degree of weather protection and are safer in the event of an accident.

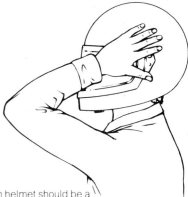

Helmet checks
For comfort and safety, a crash helmet should be a good fit. Do up the chin strap and then try and push the strap off over your chin (left). If you can, the helmet is too big. Next, hold the helmet steady with both hands (right). Try and rotate your head within it, or try and push it off from the back. If you can do either of these, the helmet is too big.

the BS2495:1977 standard.

There are two basic helmet designs from which to choose – full face (integral), or open face (jet style). The choice between the two boils down to your individual preference. Though there is little doubt that the full face design offers more comprehensive protection, some riders simply do not like the 'enclosed' feeling a full face helmet imparts.

Helmets are available in three types of shell material – glass fibre, plastic or Kevlar, the

material used in the making of bullet-proof vests. Choosing between them can be a complex business, since even experts disagree over which is superior. Generally speaking, a glass fibre helmet absorbs crash shock by delaminating – that is to say the layers of the fibre mat come apart as they absorb the energy of the shock. A plastic helmet absorbs shock through the tearing of the shell. Kelvar, a very tough material indeed, is more akin to glass fibre in its reactions when stressed.

Clothing/2

To make matters simple, stick to the highest BSI standard. If you do this, you can be assured that the helmet will give you good protection, regardless of the shell material used in its construction. Many owners opt for glass fibre helmets simply because they can be painted. You should never paint a plastic helmet, since any solvents in the paint may weaken the shell.

It is vital that any helmet you buy fits snugly and is comfortable to wear. For these reasons, never buy a helmet through the post – you must be able to try it on. If it is too tight, it will cause a pressure point to form while you are riding, which will get on your nerves and impair your concentration. If it is too loose, it may come off in the event of an road accident.

Helmet checks

Put the helmet on and do up its strap. Now try to pull the strap over your chin – you should not be able to do this. Next, grasp the neck section of the helmet and try to pull the helmet over and off your head. You should not be able to do this either. If you can, the helmet is valueless, since it is likely to come off in an accident.

Ask yourself if the helmet feels comfortable and if you are happy with the field of vision it provides. If you need to wear goggles with the helmet, make sure that they fit properly. If you are choosing a visor, make sure that it opens and closes to your satisfaction. In general, try to visualize yourself wearing it on the road – this will help you greatly in making your final choice.

Check that spare visors, where applicable, are readily available and ask about special features.

Some manufacturers, for example, offer a replacement inner trim for smartness.

Buying second-hand

Do not buy second-hand if you can avoid it. If this is forced on you, check the helmet over extremely carefully. Any signs of scratches or accident damage mean that it has done its job, but has been weakened because of this. For instance, the inner expanded polystyrene shock absorption liner may have already been compressed through a fall and the helmet inevitably will not be able to offer the same amount of protection as a result.

Helmet maintenance

Always keep your helmet and visor or goggles clean. Do not hang the helmet up by the chin strap when not in use. Always keep the helmet in the house – not in a garage, where it might become damp, with consequent rotting of stitching and fabrics.

Clothing requirements

Any clothing you choose should be practical. It must keep you warm, protect you against the weather and cushion you in the event of an accident. These demands do not mean that the clothes you wear need not be colourful and smartly cut – in recent years, fashion and style have become an integral factor in the design of motor cycling clothing.

At the bare minimum – for short distance commuter riding, say – you will need gloves, a scarf or balaclava helmet, a one-piece oversuit and riding boots. How you build on this depends on how much riding you will be doing and what you can afford.

For all-year riding, the ideal wardrobe consists of a leather riding suit, lined two-piece oversuit, heated gloves and jacket, leather boots with rubber over-boots, overmitts, balaclava helmet, scarf, neck protector and a reflective waistcoat.

Summer clothing

Even on the warmest of days, never be tempted to ride bare armed, or without gloves. In the event of an accident, it is pure instinct to put your hands out to seek protection. Even at a very low speed, you are likely to loose quite a large skin area if you tempt providence in this way.

Suitable wear for summer riding includes a one- or two-piece leather suit, leather boots, leather gloves, a scarf and, of course, a helmet. In addition, it is always a prudent precaution to carry a lightweight one-piece oversuit, lightweight overmitts and lightweight overboots, or spats. These will protect you if it rains and also keep you warm when riding at night.

Leather is the traditional material for all protective clothing. It is long lasting, resistant to tearing and surprisingly resistant to friction. It is also comfortable to wear, because it breathes and stretches, and is not as easily tugged by the wind as, say, a nylon anorak would be. Though not strictly waterproof, when properly treated, leather is water resistant and so will keep you dry through a shower.

Lightweight leather boots and gloves are also good buys. Buy boots which cover the ankles as these provide wind as well as accident protection. Plastic coated gloves may look smart when new, but they crack and

Summer A one-piece leather suit, together with strong boots and gloves, offers good protection against wind and will cushion you in an accident.

Spring It is worth carrying a lightweight, waterproof jacket and trousers to give you extra protection against sudden light showers.

Winter A balaclava, heavy gauntlets, rubber overboots and heavyweight waterproofs are all winter essentials. A reflective belt is a good safety feature when visibilty is low.

Clothing/3

fray with wear and tear so easily that they offer little protection in the event of an accident. For the same reason, training shoes, or similar, should not be worn.

Choosing your suit

When choosing a leather riding suit, may riders find a two-piece suit more convenient, because the jacket can be removed without fuss. If, however, your goal is the ultimate in protection, a one-piece leather race style suit is preferable. With a two-piece – even if the suit is of the zip-together type – the jacket may ride up in an accident, leaving the abdomen exposed.

The nature of the lining material is also worth taking into account. A satin or silk lining is best for comfort and protection. Many leather suits, however, have nylon linings, which are less satisfactory. In some cases, the nylon can burn into the skin as a result of the friction generated by sliding along the road after a fall. For this reason, nylon lined leathers sometimes may not be used for racing.

You can buy a leather suit off-the-peg, or have one made. Whichever route you choose, make sure that the suit allows you sufficient freedom of movement, particularly if you ride a machine with low race style handlebars.

Winter clothing

In winter, you need extra clothing in addition to your summer riding gear to keep out the cold. Though the greatest loss of body heat is via the head, you feel the cold in your fingers and toes first, followed by the chest and knees.

A lined one- or two-piece waterproof overproof is essential for warmth. Worn over the top of

a leather suit, it will keep the cold at bay for many miles. Wool lined mitts with nylon overmitts will allow fingers to share warmth and so to remain warmer longer. Though some finer points of touch will be lost, keeping your hands warm more than compensates for this – the alternative is them 'seizing' altogether. Riding boots (fleece lined types are available), worn with one thick pair of seaman's socks plus pull-on rubber overboots, should keep your feet and toes warm.

Keep your head warm by wearing a balaclava under your helmet, plus a scarf and neck protector. The latter is sometimes called an 'apple warmer', because it keeps the Adam's apple warm.

Maximising protection

To make the most of your protective clothing, it is essential that none of these garments are tight fitting. They must be comfortable, but fairly loose, so that there are heat insulating air layers between each separate layer of clothing.

Some riders, for instance, wonder why their feet are still cold even though they are wearing three pairs of socks. The answer is that the socks are so tightly packed that there is no air space between them, while the blood circulation is also restricted. One pair of thick socks, which allow the feet to move, is much better, while, if you leave enough room for thermal insoles, these will conserve heat still further.

Knees will get cold if you pull your oversuit tightly over them. Again, an air space is vital. Create this by sliding a pair of moto-cross style plastic knee and

shin pads down the front of your boots and then put on your overtrousers.

If the weather becomes severe, thermal underwear will help you to cope with it. Such underwear is purpose designed to retain body heat to maximum effect. A less expensive alternative is to wear ordinary long johns with matching vest.

A string vest is also worth considering. Though this may sound strange in theory, in practice this type of vest rubs against the skin as you move, so stimulating blood circulation and hence body heat. A T-shirt should be worn over the top in addition to other garments.

If you cannot afford a leather suit, then a lightweight one-piece suit, worn under a two-piece, will conserve body heat. However, a waterproof suit is vital. If dampness gets through to the skin, then you will get cold all the sooner. Overboots and overmitts are also essential to stop feet and hands from getting wet.

Coping with cold

If, despite your clothes, you find that you are getting cold, then you must stop and warm up again. Run up and down a few times to stimulate the blood circulation. When you are warmed up, you should find that you can ride for a longer stretch than you first could before getting cold again.

To continue riding when extremely cold is foolhardy. Your muscles become stiff, your riding wooden and your reactions dangerously slow. Remember that an icy wind can be extremely penetrating, especially if you are riding into it at speed.

Exercise your fingers and toes

as you ride along to help blood flow. They will also act as an early warning system, since you will know when they are getting too cold to allow you to work the controls.

Electric heating

The clothing discussed here can cope with most conditions. However, the best it can do is to conserve body heat – it cannot generate heat itself. Thus, for long rides in cold weather and short ones in extreme condition, there is no beating electrically heated garments, which allow you to defy the cold completely. Once you have discovered the benefits of heated clothing, you may well wonder how you managed before.

Electrically heated gloves, glove inners, insoles, jackets, waistcoats and long johns are all available. Before investing in them, however, check that your machine's generator output is sufficient to power them. Your dealer will be able to advise on this. Most riders find that heated gloves and waistcoat are all they require.

Electrically heated visors are also obtainable. They are designed to stop the visor misting and so keep your vision clear. Such visors can prove invaluable in foggy or snowy riding conditions.

Clothes care

As mentioned earlier, it pays to buy the best garments you can afford. Over the years, quality clothes, especially those with a guarantee, work out to be more cost effective in the long run.

However, whatever clothes you choose, you must care for them properly if they are to give years of good service. After a

Electrically heated garments, such as the jacket (left) and the gauntlets (below), can be plugged into the bike's electrical system. They provide the best level of protection against cold, especially on long, fast runs.

ride, wipe off the inevitable road grime and salt with a lightly wetted cloth and then hang your clothes up to dry in a well aired warm room.

Do not screw your clothes up and thrown them in a corner when wet, or go to the other extreme of hanging them in front of a blazing fire. Both are equally harmful. What you should so is to allow garments to dry gradually.

All riding garments should be kept in the house. If you store them in a garage, they will retain moisture and so be cold and uncomfortable when you put them on. In addition damp means that their stitching will start to rot, while the fabrics themselves may start to collect mould.

Follow manufacturers' instructions on cleaning, proofing and so on. If you take sufficient pride in your riding gear, you will not go far wrong.

Bike security

Bike thefts are on the increase. As every policeman or insurance company will tell you, it pays to secure your machine against theft.

On most modern machines, steering locks are a standard fitting. These should be kept oiled and in good working order. Otherwise manufacturers have largely ignored the problem – at least until recently. Now, however, in response to consumer demand, more and more of them are becoming security conscious.

In 1982, for instance, Honda introduced its VF750 model, which was fitted with a cable lock in addition to an ignition key operated steering lock. The cable has the further refinement of a fibre optic centre. This means that you can lock the cable into a sensor on the bike to activate a light beam, which passes through the fibre optic core. If the cable is cut, the light beam is broken and an alarm sounds. The net result is a one piece lock and alarm system.

Lock logic

Such a combination – plus the use of the steering lock – should deter all but the most determined thief. You will find that most dealer and auto accessory stores stock a wide range of anti-theft devices from which you can make your choice. In this case, economy should not be your prime consideration; in general, the more expensive the device, the more effective it is likely to be.

The simple padlock and chain is an extremely popular anti-theft device, its visual presence making it a positive deterrent as far as the majority of amateur joy riders are concerned. To use it to

greatest effect, you should secure the machine to an immovable object, such as a lamp post, via its frame tubing. When not in use, it can be wrapped around a rear rack, or safely attached to a part of the machine where it will not impair rider control.

Generally speaking, the larger the chain, the more of a problem it presents to a thief. The links should be made of hardened steel and it will pay you to establish whether or not they have been hardened all the way through. Some chains only have a thin veneer of hardened steel and so are comparatively easy to saw through with a hacksaw once the hardened layer has been penetrated.

Cable locks can be used in a similar fashion, but try to avoid securing just one part of the bike – the front wheel to a set of railings, for example – as this only protects the part you have secured, rather than the whole machine. If, for instance, a thief decides to steal your engine, all he has to do is to unbolt the front wheel and remove the rest of the bike.

Some of the U-locks on the market are extremely tough, but, because of their rigid shape, you will have to think carefully about how they can be employed to greatest effect. You may be able to lock the front wheel to a frame downtube, a fork leg to a railing, or the mainstand to a frame tube, so that the machine cannot be rolled off its stand.

Padlocks on their own can also be extremely effective. You may be able to padlock the main stand directly, for instance, or to secure it by using small padlocks fitted through drilled discs. This makes the machine impossible to

The simplest and cheapest form of bike security is a strong chain and padlock looped through a wheel *(above)*. However, since chains can be cut through, a U-lock *(below)* may be a safer investment. Their manufacturers claim that they are impossible to cut through.

ride, since the locks jam against the disc calipers.

One scooter locking device can also be adapted to suit most mainstands. One section of the device is bolted or welded to the mainstand, another one being attached to the frame. When the machine is pulled on to the mainstand, the holes in both of these sections align. Simply pass a padlock through them to lock the mainstand in place.

Other locking anti-theft devices include the locking twistgrip and locks designed to fit over spark plugs. The latter

The plug lock (right) is an ingenious device for immobilising your bike. (right). With the HT lead removed, a cap is fitted over the spark plug and locked with a key. This will prevent the bike being started, but, unfortunately, will not stop a thief wheeling the bike off to a garage to have the lock removed.

Electronic alarms are a great deterrent to a motor cycle thief, especially if the alarm itself is visible on the frame (left). If you are anxious not to spoil the look of your bike, alarms can be fitted out of sight, perhaps under the seat (below left).

prevent the HT cap from being attached, thus making it impossible to start the machine. Alternatively, you can insert a piece of rubber between the HT cap and spark plug contact. Replace the plug cap, so that everything looks normal. The rubber will stop the HT current reaching the plug.

Inserting a hidden switch to cut off the primary current to the coil is also a low cost and effective way of stopping joy riders from starting the machine.

Alarms
Fitting an alarm is the next step. The alarms on the market range quite considerably in price, some being self-contained while others have to be wired into the bike's wiring loom.

A typical self-contained type works off a dry cell battery and fits behind the rear number plate. If the machine is moved, a mercury switch triggers the alarm, whose sensitivity can be adjusted.

More sophisticated alarms must be powered by the bike's battery, so obviously are unsuitable for battery-less machines. Some can be used to protect accessories; for instance, they can be wired to trigger if a top box is opened, or the seat lifted.

Further precautions
In addition to using locks and fitting alarms, it is worthwhile marking the engine and frame. The marks will enable both to be identified easily if the machine is stolen and then recovered.

This is especially useful if your machine is stolen by a 'professional' thief. In such a case, standard practice is not only to grind off the manufacturer's engine and frame numbers and stamp in fresh ones, but also, in many cases, to dismantle the machine and sell the engine separately. If you engrave the registration number of the engine, say, out of sight on the lower crankcase, this can be an invaluable way of proving ownership even if the engine is all that is recovered. Mark the frame and wheels in similar fashion, keeping a note of exactly what the markings are and where you have made them.

Finding yourself stuck without transport, or recovering your machine after it has been joy ridden and vandalised, are both sickening experiences. Locking your bike securely and fitting an alarm should deter all but the most determined bike thief.

In addition, be careful where you park your machine. Try to keep it in sight, if at all possible. And, at night, try to park it in a well lit area.

Cleaning your bike

No bike or scooter owner worth his or her salt likes riding a dirty machine through choice. Strange though it may seem to the uninitiated, there is a great deal of pleasure and satisfaction to be derived from keeping a bike's bodywork in tip-top condition through through washing and polishing.

If you disbelieve this – or consider a regular wash and polish too time consuming – think of the following benefits:
*The first tell-tale signs of a potential problem are more easy to detect, if not masked by road dirt and grime. These include hairline fractures, which can affect the engine case, frame lugs and gussets, oil leaks, loose or missing screws and bolts and so on.
*The job itself is made easier if done on a regular basis, since dirt and grime are not given the time to harden on to surfaces, so becoming difficult to remove.
*Rusting is reduced because mud and road grime – both of which hold moisture and thus are prime causes of the problem – are removed before they have the chance to do their worst.
*If not washed off immediately, the salt spread on roads during the winter months will attack alloy components, such as engine cases, wheels and fork legs, severely.
*Keeping a machine smart helps to maintain its resale value.
*When routine maintenance has to be carried out, time will be saved because it should be possible to tackle the job swiftly, as there is much less risk of parts being contaminated by dirt.
*Deterioration of finishes, such as lacquer protection on engines and decorative graphics on tanks and sidepanels, can be spotted

quickly and attended to before it becomes serious.
*Keeping a bike looking smart helps keep pride of ownership at a high level.

Cleaning routines
You should set aside at least two hours a week to thoroughly clean down your bike. When salt is on the roads during winter months, the machine should be washed every night as well to get the salt off, as otherwise expensive alloy components will become severely pitted.

It is best to use a proprietary cleaning fluid containing a degreasant. Give the degreasant time to dissolve the grease and then wash it off with a sponge and brush soaked in warm soapy water. If you have a hose pipe, so much the better, since the spray can be used to dislodge stubborn grease spots and to reach parts that would otherwise be difficult to clean by hand.

Take care, however, not to get water into places you do not wish it to penetrate, such as the air box and carburettors. Also, take care not to wash away essential protective grease, such as that in the headstock, wheel bearings and swinging arm. This warning especially applies if you are using a pressure washer.

If, like most owners, you rely on cleaning your bike by hand, you should consider building up a selection of brushes to ensure that you do a really efficient job. A small brush with fairly stiff bristles is ideal for cleaning the engine and alloy wheels. A larger, stout brush with an angled handle will help you tackle the underside of the rear mudguard, while a toothbrush will be found useful for cleaning carburettors and between fins.

Chrome
Polish this with a good non-abrasive cleaner. To remove stubborn rust spots, rub down with aluminium kitchen foil.

You should work carefully and methodically, making sure that the cleaning implements you use are not likely to cause scratches. Use plenty of warm, soapy water – washing-up liquid is ideal – at the same time taking care not to wet the top of the battery, headlight lense and so on.

To carry out the job really thoroughly, remove the seat and side panels. These should then be washed separately.

After washing
Once the machine has been washed, it should be rinsed down with clean water and allowed to dry. Using a chamois leather will help to speed up the drying process. Wet the leather with clean water to soften it and then go over the bodywork, tackling this in the same order in which you tackled the original washing. Remember to rinse out

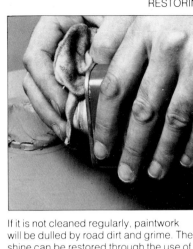 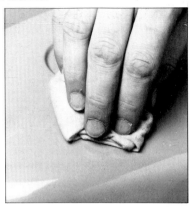

If it is not cleaned regularly, paintwork will be dulled by road dirt and grime. The shine can be restored through the use of a cutting fluid, such as T-cut. This is a mildly abrasive fluid that takes off the top layer of paint and grime, revealing the shiny surface underneath. Apply the fluid with a lint free cloth *(left)*. Rub it on to the paintwork gently, concentrating on small areas at a time. Allow the fluid to dry and then polish off *(right)*.

Engine

There are several engine cleaning fluids available that can be sprayed or brushed on. They loosen dirt and grime, which can then be cleaned off with water. If you use a hose, cover the ignition and coil to protect them from damp.

Paintwork

Wash paintwork regularly to stop the build up of dirt and grime. Use a car shampoo if you are not waxing, as this often contains a protective agent.

Polishing kit

Wax polishes are available in sprays or paste form. A spray makes application easier and quicker, but tends to cover areas that should be left unwaxed. A cutting fluid, such as T cut, can be used to remove ingrained grime and restore the shine.

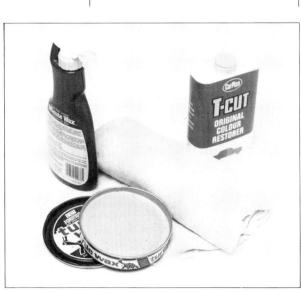

the leather frequently during the course of the job.

When the bike is dry, you can begin to polish it. The drying should take around half an hour or so. Do not attempt to polish wet bodywork, as the polish will smear. Check the instructions on the polish container. It is also best not to use most polishes in direct sunlight; if you do, the polish will dry too quickly and so cannot be spread evenly. So, whether you use a paste, cream or aerosol polish, follow the maker's instructions and apply the polish evenly with a clean rag, using a circular motion.

Allow the polish to dry for the period specified by its maker and then polish off the surface with a soft, lint-free, cloth. The final result will reflect the quality of the polish and the care with which it has been applied.

Use specific polishes for specific jobs – alloy polish for alloy components, wax for painted surfaces, chrome polish for chrome plate, plastic polish for fairing screens and so on. Always follow the instructions on the containers.

Dealing with chrome

Heavily rusted chrome cannot be restored satisfactorily, but you can eliminate surface pitting through the use of an abrasive chrome cleaner paste, or a paste cutting compound. Apply either of these to the chrome just as you would apply cutting compound to paintwork. Finish by applying a good quality chrome sealer to provide extra protection.

Anatomy of the motor cycle

Many bikers – whether newcomers to two-wheels or even experienced enthusiasts – have never come fully to terms with the mechanical anatomy of their machines. This chapter of You and Your Bike fills this gap. By taking the various component systems one at a time, it fits together the pieces of the jigsaw to form a complete whole. With its aid, you will understand not only how each system works, but how the various systems inter-relate, thus building up a clear picture of your bike's inner and outer workings. As a result, you will be able to maintain it at the peak of efficiency and cope confidently with problems if and when they occur.

Bike background
A century ago, in 1885, the ancestor of today's motor cycles made its maiden run. It was a timber framed bicycle with a half-horsepower single cylinder engine built by Gottlieb Daimler in Germany. The engine unit was a four-stroke Otto cycle design, so-called because it was invented by Nikolaus Otto, who had patented the design in 1876.

What is interesting is that, despite all subsequent developments and refinements, Daimler's pioneer would be immediately recognizeable as a motor cycle to the enthusiast today. As the wheels of motor cycling power into a second century, the term 'motor cycle' remains as descriptive as ever. Underneath their diverse and dazzling exteriors, the machines of the 1980s fundamentally remain cycles with motors.

Of course, progress over the decades has led to the development of machines of fantastic capabilities, insofar as of acceleration, cornering and braking are concerned. Engine design, too, has progressed with the development of the two-stroke engine, the original design of which is credited to England's Edward Butler, who patented a horizontal two-stroke twin in 1884.

The two-stroke came of age after the Second World War, when its simple design was refined to make it totally reliable. Because it is lightweight and easy to manufacture, it is now widely used on smaller machines. In the scooter world, for instance, Vespa and Lambretta of Italy relied on it entirely. In Japan, Suzuki introduced its first two-stroke in 1954 and marketed nothing else until the advent of its 750cc four cylinder four-stroke in 1976.

During the early 1970s, the two-stroke became the performance ideal. Now, however, legislation has forced designers to put more effort into the cleaner running four-stroke, which has regained its hold on the market as a result. Thanks to the Honda 50, it has also been the most popular moped engine for the past 30 years.

Enthusiasts still argue for hours as to which of the two systems is best. In this chapter, both types of engine are explained, while elsewhere in the book their comparative merits are assessed.

Understanding the engine
If you bear in mind the original Daimler motor cycle was nothing more than a bicycle with an engine attached to it, you will find it easy to understand the workings of a modern machine if you think of it in exactly the same way – irrespective of whether the engine is two-stroke, or four-stroke.

Put at its most simple, the driving force of the engine is provided by a piston, or pistons, which move up and down inside a bore within the crankcase. The thrust this produces is converted into circular motion by a crankshaft and the resultant energy is then passed to the gearbox via a clutch, which allows the energy to be engaged or disengaged at will.

The gears contained within the gearbox are used to alter what is technically termed the leverage ratio from crankshaft to rear wheel. Two examples will demonstrate why this needs to be altered to suit driving needs. You need a considerable leverage ratio – that is, a low gear – to get up a steep hill, for example. In low gear, the crankshaft spins many more times than the rear wheel. On the other hand, you select a high gear for cruising on a flat road. In this case, the engine – and hence the crankshaft – revolutions are reduced in relation to the number of times the rear wheel turns. Thus the leverage is less.

In most cases, the gearbox passes the energy on to the rear wheel via a chain. On some large touring machines, a drive shaft is used, while some mopeds are fitted with a rubber drive belt.

How does the energy required to drive the piston down the bore originate? It comes from a mixture of fuel and air – the mixture being created inside the carburettor – which is ignited within the space above the piston. The gases the ignition produces naturally expand, so driving the piston down the bore, the waste gases leaving the engine via the exhaust pipe.

Understanding the frame
Just as the term implies, the 'cycle' part of a motor cycle or scooter is very similar to that of a bicycle. All it basically consists of is two wheels attached to a frame The rear wheel is used to turn the energy provided by the engine into a forward driving motion, while the front wheel is allowed to pivot to provide the steering.

For comfort and safety, the wheels are fitted with spring suspension. This allows them to move up and down, so that they can cope with the bumps and undulations that are inevitably an integral part of any road surface. To slow the machine down, each wheel is provided with a brake.

The frame itself carries the engine, plus all the ancilliaries the machine requires. These can vary from bike to bike, but essential basics include the fuel tank, lighting, wiring, instruments and seat.

Frame design
Frames come in various designs, the most common being what is termed the full cradle frame. In this case, the frame tubing surrounds the engine – just as a picture frame surrounds a picture. On models fitted with small engines, the spine, or backbone, frame is popular, the

frame consisting of one main section. The frame is rather like the spine of a horse, the engine hanging below it.

In recent years, many manufacturers have adopted the 'integral' frame. In this design, the engine is a stressed member of the frame – thus eliminating the bottom rails of the cradle arrangement. Instead, the frame tubes in front and behind the engine are bolted to the engine casing. Thus, the design saves space and weight; however, it is not suitable if the engine produces marked vibration.

For this reason, all the manufacturers favouring this form of design plan frame and engine as one integral unit. The demands of the frame also influence engine design – in the case of the Ducati V-twin, for instance, the engine is designed from the start to ensure maximum inbuilt smoothness, while, on the Honda RS250 four-stroke single, balancers within the engine damp out vibrations. In this case, the Honda engineers have been able to keep the weight of the frame down to just 23lb (10.2kg) precisely because the stress produced by vibration has been reduced so substantially.

The engine

Motor cycles are fitted with one of two basic forms of engine – four- or two-stroke. The four-stroke system uses valves to control the movement of the fuel and air mixture on which combustion depends. The two-stroke engine relies on a number of holes, or ports, in the cylinder to provide passages for the mixture, the ports being opened and closed by the movement of the piston.

Whether four- or two-stroke, the most basic types of engine have a single cylinder and piston. Since a small cylinder size tends to be most efficient, larger capacity engines are made up of several cylinders joined together.

The four-stroke cycle

The four strokes (vertical movements of the piston) of this cycle are induction, compression, power and exhaust. The induction stroke begins with the piston moving down the cylinder to draw in the fuel and air mixture. The inlet valve is open at this stage. At the bottom of the stroke, the inlet valve closes and the piston returns back up the cylinder, compressing the mixture.

The spark plug then produces a spark to ignite the mixture, the resulting expansion forcing the piston down the cylinder. This is the power stroke. Due to the momentum of the crankshaft flywheel, the piston then moves back up the cylinder, the exhaust valve opens, the spent mixture is forced out and the sequence starts again.

The two-stroke cycle

In the two-stroke cycle, the stages in the four-stroke cycle are combined in two strokes. The system works by using the crankcase, the space underneath the cylinder, as an induction chamber. The cycle starts as the piston moves up the cylinder. The charge is drawn through the inlet port into the crankcase. At the same time, it is compressing the previous charge in the cylinder.

The ignition of this charge forces the piston down and, at the same time, the fresh charge is forced out of the crankcase up through a passage in the cylinder wall – the transfer port – into the cylinder. Here it helps expel the burnt charge from the previous ignition stroke through the exhaust port, which is now exposed.

Thus, the power and exhaust strokes are combined. The piston now starts its upward travel, sucking a fresh charge into the crankcase, compressing the charge in the cylinder ready for ignition, and the cycle continues.

This means that a two-stroke produces a power stroke twice as often as a four-stroke engine. However, this does not mean that the two-stroke produces twice as much power.

The cylinder head

In a four-stroke engine, the cylinder head carries the valves, the number depending on the design of the engine. Sometimes, the valves are doubled up. Thus, instead of just one inlet and one exhaust valve per cylinder, there are two of each.

This arrangement is referred to as a 'four-valve head'. It is more efficient, because the larger surface area allows more mixture into or out of the cylinder.

In many motorcycle engines,

the camshaft is also carried on top of the cylinder head, a design arrangement known as 'overhead cam' (OHC). The camshaft is basically a long shaft with eccentric lobes mounted on it. As the shaft rotates, the lobes bear directly on the valves, or on levers known as rocker arms, and force them open.

If the camshaft is mounted below the head, then a series of rods and rockers are needed to operate the valves. This type of engine is known as a 'push-rod' or 'overhead valve' (OHV) engine. The valves are closed automatically by strong springs fitted over the valve stems.

Two-stroke cylinder heads are much simpler. Basically a two-stroke head is just a piece of aluminium with the combustion chamber formed in it. The chamber's design – that is, its shape – is very important. There is often a deep section to carry the spark plug, with a shallow ring around the outside. This

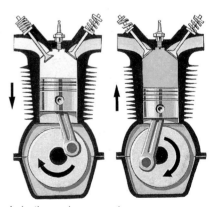

THE FOUR-STROKE CYCLE

Induction and compression
With the inlet valve open, the fuel/air mixture is drawn into the cylinder. *(left).* The inlet valve closes and the rising piston compresses the mixture into a small space at the top of the cylinder *(right).*

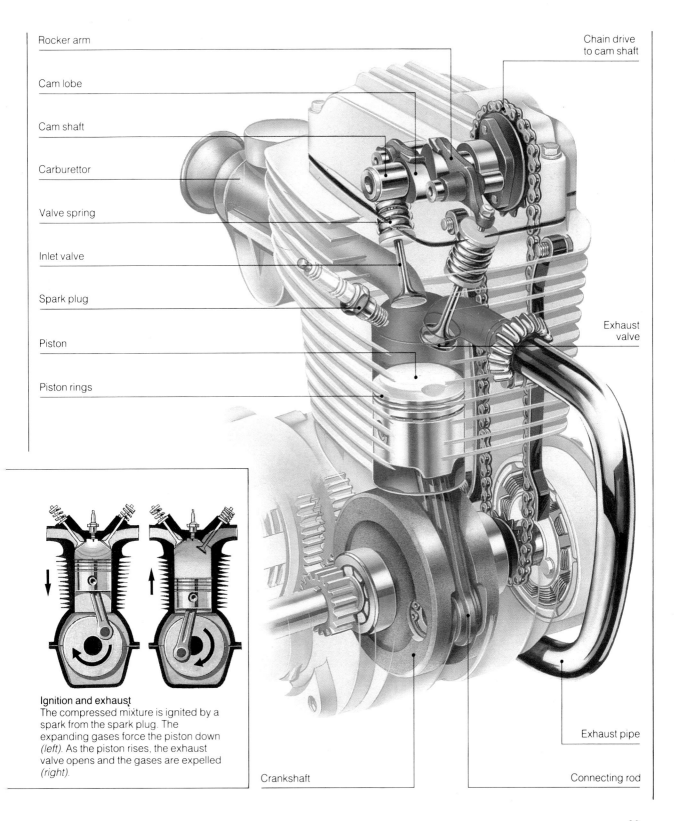

Rocker arm

Cam lobe

Cam shaft

Carburettor

Valve spring

Inlet valve

Spark plug

Piston

Piston rings

Chain drive
to cam shaft

Exhaust
valve

Exhaust pipe

Crankshaft

Connecting rod

Ignition and exhaust
The compressed mixture is ignited by a
spark from the spark plug. The
expanding gases force the piston down
(*left*). As the piston rises, the exhaust
valve opens and the gases are expelled
(*right*).

Engine/checklist

ring, or band of metal, is known as the 'squish band'. The idea is that, when the piston comes in close proximity to the head, the mixture trapped between piston and head is 'squished' into the main combustion chamber areas. This turbulence improves the combustion of the mixture.

One further design feature depends on whether the engine is water- or air-cooled. If the engine is water-cooled, the head and block have a jacket cast around them, allowing the coolant to flow around the hot spots. An air-cooled cylinder head has a series of fins, which provide a large surface area to dissipate engine heat to the atmosphere.

Cylinders and pistons

There are two types of motor cycle cylinder block. The basic block consists of a simple metal casting with a hole in it to take the piston, while an aluminium block has a suitable liner fitted in which the piston runs. In either case, it is important that the piston is a good fit; otherwise gas leakage would impair performance.

As the piston is often made from aluminium and the block is of cast iron – or the liner of steel – there must be an adequate working clearance between the two. As the engine heats up, the piston expands more than the surrounding metal, so, if the clearance were to be inadequate, the two components would seize. However, when the engine is cold, there is often excessive clearance between piston and block.

To seal the piston against the cylinder, the piston is fitted with sealing, cast iron, piston rings, which fit into grooves in the piston. The rings are squeezed against the cylinder wall to provide a seal against combustion pressure.

Lubrication

In principle, two-stroke lubrication is extremely simple. On older machines, the oil is mixed with the fuel and, as the fuel passes through the engine, it carries the lubricant with it. This method is known as 'total loss', since the lubricant is burnt and passed out with the fuel. Modern two-strokes are generally fitted with a system based around a separate oil pump and metering device, as opposed to mixing the oil in the fuel tank.

In a four-stroke engine, the oil is not burnt, but constantly pumped around the engine. There are two systems in general use. The commonest is called 'wet sump', in which the oil is carried in the crankcase. As the engine operates, the oil is splashed around freely inside the case, as well as being pumped around the engine. Because the drag on moving parts reduces power, many high-performance engines use an alternative system. In this 'dry sump' system, the oil is held in a separate tank and special oil drillings are used to squirt oil where it is needed. In all other respects, the two systems are the same.

THE TWO-STROKE CYCLE

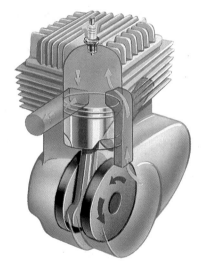 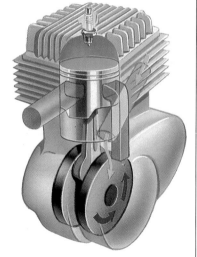

Ignition and exhaust
The compressed mixture is ignited and the expanding gases force the piston down. The exhaust port is exposed, allowing the burnt gases to escape. As the piston moves down, it exposes the transfer port and closes off the inlet port. The descending piston forces fresh mixture from the crankcase through the transfer port and into the cylinder, where it helps to expel the exhaust gases.

Induction and compression
As the piston moves up, the fuel/air mixture is drawn into the crankcase through the inlet port. At the same time, the mixture transferred into the cylinder on the previous stroke is compressed by the piston into a small space at the top of the cylinder.

CHECKLIST

Check the engine oil level. With wet sump lubricated machines, you can check this by looking through a small window set into the crankcase, or via a dip stick. With a dry sump machine, the level in the oil tank must be checked. In all cases, the machine should be standing on level ground, and, in the case of a crankcase window checking system, off the centre stand.

On two-stroke machines fitted with an automatic oiling system, the level of the tank must be topped up whenever necessary. A low level warning light (where provided) will operate when the oil in the tank is below the normal operating level.

Check for oil leaks around the underneath of the engine. On four-stroke machines, pay particular attention to the oil filter. Regular cleaning with de-greasant and clean water is recommended.

Check the tightness of the engine mounting bolts, especially on single cylinder machines, which are prone to heavy vibration, and motorcycles uses off-road.

Check the condition and setting of the spark plugs. These should be in good condition and gapped correctly.

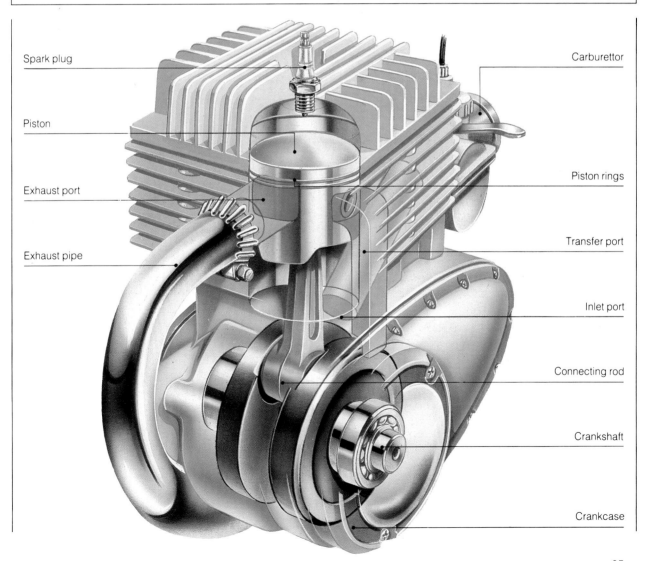

Spark plug

Piston

Exhaust port

Exhaust pipe

Carburettor

Piston rings

Transfer port

Inlet port

Connecting rod

Crankshaft

Crankcase

The electrical systems

You cannnot see, smell or hear electricity, but you certainly can feel it, as anyone who has received a high voltage shock form their bike's ignition system will tell you. This happens more frequently than should be the case, since, for many bike and scooter riders, the electrical system on which their machines rely is something of a mystery. There is absolutely no reason for this, however, since the basic principles of wiring, ignition and lighting are not difficult to follow and understand.

Electrical basics
The first idea to fix in your mind is that electricity has direction. This means that it 'flows' from one component to another along a wire.

There are two types of electric current. Electricity which is continually flowing in one direction is known as direct current, or DC. This is the type of electricity a bike's battery produces. If the electricity flows first one way and then the other, it is termed alternating current, or AC. This is the type of current that a bike's alternator produces.

From DC to AC
While an alternator will produce AC current for as long as it is being turned by the engine, a battery will produce DC current only while it retains an adequate charge. On most modern bikes, a fresh charge is provided by taking alternating current from the alternator and converting it to direct current through an electronic device known as a diode. The diode acts just like an electrical one-way valve. Its presence in a circuit means that electricity can flow in only one direction, which means that only

the pulses of the AC current travelling in the same direction get through to become direct current.

Current regulation
The alternator produces current while the engine is running; obviously, the faster the engine runs, the more current it produces. On most modern machines, this output is controlled by an electronic regulator, which ensures that the alternator does not produce more electricity than the electrical circuits require. On 12 volt machines, the regulator normally switches off the battery's charging flow if the alternator's output reaches above 14.5 volts; on a six volt machine, the corresponding figure is eight volts.

In addition, each circuit on your bike is further protected by a fuse or fuses. These are

deliberate weak links, designed to blow and so cut off the flow of current should the circuit become overloaded, protecting the wiring and the component it serves. Because these fuses come in different ratings, it is important to fit the fuse rated for the job to a specific circuit. An underrated fuse will blow, while

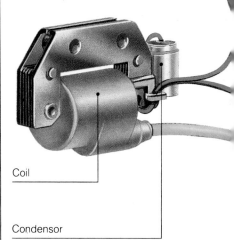

Coil

Condensor

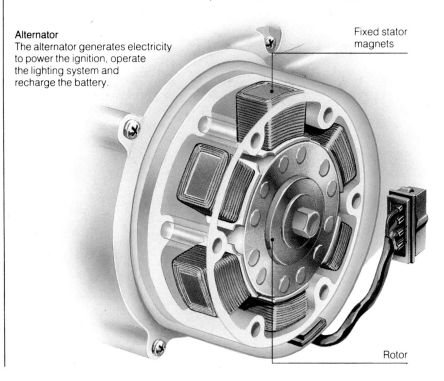

Alternator
The alternator generates electricity to power the ignition, operate the lighting system and recharge the battery.

Fixed stator magnets

Rotor

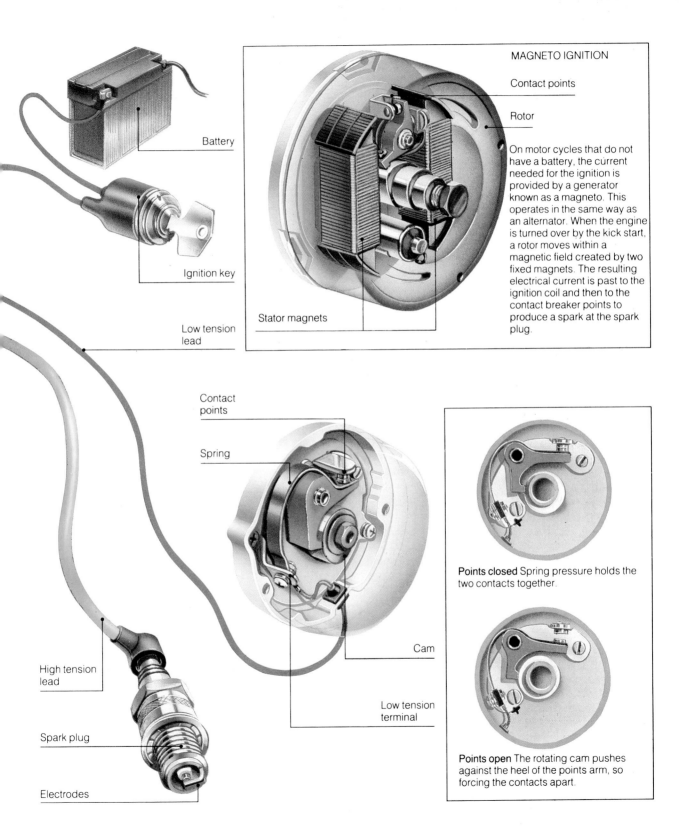

Battery

Ignition key

Low tension
lead

MAGNETO IGNITION

Contact points

Rotor

On motor cycles that do not
have a battery, the current
needed for the ignition is
provided by a generator
known as a magneto. This
operates in the same way as
an alternator. When the engine
is turned over by the kick start,
a rotor moves within a
magnetic field created by two
fixed magnets. The resulting
electrical current is past to the
ignition coil and then to the
contact breaker points to
produce a spark at the spark
plug.

Stator magnets

Contact
points

Spring

Cam

Low tension
terminal

High tension
lead

Spark plug

Electrodes

Points closed Spring pressure holds the
two contacts together.

Points open The rotating cam pushes
against the heel of the points arm, so
forcing the contacts apart.

Electrical systems/checklist

an overrated one may well allow the circuit to become overloaded.

'Earth return'

In order for electricity to flow, there must be an unbroken circuit – from one side of a battery to the other, for instance. This, however, is theory rather than practice, since it would mean running one wire to a component and another back to the other battery terminal.

To avoid this, a system known as 'earth return' is used. The negative battery terminal is wired to the frame of the machine. This is the earth terminal. This means that only one wire needs to be run to each component, the return circuit being completed by connecting the return cable to the frame, which acts as a return path for the current. The frame is large enough to handle all the return circuits your bike's electrical system requires.

The ignition system

Your bike's ignition system is designed to fulfill one simple purpose – to create an electric spark. The high voltage current created by the system jumps the gap between the electrodes of the spark plug, so creating the spark, which starts the fuel and air mixture burning. This current can be produced in either of two ways – one using a battery and the other not.

Battery ignition

The heart of this type of ignition system is the ignition coil. This is designed to take electrical energy from the battery and compress it into a high voltage spark of very short duration at the plug.

The low voltage, low tension (LT) current passes from the battery to the coil. This current is passed around a soft iron rod and a magnetic field is built up within the coil as a result. When the current is switched off, the magnetic field collapses and a burst of high voltage, high tension (HT), current is produced.

The device that controls the switching on and off of the low tension current is known as the contact breaker points. A cam, which rotates with the engine, forces two contacts apart at regular intervals. When the contacts are touching, the low tension current can flow through the circuit – when they are pushed open, the circuit is broken and the coil produces its burst of high tension current.

This current travels down the high tension lead attached to the coil and through the spark plug until it comes to the gap between the plug's centre electrode and earth electrode. It then jumps the gap to create a spark. This ignites the fuel and air mixture surrounding the spark plug.

The timing, as well as the creation of the spark, is all important, as the burst of energy the coil produces must arrive at the spark plug gap at exactly the right time. Again, the principle is simple.

The contact breaker points are set to open just before the piston reaches the top of its compression stroke. This is achieved mechanically by an engine-driven cam, which opens the points at the required moment in relation to piston travel.

The same principle applies when an electronic timing device is used in place of

mechanically operated points. The flow of current to the coil is regulated electronically, the timing of the spark usually being controlled by a magnetic pick-up, which is triggered as the engine crankshaft rotates.

Battery-less ignition

Some bikes are not fitted with batteries, usually for reasons of manufacturing cost. In such cases, the same principle of coil ignition is used, but the initial current has to come from another source – a small generator mounted on the engine. This is called a magneto.

In common with an alternator, the magneto only produces electricity when the engine is turning. You create this current physically by turning the engine over via the kickstart. As a result, the magneto supplies a small current direct to the ignition coil. From then on, the spark is produced exactly as before.

Advantages and disadvantages

The main disadvantage of battery-less ignition – or 'energy transfer' ignition, as it is sometimes termed – is that the magneto does not produce a strong current until the engine speed increases. When you turn the engine over to get it started, the current passed from the magneto through the coil is weak and hence the spark at the spark plug tends to be weaker. Once the engine has started, the spark improves.

With the battery system, on the other hand, the full ignition current flows from the moment you turn the ignition key – even if you are kicking the engine over to start it. Thus, bikes with battery ignition are generally easier to start than battery-less types. Once the engine is running, the two systems are equally efficient.

Bulbs and reflectors

Most motor cycles, especially lightweights, are fitted with separate headlight bulbs and reflectors. Some fast or large capacity machines have high

intensity quartz-halogen bulbs, while a few have car-type sealed beam headlight units.

In the case of the high intensity quartz-halogen bulb, inert gas under high pressure within a quartz 'envelope' provides superior lighting. The quartz must be kept free from dampness and grease and

should be handled by its metal base.

The sealed beam unit has the advantage of keeping out dirt, dust and moisture, protecting the reflector from deterioration. While the design is efficient, its size means that it can be inconvenient to carry a spare on your bike.

CHECKLIST

Check the battery before any other electrical component. Apart from ensuring that the connections are clean, the electrolyte level must be maintained. Most motor cycle batteries have a clear case, which allows you to visually check this clearly, but you may have to remove the battery from the machine.

Only use distilled water to top up the battery – this prevents internal corrosion – and do not over-fill the cells. When re-fitting the battery, make sure the breather pipe is re-fitted as well and that it is correctly routed and not kinked. If fitted, any sponge or padding around the battery must be replaced as well, since this protects the battery from machine vibration. Excessive vibration will shorten the battery's life severely.

Check the wiring loom at the connector block and plugs. Where one part of the loom is connected to another with a plug, or other connector, check that the joint is clean and dry. Wipe a little silicon grease – normal lubricating grease must not be used – into the connectors to keep out water.

Check the connecting cable at

the starter motor (if fitted). The joint must be clean and tight. Follow the run of the cable back to the starter solenoid and check these connections as well.

Check handlebar switches for security. Many of these can be taken apart, so that you can clean and check the contacts. Use a little silicon grease to seal around the switches when re-assembling them.

Check bulb connections and bulb holders. If water gets into a bulb holder, the bulb can rust into position, so causing a bad earth. When replacing bulbs, make sure that their protective covers are refitted correctly and that any waterproofing seals are intact.

Check the condition of the reflectors in headlights and rear lamps. Water can cause rusting and consequent loss of lighting performance.

Check the battery connections (if battery is fitted), making sure that they are tight and free from corrosion. If they are corroded, clean the terminals with a wire brush. Smear the terminals lightly with petroleum jelly to prevent further corrosion.

Check the coil's low and high tension connections. These should be clean and tight. A thin smear of silicon grease will help to waterproof them,

Check the spark plug connection at the high tension lead. This should fit tightly to the top of the plug. Examine the lead at the point where it enters the plug cap and check that it is secure. Smear lightly with silicon grease, as for the coil connections.

Check the spark plug – this involves removing it from the engine (you may need a special plug spanner to do this). Check the gap between the spark plug electrodes with a feeler gauge. Clean off any carbon build-up with a wire brush. Check the electrodes for signs of wear. If the edges are sharp, the plug is in good condition.

Check the faces of the contact breaker points (if fitted). These should not be pitted or look burned. Check the gap between the points at maximum lift by turning the engine over until they are fully opened and insert a feeler gauge (check handbook for correct size) between them. The gauge should be a snug, sliding fit. If not, adjust the gap

The transmission system

On nearly every motor cycle or scooter the transmission system consists of several drive stages before the drive finally reaches the rear wheel. The first of these, termed the primary drive, is where the drive to the rear wheel originates.

What happens is simple. The engine crankshaft rotates under the driving force of the piston

and the drive is transmitted through chains or gears to the input side of the gearbox – normally via the clutch. This is a sliding friction device, which allows the transmission to be engaged gradually, so the bike can move off smoothly from a standstill start.

Once the clutch is fully engaged, it becomes an integral

part of the the drive, passing it on to the gearbox input shaft. From there, the drive is transmitted through different sets of gears – there are various sets suited to dufferent speeds – to the gearbox output shaft and then to the gearbox sprocket.

On most machines, a chain is used as the final link between gearbox and rear wheel

Shaft drive
On some larger motor cycles, the final drive is transmitted to the rear wheel through a shaft. This gives smoother power transmission and is longer lasting than chain drive.

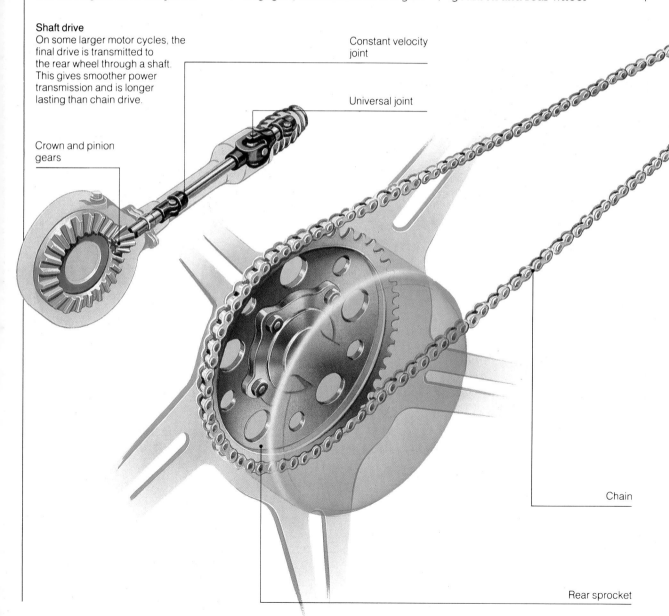

Constant velocity joint

Universal joint

Crown and pinion gears

Chain

Rear sprocket

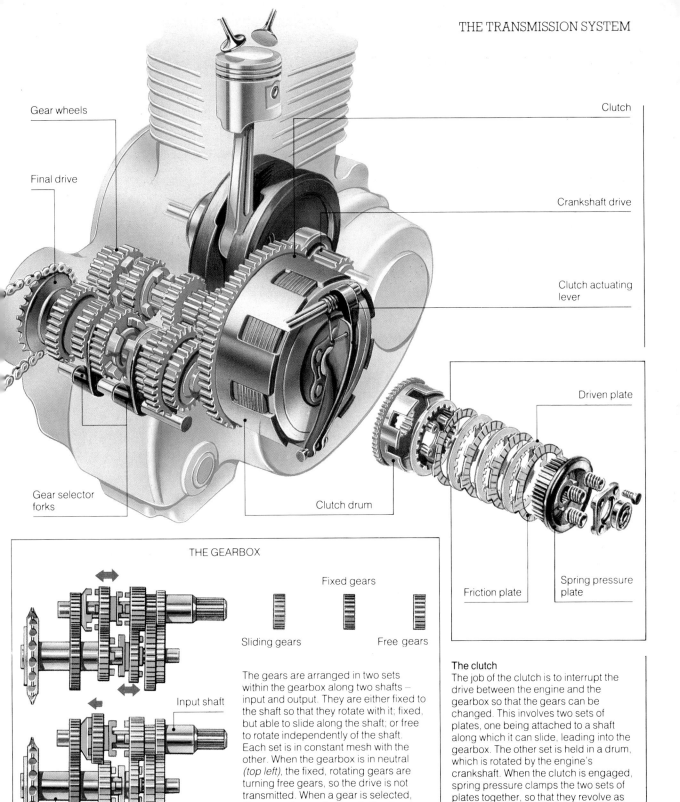

Gear wheels

Final drive

Clutch

Crankshaft drive

Clutch actuating lever

Gear selector forks

Clutch drum

Driven plate

Friction plate

Spring pressure plate

THE GEARBOX

Fixed gears

Sliding gears

Free gears

Input shaft

Output shaft

The gears are arranged in two sets within the gearbox along two shafts – input and output. They are either fixed to the shaft so that they rotate with it; fixed, but able to slide along the shaft; or free to rotate independently of the shaft. Each set is in constant mesh with the other. When the gearbox is in neutral *(top left)*, the fixed, rotating gears are turning free gears, so the drive is not transmitted. When a gear is selected, like second gear *(bottom left)*, a fixed, sliding gear is moved along the shaft to lock with a free spinning gear and so transmit the drive to the output shaft.

The clutch
The job of the clutch is to interrupt the drive between the engine and the gearbox so that the gears can be changed. This involves two sets of plates, one being attached to a shaft along which it can slide, leading into the gearbox. The other set is held in a drum, which is rotated by the engine's crankshaft. When the clutch is engaged, spring pressure clamps the two sets of plates together, so that they revolve as one and transmit the crankshaft's motion to the gearbox. When the pressure is released, the plates separate, leaving one set to rotate freely while the set on the gearbox shaft remains stationary.

Transmission system/checklist

sprocket. On some, however, a gear-driven shaft is used, with the gears at either end of the shaft at 90° to one another.

The clutch

The clutch can be best described as two drums, one rotating inside the other. The outer drum is connected to the primary drive and the inner drum to the gearbox input shaft. Between the two lie two sets of friction plates, known as clutch plates. One set of these is splined to the outer drum. This means they rotate with the drum, but can be moved laterally at the same time. The other is splined to the inner drum.

Both sets are arranged so that each alternate plate is fitted to the inner, then the outer, drums. One set is faced with a friction material, while the other set is of plain steel.

When the clutch is engaged the two sets of plates are clamped together by the spring pressure of the clutch cover plate. This forces the drums to rotate together as one unit. When the clutch spring pressure is released, however, the plates separate and the drums can rotate independently. You do this via a lever on the handlebar which pulls a cable that activates a push rod. This literally pushes the cover plate away from the clutch friction plates and releases the spring pressure.

When you pull the handlebar lever in, you release the clutch. This means that the engine can rotate and drive the clutch's outer drum via the primary gear, without the gearbox input shaft turning. When you release the lever you engage the gearbox input shaft.

This type of clutch system is common to the majority of bikes. On some small machines, however, an automatic clutch may be used. Designs vary, but many models rely on a centrifugal type. Shoes lined with friction material are thrown outwards by centrifugal force as the engine revs rise and engage with the inner surface of a circular drum to transmit the engine power.

The gearbox

Basically, the common term 'changing gear' is misleading as far as motor cycle gearboxes are concerned, since you do not physically change from one gear into another.

The gearbox is made up of two shafts – input and output – lying alongside each other. The input shaft carries a set of gear wheels – some fixed to the shaft and constantly driven, some that are constantly driven but can slide along the shaft and some that can rotate independently of the shaft. The output shaft carries a matching set of gears, arranged in a similar fashion.

To select a gear, you operate a foot lever. This works a selector mechanism, which will engage a sliding gear on the input shaft to a free spinning gear. It does this by pushing the two together, so that the lobes on the sides of both the gears lock.

The free spinning gear is in what is termed constant mesh with a fixed gear on the output shaft. Now that it is locked to a gear locked to and being driven by the input shaft, the rotation is transmitted to the output shaft.

Changing gear

To change gear, you simply operate the gear lever with the clutch disengaged. The selector mechanism then disconnects the previously engaged gear from the drive and locks another pair of gears to the spinning output shaft. The drive is then passed to the gearbox (drive) sprocket, which is usually mounted on the end of the output shaft.

The whole purpose of the gear change mechanism is to convert the up-and-down motion of the rider's foot into a circular motion of the selector drum. This, in turn, moves selector forks, which slide the moving gears along the splined shafts to pass the drive from input to output shafts. All bike gearboxes work on this principle, though some have an intermediate gear shaft on the primary drive, while others have an intermediate shaft on the output side of the gearbox.

Types of primary drive

In the primary drive, the general terms chain drive and gear drive cover a multitude of different types of transmission. The final drive chain is always a single row, but a primary chain may have two, or even three rows.

Triplex (three row) chains used to be very common on British motor cycles. On Japanese machines, the use of a hybrid chain, known as a 'Hy-vo' chain, is quite common. This is made up of flat plates, the chain running over a form of gear wheel rather than over a sprocket. Because the driving force is spread over a relatively large area, these chains have a long life.

Final drive

On most bikes, the final drive between gearbox and rear wheel is by chain. A chain is a simple and cheap way of transferring power to the rear wheel and, as it is set up with a certain amount of slack, can accommodate the changes in distance between the gearbox drive sprocket and the rear wheel sprocket. This occurs as the rear wheel moves up and down on its suspension travel, whereas the gearbox does not move in relation to it.

For this reason correct chain tension, correct sprocket alignment and thorough lubrication are essential to chain life. For a chain to function efficiently, it must run with a pre-determined amount of slack along its length. This means that you must be able to adjust the chain to compensate for wear. The simplest method allows you to move one of the sprockets in relation to the other one by moving the rear wheel further away from the engine.

A second system involves what is termed a 'slipper' tensioner, which the chain passes over when running from one sprocket to the next. This tensioner is always fitted to the non-driving side of the chain's run. It can be spring loaded, or moved manually by a lockable adjuster on a threaded screw.

On some larger bikes, the final drive is achieved with a drive shaft. The drive from the gearbox is turned through 90°, transmitted along the shaft and turned back 90° at the rear wheel.

The advantages of shaft drives are twofold. They give longer final drive life and smoother running than chain equivalents, but they are more expensive to produce. To accomodate the up and down movement of the rear wheel, the shaft has to have two universal joints built into it, which allow the shaft to transmit its rotation through an angle, as well

as joints, known as constant velocity joints (CVs), which allow the shaft to transmit its drive as it is shortened or lengthened by the movement of the rear wheel. At these joints, the shaft is split and a splined collar fits over either end. The collar allows the ends of the shaft to move in and out, while still rotating.

Many mopeds and small scooters use V-belts, similar to a car fan belt, to transmit the drive. These belts are cheap to produce, silent in operation and do not require lubrication. However, they would slip if they were used with more powerful engines.

Gear sets

Only two types of gear set are commonly used on motor cycles. The first type, normally used in the gearbox, is the straight cut gear. As the name suggests, this type of gear has a straight cut tooth on the gearwheel. This form of drive is efficient, but it is noisy.

Helical cut gear sets – a helical gear set has its teeth cut at an angle – are often used to transmit the primary drive. This type of gear gives gradual engagement and reduces drive noise, but it does create what are technically termed side load forces, which absorb more engine power than straight cut gears.

Lubrication

Most gear sets are lubricated with normal engine oil, but the gear set which takes the final drive through its 90° turn needs a special high pressure gear oil. This is because there is a great deal of pressure between the teeth of the gear set. EP (extreme pressure) or 'Hypoid' oil should be used.

CHECKLIST

Check that the tension of the final drive chain is correct. This may have to be done with the machine off the centre stand and the suspension partly compressed.

Check that the final drive chain is adequately lubricated. Check in your handbook to see whether a special lubricant is needed.

Check the final drive chain sprocket for wear. A visual check should not reveal signs of 'hooking' in the direction of wheel rotation.

Check primary chain adjustment and the lubricant level in the chaincase.

Check clutch operation and settings. A certain amount of free-play must be maintained at the handlebar lever. Check your handbook for the setting.

Check the gearbox oil level. When you do this, make sure that the machine is standing on level ground, or follow the recommendations in your handbook. Only top up with the recommended oil.

Check the oil levels in the final drive gearbox on shaft-drive machines. Special EP or 'Hypoid' oils may be needed for topping up – check your handbook.

The cooling system

When a motor cycle or scooter engine burns fuel, a great deal of heat is produced by the expanding gases as they exert pressure on the piston to force it downward. However, not all of this heat is harnessed to propel the vehicle. A large part of it disappears down the exhaust pipe, but a significant amount is absorbed by the cylinder head, the cylinder barrel and the piston.

In order to prevent these components overheating, which will lead to the engine seizing as an end result, some form of cooling system is essential. Basically, there are two types of system – air cooled and liquid cooled.

Air cooling

All conventional modern motor cycles are air cooled to some extent, since all of them have their engines positioned in the open, between the wheels. This means that the passing air stream will help to dispose of surplus engine heat, regardless of whether the engine is air cooled or liquid cooled.

An air-cooled engine can easily be identified by the large cooling fins around the cylinder barrel, or barrels and cylinder head. The fins effectively enlarge the surface area of the engine, allowing a greater volume of air to absorb the heat. They are normally cast as part of the component, the heat inside the engine being conducted along them. Some larger, more powerful bikes have fins cast on the underside of the crankcase to help to dispel the heat from the engine oil.

Though the surface area of the fins is large enough to cool the engine even when the bike is stationary, the system is at its most efficient when the bike is in motion. The faster the bike travels, the greater the cooling effect of the air. This makes such systems very efficient, especially during high speed runs in the heat of high summer.

Some scooters are fitted with enclosed air-cooled engines. In such cases, a fan may be fitted to blow the cooling air over the engine, while ducting may also be used to channel the air to places it otherwise could not reach. The drawback here is that some engine power is required to drive the fan.

Liquid cooling

Liquid-cooled systems are much more efficient than air-cooled ones. For a start, the engine designer can arrange to have a considerable amount of liquid in the areas that need cooling the most – around the exhaust port, for instance – and very little in cooler areas, such as the inlet port. A liquid coolant has one further advantage. It can be maintained at a fairly constant temperature – one at which the engine performs most efficiently. This means that the engine temperature is similarly maintained near that constant, irrespective of speed, load or air temperature. The system depends on the coolant 'jacket' around the cylinder barrel and cylinder head, which, through its

AIR COOLED ENGINE

The majority of motor cycles are fitted with air cooled engines. This means that the heat created by the combustion of the fuel/air mixture and the friction of all the moving parts, is dissipated into the surrounding air. The amount of heat lost depends on how much surface area of metal is in contact with the airflow. This is increased by casting metal fins into the cylinder block and cylinder head, the parts of the engine subject to the most heat. On some large motor cycles, the oil sump is also 'finned' to dissipate heat.

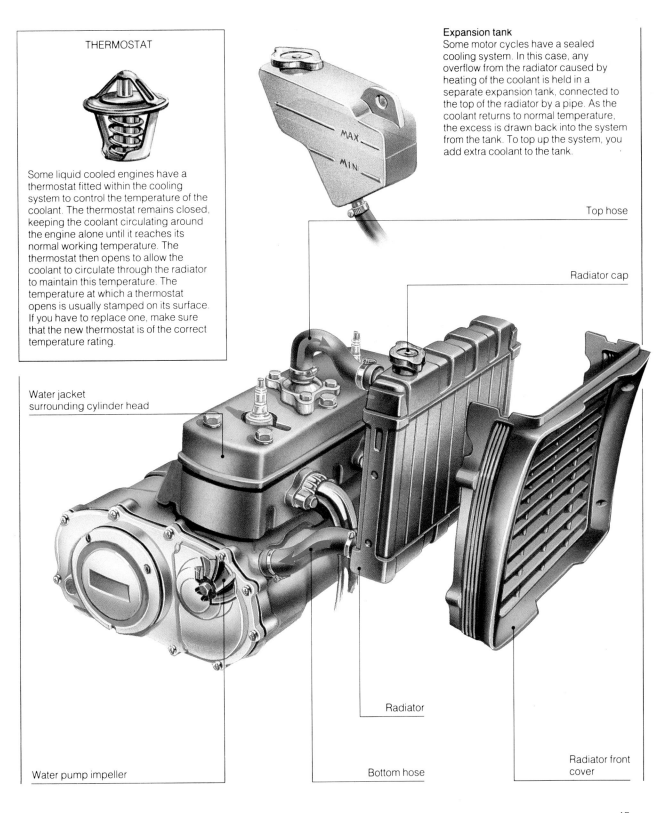

THERMOSTAT

Some liquid cooled engines have a thermostat fitted within the cooling system to control the temperature of the coolant. The thermostat remains closed, keeping the coolant circulating around the engine alone until it reaches its normal working temperature. The thermostat then opens to allow the coolant to circulate through the radiator to maintain this temperature. The temperature at which a thermostat opens is usually stamped on its surface. If you have to replace one, make sure that the new thermostat is of the correct temperature rating.

Expansion tank
Some motor cycles have a sealed cooling system. In this case, any overflow from the radiator caused by heating of the coolant is held in a separate expansion tank, connected to the top of the radiator by a pipe. As the coolant returns to normal temperature, the excess is drawn back into the system from the tank. To top up the system, you add extra coolant to the tank.

MAX

MIN

Top hose

Radiator cap

Water jacket
surrounding cylinder head

Radiator

Water pump impeller

Bottom hose

Radiator front
cover

Cooling system/checklist

channels, directs coolant past all the engine's hot spots. The coolant flows from the engine to the bike's radiator through rubber hoses, whose flexibility absorbs the engine's vibration and stops it reaching the rigidly mounted radiator. The constant vibration that the hoses endure will eventually have its effect and the rubber will crack or split.

The coolant is normally forced around the engine and through the radiator by an engine driven pump. The hot coolant enters the radiator at the top and from there, it drains through to the bottom, being cooled by the air flow through the radiator as it does so, and then is fed back to the engine again.

The radiator itself is made up of two separate coolant reservoirs, joined together by a series of fine bored tubes. These tubes incorporate a series of very fine fins, which, like the fins on an air cooled engine, transfer the heat from the coolant into the air stream passing through the radiator. From this, you can see that even a liquid-cooled engine depends on air-cooling to a great extent. It only uses the liquid to collect the heat initially; the heat then passes into the surrounding air as in the air cooled system.

The top tank of the radiator has a removable cap that allows extra coolant to be added. This cap, however, serves a duel purpose. It has a spring-loaded valve at its base that seals the neck of the filler tube. As the coolant heats up, its pressure increases and the valve allows that pressure to be maintained. Water, at atmospheric pressure boils at 212°F (100°C), but with the pressure raised, it boils at a higher temperature. This allows the engine to run efficiently even at a high temperature.

For example, the coolant of Honda liquid-cooled engines is allowed to build up to 13psi (0.9kg-cm) pressure. This allows the coolant to reach 260°F, (127°C) before boiling. For this reason, the radiator cap of any bike should never be removed when the engine is hot. You should always allow it to cool for a moment. Then wrap a rag around the cap and release it slowly, allowing the pressure to escape before removing the cap fully. Also, if you ever have to replace the filler cap, ensure that the new one is of the correct pressure rating.

Another refinement found on some liquid-cooled motor cycles is an electric cooling fan. When the bike is stationary, or moving slowly, the air passing over the radiator may be insufficient for adequate cooling. In this case, the fan comes on automatically – usually between 194°F and 212°F (90°C and 100°C) – to pull more air through the radiator. When the temperature is reduced, the fan cuts out.

A refinement of this system involves the fitting of a separate expansion, or 'header', tank, which carries a reserve of coolant. As the coolant expands and cools down, it is allowed to overflow into the expansion tank before it is returned to the radiator. In this case, the radiator does not have a removeable cap; the coolant is topped up in the expansion tank. However, the same safety rule applies – do not remove the expansion tank's cap until the bike's engine has cooled down.

Thermostats
On some bikes, a special valve, called a thermostat, is fitted in the coolant passage. Its job is to keep the flow of coolant circulating around the engine until the engine has reached optimum operating temperature. The thermostat then opens automatically to allow the coolant to flow through the radiator and so maintain the correct temperature. The device is particularly useful during the winter, since it prevents over-cooling.

A thermosat operates by means of a rubber diaphragm, which has a rod attached to it. The rod's base is surrounded by wax, held in a sealed container. As the surrounding coolant heats up, the wax gradually melts and expands. The expansion pushes the rod up to open the diaphragm, so allowing the coolant to flow.

The temperature at which the thermostat opens to allow coolant to enter the radiator is carefully pre-determined. If your thermostat fails, you must ensure that the replacement is of the correct temperature rating. Otherwise it may open too soon or too late – if at all – with the risk of engine damage as the result.

On bikes not fitted with a thermostat, the total volume of coolant is carefully calculated so that the optimum temperature is reached through normal operation.

The problem of corrosion
Corrosion is the chief problem that all liquid-cooled systems face. Water tends to rust steel and causes alloys to corrode. For this reason, a corrosion inhibitor should be added to the water.

Water can also freeze during the winter months. As the water freezes, it expands and can burst hoses or at worst, crack the metal of the water jacket and another additive is needed to prevent this.

Normally the two additives are combined in the form of an anti-freeze mixture. Check your handbook for the recommended mix between this and water, but a safe average is 50% water to 50% of anti-freeze.

Most modern anti-freeze mixtures will remain effective for more than one year. However, if the coolant is topped up regularly, the mixture will become diluted and lose some of its effectiveness as a result. Check its strength from time to time to prevent this.

Oil cooling

While the oil's main job inside a four-stroke engine is to act as a lubricant, it also acts as a coolant, since it can reach the hottest parts of the engine directly. As it passes around the engine, the oil absorbs heat and so helps cool the engine from the inside.

For this reason, some motor cycles are fitted with a powerful oil cooler. This works in exactly the same way as a radiator, the only difference being that oil – not coolant – is pumped through it. In the majority of cases, however, the oil capacity of the machine is purpose-planned to be sufficient to cope with these demands without the refinement of an oil cooler.

Cooling modifications

If the motor cycle bodywork is modified from standard in any way, the extra demands such changes may impose on the cooling system must also be taken into account. For example, a fairing should not be allowed to restrict the air flow to the cylinder fins on an air-cooled

engine, or to the radiator on a liquid-cooled machine.

If a liquid-cooled bike has a fairing as a standard fitting, you will find that the fairing often incorporates special air scoops, which direct cooling air into the radiator. Such a fairing should not be removed, or modified, as any modification may disturb the bike's aerodynamics and reduce the radiator's air flow.

CHECKLIST

Check that road dirt or mud is not blocking the gaps between the cooling fins on air-cooled engines. Clean any dirt or mud out with a scraper.

Check that the radiator fins on a liquid-cooled engine are not blocked by road dirt or mud. Clean out by washing with a hose pipe and water.

Check the level of the liquid in the cooling system. Depending on your machine, you should check this at the radiator, or at an expansion tank. Consult the handbook.

Check that the coolant has sufficient anti-freeze content. This can be done by using an inexpensive anti-freeze tester, or a hydrometer.

Check the condition of the seals on the radiator or expansion tank sealing caps. If they are perished, fit replacements.

Check the condition and security of the cooling hoses connecting the engine to the radiator and from the engine to the pump (if fitted). If they are worn or perished, replace them,

Check around the engine and radiator area for signs of leakage. Leaks can often be pin-pointed by the corrosion found at their source.

Check that the engine oil level is correct on four-stroke engines.

The fuel system

The fuel system provides the charge – a mixture of fuel and air – burnt in the engine's cylinder to produce the driving force for the cylinder's piston.

In order to burn, the fuel must first be mixed with air in the right proportion. In normal conditions, this is usually in a ratio of 15 parts of air to one part of fuel. The component that does the mixing is known as the carburettor.

The fuel feed

Fuel is fed into the carburettor from the fuel tank, usually by gravity feed since the tank is nearly always mounted above the engine. In cases where the tank is below the level of the carburettor, a fuel pump is required.

On conventional gravity feed tanks, a tap can be turned off to stop the flow of fuel when the machine is not in use. The tap is often designed so that, when it is switched to the 'on' position, it will allow the tank to drain down only to a certain level. At this point the petrol ceases to flow. You have to physically move the tap again to the 'reserve' position in order for the tank to drain to its bottom.

The carburettor

Since it is not truly possible to mix petrol and air, the carburettor turns the petrol into a fine spray, and mixes this with the air that entering the engine. The way in which a spray aerosol works is a good analogy.

The main section of the carburettor consists of a tube open to the air at one end and connected to the engine inlet port at the other. The tube narrows in the middle – this narrowing is known as the 'venturi'. Air drawn through the

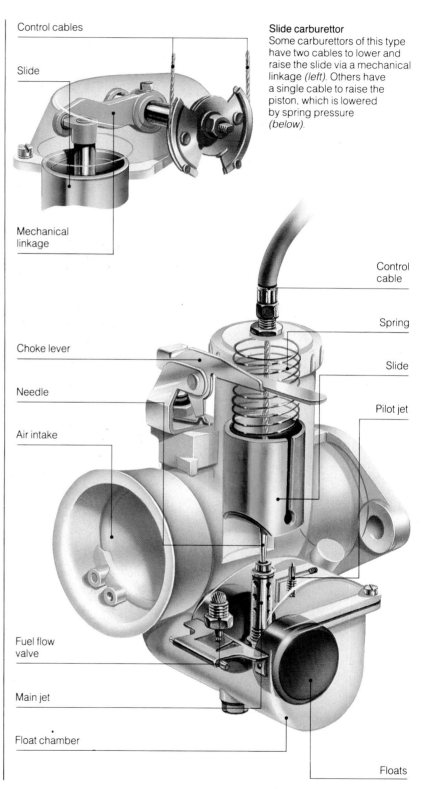

Control cables

Slide

Mechanical linkage

Slide carburettor
Some carburettors of this type have two cables to lower and raise the slide via a mechanical linkage *(left)*. Others have a single cable to raise the piston, which is lowered by spring pressure *(below)*.

Choke lever

Needle

Air intake

Fuel flow valve

Main jet

Float chamber

Control cable

Spring

Slide

Pilot jet

Floats

Constant vacuum carburettor

In this type of carburettor, the movement of the needle is controlled by the amount of air being drawn into the engine. Air enters a chamber, which is sealed by a flexible diaphragm, and the resulting pressure pushes the piston up. Spring pressure forces the piston down when the air pressure decreases.

Instead of a rubber diaphragm, some carburettors have a collar cast around the cylinder holding the needle. This forms the seal necessary for the air pressure to raise the needle *(left)*.

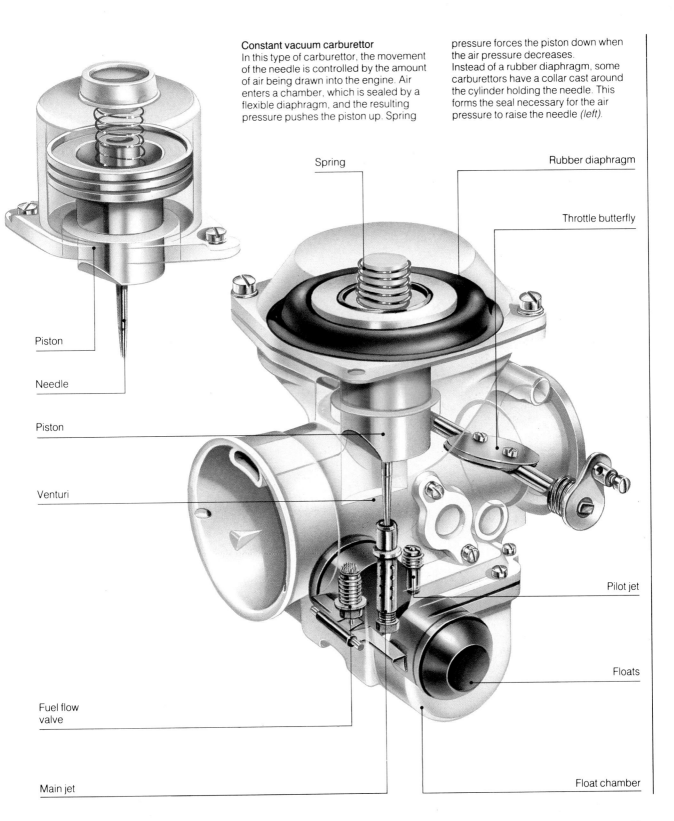

Piston

Needle

Piston

Venturi

Fuel flow valve

Main jet

Spring

Rubber diaphragm

Throttle butterfly

Pilot jet

Floats

Float chamber

Fuel system/checklist

tube by the engine is forced to speed up as it passes through the venturi. As a result, its pressure is lowered. This low pressure area effectively 'sucks up' the fuel from a chamber in the base of the carburettor. As the fuel enters the venturi, it forms a spray that mixes with the passing air to create a mist.

A correct mixture of air and fuel is maintained for the most part since the more air that passes, the greater the low pressure area and the more fuel that is drawn up. The level is maintained in the chamber, just below the outlet point, by a float. This operates a valve that can shut off the supply of petrol coming into the carburettor. As the chamber fills with fuel, the float rises and pushes the valve closed – as the fuel is used up, the float lowers itself and the valve opens.

Power control

As the amount of fuel/air mixture entering the engine governs the speed at which it runs, the carburettor must be regulated. This is the job of the handlebar twist grip. The twist grip is linked to the carburettor by a cable. Depending on the type of carburettor fitted to the bike, the cable acts directly, or indirectly, on the mechanism that controls the amount of fuel entering the carburettor venturi.

Basically, this mechanism operates as follows. Fuel from the float chamber is drawn up through the carburettor's main jet. The size of the jet is calculated to allow sufficient fuel to pass through it to run the engine at full power.

A tapered needle is fitted into the jet – this can be raised and lowered to control the flow. At the needle's lowest point, the jet is closed off. As the needle is raised, its taper effectively increases the size of the hole in the jet, so allowing more fuel to pass through it.

Types of carburettor

Most bikes are fitted with a carburettor or carburettors of one of two types. The simplest type in common use is the so-called slide carburettor.

In this case, the action of the tapered needle moving up and down in the main jet is controlled by the twist grip via a mechanical linkage and cable. As the grip is rotated, a cylindrical slide, to which the needle is attached, is raised by the mechanical action.

Most modern bikes, however, are fitted with a 'constant vacuum' (CV) carburettor. In this case, the raising and lowering of the needle is controlled by air pressure in a chamber below the piston that holds the needle. The operation of the twist grip rotates a circular plate, known as the throttle butterfly, which covers the engine intake end of the venturi.

As the throttle is opened, the butterfly rotates to allow more of the fuel/air mixture to enter the engine. As the engine speed increases, the suction from the piston increases the air flow – it is this pressure that is channelled to the chamber below the needle to raise it. Spring pressure pushes the piston down when the butterfly closes.

Other jets

Whereas the main jet and needle control the fuel/air mixture during most of the throttle commands, both types of carburettor have auxiliary jets,

called pilot jets, to assist the fuel flow when the engine is at tickover or at small throttle openings.

These jets are connected with small outlets in the venturi and supply fuel at low air speeds. Once the throttle is a quarter opened, the main jet takes over.

The choke

The choke that you operate for cold starting has only one purpose – to alter the balance of the mixture by adding more fuel to it. Whereas normal running requires a mixture of about 15 parts of air to one part of fuel, cold starting needs a mixture of about eight parts air to one part fuel. This is necessary because much of the fuel condenses along the cold inlet passage and so does not reach the combustion chamber.

There are two ways to enrich the mixture. Either the amount of fuel can be increased, or the amount of air decreased. The simplest method involves the use of a second flap – similar to the throttle butterfly, but placed at the intake side of the venturi – to reduce the amount of air entering the venturi.

This choke flap normally has a simple lever or a cable connected to it. Fully closing the flap would obviously stop all air entering the engine, so the flap often has a spring loaded door which allows air to pass through it as required.

An alternative to restricting the air supply is to build a separate cold start system into the carburettor body. This involves an enriching cold start jet, which is almost like a miniature carburettor. This jet supplies fuel to the main body of the carburettor, independent of the main operating system, and so adds to any fuel being drawn from the main jet system.

Fuel injection

Fuel injection has been made possible by modern electronics. In this system, a meter checks air flow to the engine and sends a signal to an injector, a small jet fitted directly to the inlet pipe of the cylinder. The injector squirts precisely the right amount of fuel into the air stream. No float system or venturi is needed as fuel injection depends on the accuracy of the air flow metering, fuel measurement and the pressure at the injector to atomise the fuel into the air stream.

Fuel injection, though more efficient than the conventional carburettor, is a more expensive system to manufacture. Hence it is fitted to few machines.

Air filters

One important part of the fuel system that is often overlooked is the air filter. If air was allowed to enter the carburettor and engine directly from the atmosphere, the particles of dust and dirt that would be drawn in with it would eventually clog the small orifices of the jets and increase the wear on the component parts of the carburettor and engine. For this reason, a filter is placed over the air intake of the carburettor.

Your air filter is usually made of corrugated paper, or sometimes of foam sponge. Though it will allow air to pass through it, it will trap any small particles the air is carrying. It is important to change the air filter regularly, because it will restrict the air flow as it traps more and more dirt and will in effect put the fuel/air mixture out of ratio.

CHECKLIST

Check the fuel filter(s) in the supply line from the tank to the carburettor. Usually a filter is fitted to the inlet side of the petrol tap inside the fuel tank.

Check that no debris has built up in the float chamber of the carburettor where it may be drawn up to block the jets. On many machines this can be done by unlocking the float chamber drain cock and allowing the petrol to drain. This should be done with the petrol supply turned off.

Check that the float level is correct. This involves removing the carburettor from the engine. A special measuring tool may also be required. Check your handbook for correct procedure.

Check the operation of the carburettor controls. Ensure the throttle cable has a smooth run and is lubricated. The throttle stop screw should be adjusted to give the recommended engine idle speed.

Check that the idle mixture screw is positioned for optimum idling mixture. On engines with more than one carburettor this may only mean ensuring that each screw is a set number of turns out from the fully closed position.

Check the operation of the choke flap (if fitted). It must be returning to the fully off position (at 90° to the air intake orifice). Operating links should be lubricated.

Check that the air filter is clean and not clogged with dirt. If so, it should be cleaned or replaced.

Brakes

Motor cycles and scooters can be fitted with either or both of two braking systems. These are disc brakes and drums. Both work on the same principle – through friction, they convert the energy of movement into heat, which is then lost to the motor cycle's airstream. It is the system's job to apply and control this friction.

Disc brakes

The majority of modern motor cycles are fitted with disc brakes, especially on the front wheel. They are more efficient than the conventional drum brake for several reasons. They are better at transferring heat into the airstream, simpler to construct and do not require mechanical adjustment to compensate for the inevitable wearing down of the friction material. As the pads wear down, the pistons simply move closer to the disc to take up the wear automatically, though the brake fluid may need topping up to compensate for this.

Disc brakes operate in an extremely simple way. The easiest way of stopping a spinning disc is to press the edge between your fingers. This is the basis of the disc system. Two pads, covered with friction material and held in a caliper grip a metal disc bolted to the wheel hub and thus stop the wheel turning.

Hydraulic or mechanical pressure forces a piston against the pads and they press against the disc. The greater the pressure, the more friction – and therefore the more braking force – generated.

The design and operation of the caliper varies from one machine to the other, the disc

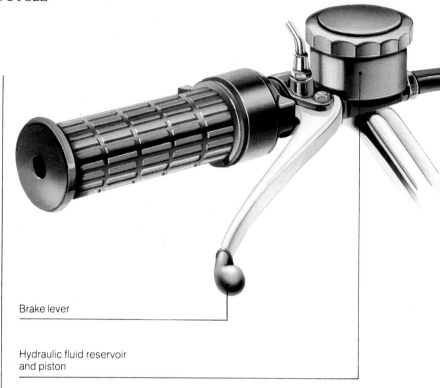

Brake lever

Hydraulic fluid reservoir and piston

itself being of standard design. A 'twin piston caliper', for instance, has two pistons, one on either side of the disc.

The 'four piston caliper' is a refinement of this. In this case, there are two pistons either side of the disc, each pair operating against a larger friction pad. This arrangement means that a larger area of friction material can be used without increasing the overall diameter of the disc.

However, the caliper system most commonly found on motor cycles is the 'single piston', or 'sliding caliper', unit. Here, the caliper is fitted in a sliding cage, which is bolted rigidly to the machine. A friction pad is fixed to one side of the caliper, the second pad being fitted against a single moving piston on the other side of the caliper.

As the piston moves out, the pad comes into contact with the disc. Further piston movement causes the caliper to slide

TWIN PISTON CALIPER

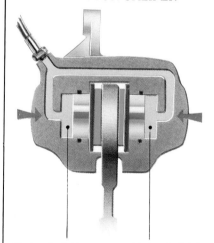

Hydraulic fluid   Hydraulic fluid

The twin piston caliper system (*above left*) depends on the action of two pistons, one on each side of the brake disc, which are moved by hydraulic pressure to apply equal force to the brake pads. The friction material on the pads applies a braking force to the disc. In the sliding caliper system (*above*

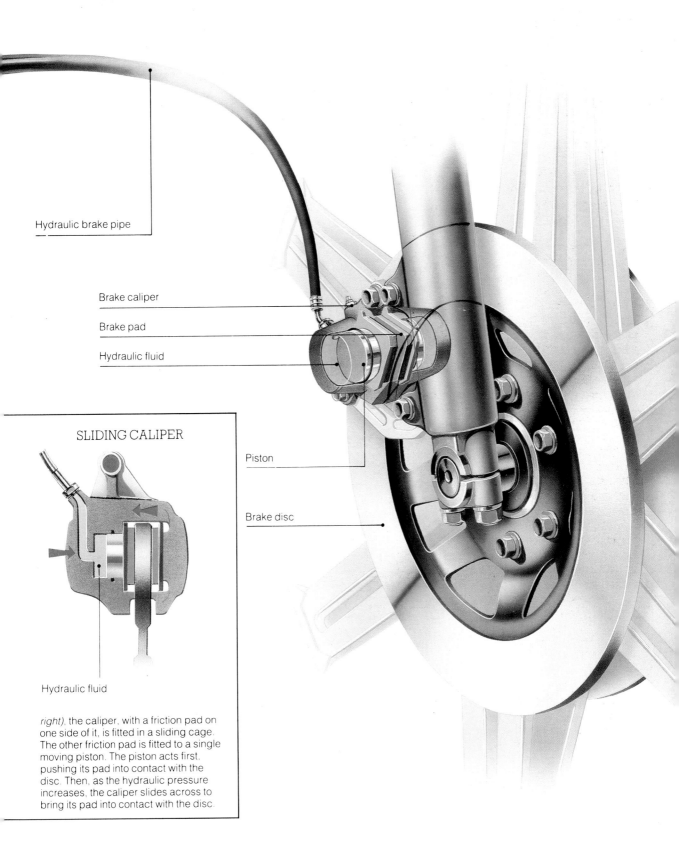

Hydraulic brake pipe

Brake caliper

Brake pad

Hydraulic fluid

Piston

Brake disc

SLIDING CALIPER

Hydraulic fluid

right), the caliper, with a friction pad on one side of it, is fitted in a sliding cage. The other friction pad is fitted to a single moving piston. The piston acts first, pushing its pad into contact with the disc. Then, as the hydraulic pressure increases, the caliper slides across to bring its pad into contact with the disc.

Braking system/checklist

across, so bringing the fixed pad into contact with the other side of the disc. The disc is now clamped between the pads.

Disc brakes in operation
The force required to move the pistons can be applied either by straightforward mechanical leverage, or by hydraulic pressure. If the system is mechanical, it is normally cable operated, the movement of the cable being transferred to the caliper pistons via a ball and ramp mechanism. The obvious drawback is that the amount of mechanical leverage that can be applied is obviously limited, since a high leverage ratio would require too much movement of the handlebar lever. Hence, the system is used only on lightweight machines.

In the more powerful hydraulic disc brake system, pistons and cylinders are linked by a hydraulic brake line, or hose, which transport hydraulic fluid from a reservoir mounted next to the brake lever. The fluid can withstand high temperatures without boiling and lubricates and protects the moving pistons.

Fluid from the reservoir flows into the master cylinder, which

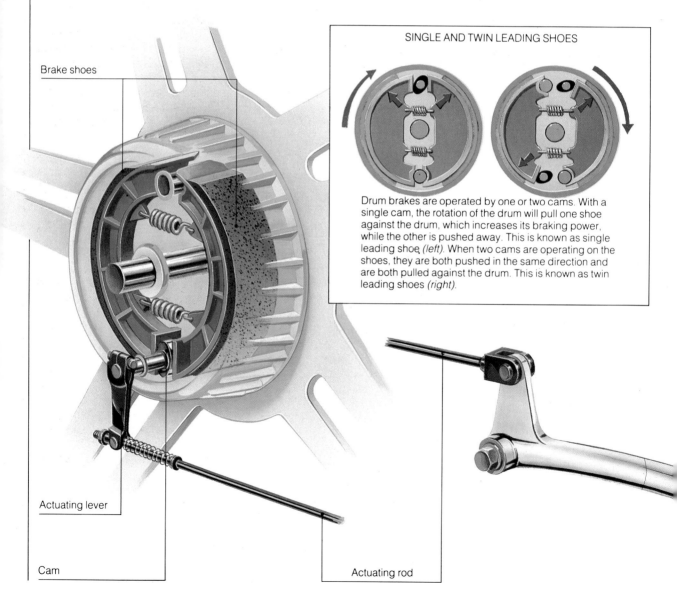

Brake shoes

SINGLE AND TWIN LEADING SHOES

Drum brakes are operated by one or two cams. With a single cam, the rotation of the drum will pull one shoe against the drum, which increases its braking power, while the other is pushed away. This is known as single leading shoe *(left)*. When two cams are operating on the shoes, they are both pushed in the same direction and are both pulled against the drum. This is known as twin leading shoes *(right)*.

Actuating lever

Cam

Actuating rod

contains a piston, operated by the brake lever. Movement of the piston applies pressure to the pistons in the caliper via the hydraulic fluid. The application of braking pressure is determined by the difference in size and travel of the piston in the master cylinder, compared to the size of the piston in the brake caliper.

Drum brakes

As the name implies, the core of the drum brake is a hollow drum in the centre of the road wheel. Inside the drum are placed a pair of brake shoes, covered in friction material. When pressed against the drum, these provide the necessary friction.

One end of each shoe is pivoted, the other can be moved by a simple rotating cam. The movement of the cam is regulated by a cable from the handlebar lever, if it is the front wheel – by a rod from a foot pedal if it is the rear wheel. The rotation of the cam brings the shoe into contact with the drum.

Single and twin leading shoes

If the direction of rotation of the drum is clockwise the left hand shoe, when moved by the cam will be pulled on to the drum's surface by the rotating action, and the braking effect will be increased as a result. This edge

is known as the 'leading shoe' and the shoe itself is said to have 'self-service action', because it grips the drum and digs into it.

Now, take the other shoe. The rotating action of the drum will tend to throw this off the drum's surface. This shoe is known as the 'trailing shoe' and does not grip the drum easily.

Designers overcome this problem by fitting a second pivot point and a second cam. The result is termed a twin leading shoe brake. This gains in efficiency because both shoes are being pulled against the drum.

The main limitation of drum brakes is that the heat the friction generates tends to stay inside the drum, causing the friction

material to over-heat. This can lead to brake fade.

Brake balance

When you brake, the weight of your machine is transferred on to its front wheel, with a subsequent reduction in the load on the rear wheel. This, in turn, means that the front wheel can produce more braking effort before the wheel locks, while it also follows that the rear wheel will lock much easier.

For this reason, motor cycles and scooters are commonly fitted with a simple single-leading shoe drum brake at the rear and a powerful disc brake at the front. On fast or heavy machines, twin discs are usually fitted to the front wheel.

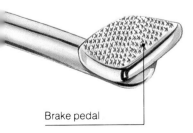

Brake pedal

CHECKLIST

Check the amount of friction material left on the brake pads. This should not be allowed to wear down below 2mm , but check your handbook for the minimum permissible depth.

Check that the fluid in a hydraulic system is maintained a the correct level. You can establish this visually by checking the transparent cover or sight window of the master cylinder. Top up only with the recommended fluid.

If you find you are having to top up constantly, check for a fluid leak. The machine should not be ridden until any leak is repaired.

Check the condition of brake pipes and flexible hoses. Apply the brake and check the hose for signs of swelling. Check the hose for surface cracks and the

junctions for leaks. Consult your handbook for the recommended renewal periods for brake fluid and hoses.

Check the condition and operation of mechanical linkages and cables. You can lubricate these, but keep the lubricant away from the brake pads and shoes.

Check that the wheels are free to spin with the brakes off. A dragging brake drum may need adjustment. Check a sliding disc caliper, the mechanism can seize as a result of corrosion. Check discs are clean and free from oil or grease.

Check the wear limit of brake shoes by dismantling them inspection, or check the brake wear indicator (if one is fitted to your bike).

The suspension system

All bikes need an adequate suspension system to absorb road shocks. By doing this, the system ensures the machine's stability by keeping the tyre firmly in contact with the road; it also contributes to rider safety.

Imagine, for example, riding a bike head-on into a kerbstone. Without suspension, the shock of hitting the kerb would be transmitted directly through the handlebars. This could be so violent that, as well as being extremely uncomfortable, the front wheel could even buckle and the rider loose control of the machine as a result.

This was often the case on some early motor cycles, which had no suspension at all. Now, however, advances in suspension design mean that modern bikes provide better road holding and rider comfort. Indeed, some of the systems in current use have gone to the other extreme. Some have become so sophisticated that they present riders with a bewildering choice of possible adjustments and settings.

Nevertheless, no matter how sophisticated the system, the job it is designed to perform remains the same as it always has been – to prevent road shocks being transmitted through the machine to affect your steering and personal comfort. It must also allow the bike's wheels to remain in contact with the road surface and the tyres to maintain their grip on it.

Coil springs

Coil springs are the heart of every bike's suspension system. Usually the springs are fitted inside the forks at the front of the machine and to the outside of the suspension unit, or pair of units,

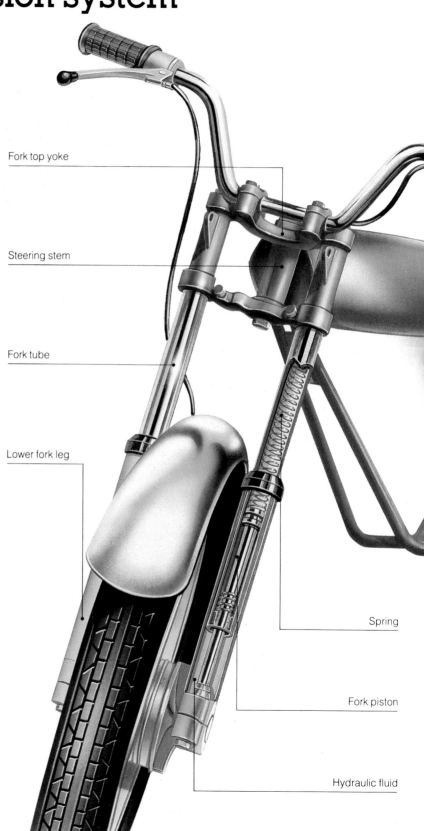

Fork top yoke

Steering stem

Fork tube

Lower fork leg

Spring

Fork piston

Hydraulic fluid

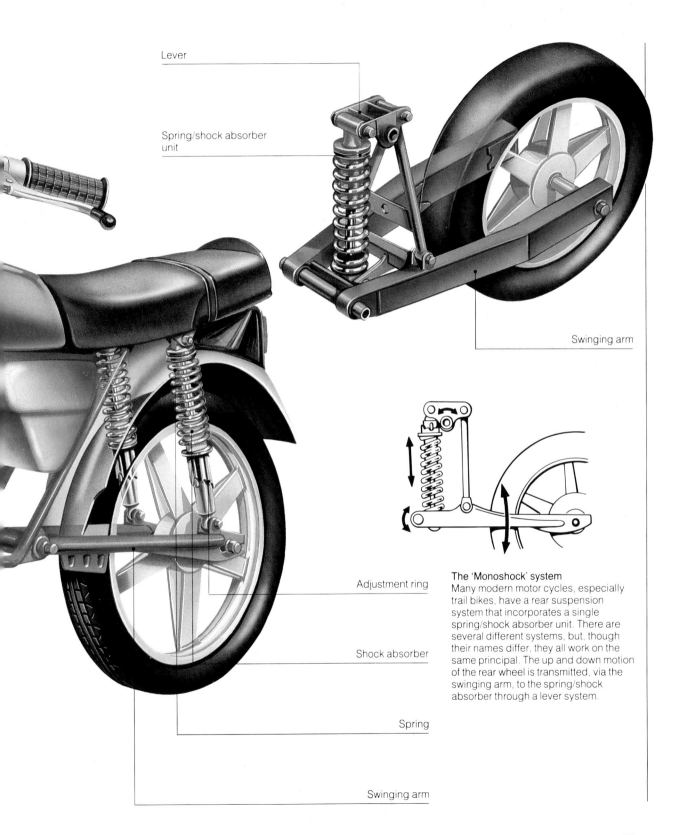

Lever

Spring/shock absorber unit

Swinging arm

Adjustment ring

Shock absorber

Spring

Swinging arm

The 'Monoshock' system

Many modern motor cycles, especially trail bikes, have a rear suspension system that incorporates a single spring/shock absorber unit. There are several different systems, but, though their names differ, they all work on the same principal. The up and down motion of the rear wheel is transmitted, via the swinging arm, to the spring/shock absorber through a lever system.

Suspension system/checklist

at the rear. While it has been common design practice to fit a pair of suspension units either side of the rear wheel over the last 30 years, the use of a single, larger unit, mounted centrally in front of the rear wheel, is now becoming more widespread. This system is popularly termed 'monoshock' rear suspension.

The 'monoshock' system

In the 'monoshock' system, as the front and rear wheels hit a bump, the springs are compressed, allowing the wheels to follow the bump's contours. If the springs are functioning efficiently, the attitude of the bike will remain unchanged and the rider will not be pitched out of the saddle.

When the spring compresses, it picks up and stores energy. It then rebounds – the tendency is for it to try to over-stretch its natural length – compresses and rebounds again, rather like the oscillations of a pendulum, until the energy imparted by the bump has been fully absorbed.

This series of reactions creates a major problem, since, if the suspension depended on the springs alone, the recoil that follows any bump might well force the bike off the ground. The harder the bump, the more likely this is to happen. For this reason, shock absorbers are fitted to absorb the energy contained in the springs after they have been compressed.

Modern shock absorbers, or dampers, fulfill this function to near perfection, dampening the recoil shock of the spring. However, they do not absorb the original shock – as already explained, this is the job the springs perform.

On a bike or a scooter, the shock absorber is normally an integral part of the suspension unit. Thus, a bike's two front fork legs contain the spring and the means of providing damping. At the back of the bike, the damper usually has the spring sleeved over the top of it.

In all cases, the principle of operation relies on the fact that, unlike air, it is impossible for the oil used to absorb the shock to be compressed. On some bikes, automatic transmission fluid (ATF) may be employed as the damping medium. The oil or fluid is housed inside the fork legs at the front of a motor cycle and inside the damper unit or units at the back.

How shock absorbers work

As the bike's wheels meet irregularities in the road surface, the springs of the suspension are compressed. Their natural inclination to recoil violently is checked by the shock absorber system, which slows recoil by forcing the oil it contains through a series of narrow passageways. Since the oil refuses to be compressed, the spring can extend only as fast as the oil passing through the passageways allows.

In this way, the spring energy is absorbed, being turned into heat as the oil is forced through the passageways. The system ensures that the spring returns to its original length in a smooth, controlled manner, leaving the wheel ready to encounter its next road shock. Thus, the wheel is kept in firm contact with the surface of the road.

Damper refinements

Many motor cycles are fitted with double acting dampers. This is a slightly more advanced damping system than the single acting version, but the principles are the same.

Double acting dampers differ from the single acting type by offering resistance to the compression (bump) stroke of the spring as well as to the extension (rebound) stroke. Thus, this type of damper helps the spring to cushion bumps.

Usually, the system of valving inside such a damper allows the oil to pass more freely on the bump stroke than on the rebound. On some bikes you can select the level of damping you require. This means that you can adjust the suspension to compensate for the weight of extra luggage, a pillion passenger, or the demands of fast riding.

Air assistance

In addition to oil, some modern suspension units use air as an extra means of assisting the damping process.

Air differs from oil in the way it resists compression, its pressure doubling as its volume is halved. This is invaluable in some driving conditions. If, say, a machine is carrying an extremely heavy load, or is being ridden over bad road surfaces, the permissible movement of the suspension may be taxed to the full for most of the time. If this happens, there is a tendency for the suspension to 'bottom' when the limit of suspension travel is reached. By introducing air pressure resistance, compression is increased and 'bottoming', the point at which there is no more compression in the springs, can be avoided.

Many sports machines are fitted with air forks, so stiffening the suspension to cater for the demands of fast riding. More costly models may also have air rear suspension units fitted, so that air may be added for fast riding or to help the bike cope with an unduly heavy load. The use of the air restores ground clearance and compensates for the extra weight and strain put on the machine, especially when being ridden hard through corners or under heavy or sudden harsh braking.

Preload adjustment

All bikes, with the exception of low-cost lightweights, provide spring preload adjustment on their rear suspension units, while some machines offer the same facility on the front forks. With preload adjustment, you turn a collar to compress the spring and so shorten its overall length to suit road conditions. Rear suspension units, for instance, usually have five adjustment positions.

By increasing preload, you can restore the ground clearance to normal when riding your bike two-up, or when carrying heavy luggage. The technique does not stiffen the spring, but it does give a harder ride over slight deflections. This is because the spring's initial movement, which would otherwise be available to cushion such bumps, has already been taken up by the preload.

How the suspension is fitted

At the front, nearly all bikes are fitted with a pair of telescopic forks, one leg of which is attached to one side of the wheel spindle and the other to the spindle on the opposite side of the wheel. The tops of the legs are clamped in a pair of yokes – these are situated at the top and bottom of the steering head respectively.

The forks are referred to as telescopic because, when a bump is encountered, the lower section, (the slider), slides over the top section, shortening the overall length of the fork in the manner of a telescope. The top section of the fork is referred to as the fork tube, or stanchion.

Although most older bikes are fitted with dual unit rear suspension, the modern trend is towards the single suspension unit system. This system is often referred to as 'monoshock', 'cantilever', or simply 'single shock rear suspension'. It is fitted to the BMW 800cc R80GS – the manufacturer's term for it is 'monolever' – and is used on many Yamaha models, from 50cc to 1000cc.

Whichever system is used, the wheel is housed in a fork, popularly known as a swinging arm, with a pivot point attached to the main frame. This allows the assembly to swing in an arc as the wheel traverses road irregularities.

Recently, some single suspension unit systems have been further developed to include what are termed rising rate characteristics. Honda, for example, include this facility on some of their models fitted with their 'Pro-Link' system.

Rising rate means that, as the wheel nears the end of its travel, resistance to movement is greatly increased in order to stop the suspension bottoming. With such a system, the suspension can be tailored to provide a very sensitive reaction to even the smallest road surface irregularities and to offer progressive resistance to more violent bumps.

CHECKLIST

Check for signs of oil leaks on fork tubes (stanchions) and on rear damper tubes. If you detect leaks from the fork tubes, have the oil seals replaced. In the case of rear suspension dampers, which cannot be dismantled, replace the affected unit.

Check for signs of pitting on fork tubes and on damper rods on rear suspension units. Renew these components if pitting is severe and causing oil loss.

Check suspension action by compressing the suspension and observing recoil. If the return is 'springy', with a tendency for the spring to rebound beyond its normal static length, then it is likely that the damping action is impaired. This may be caused by water contaminating the damping oil, or by oil loss.

The oil used in the forks should be changed at regular intervals. Consult your handbook to check the quantity and grade of oil that is required. If your rear suspension dampers are affected, consult your dealer to see if they need replacing.

Check the condition of the pivot bearings on the rear suspension swinging arm. Such bearings are usually bushes or needle roller bearings. Check condition by removing the suspension unit(s) and feeling to see whether up-and-down movement and side-to-side play is smooth. If necessary, consult your handbook for lubrication method and service intervals.

Wheels and tyres

Your tyres are one of the most vital parts of your bike. They have an enormous influence on the way your machine feels and handles, so fitting the right combination – making sure, of course, they are also inflated to the correct pressure – will make riding much more enjoyable and much safer.

The tubeless tyre is now a standard fitting on many machines, while the radial type seems to be replacing the current cross-ply. The ultra lightweight plastic wheel may also soon become standard. Nevertheless, the majority of machines are still fitted with spoked or cast alloy wheels, with treaded tyres of cross-ply or what is termed bias belt construction, used either with or without an inner tube.

Tyre facts
By law, the tread on a motor cycle or scooter tyre must be at least 1mm deep across the whole circumference of the tyre area. In fact, many tyre makers recommend that motor cycle tyres are changed when tread depth is down to 2mm. At less than this depth, handling is affected adversely.

The chief reason for this is that tyres have to cope with all weathers. The raised tread is essential if the tyre is to cut through rain water.

A tyre with little or no tread would aquaplane in the wet at speed, as the smooth tyre surface would not be able to displace water from the road surface. Thus, the tyre would skim on top of the water. When this happens, the bike quickly goes out of control.

Tread patterns vary according to the job they are intended to

fulfill. So, too, does the composition of the tyre. For instance, a tyre designed to give excellent grip for cornering and acceleration on an extremely powerful motor cycle will be a soft compound. The penalty for this is rapid wear. A tyre fitted to a low powered commuter machine will not have such superior grip qualities, but will be designed to last longer.

The tyres to suit your bike
When selecting tyres consult your tyre supplier or dealer for advice. Some tyres, such as the ribbed pattern type, are designed to be fitted only to front wheels; others have directional arrows on their sidewalls to indicate which way around they should be fitted to a particular wheel.

Take a performance block pattern tyre, for instance. This can be fitted to either the front or rear wheel, but the arrow should point in the direction of forward rotation in the case of the rear wheel and the opposite way round in the case of the front wheel. The reason for this is that the tyre is constructed to function at its best only in one direction.

Tyre markings
Tyres are marked for speed rating and size. By law, you must fit the tyres that are speed rated to match the capabilities of your bike. The rating is denoted by a code letter, which should be marked on the tyre sidewall, along with the tyre size markings. The code and maximum permissible speeds is as follows:
S: to 112mph (180k/hr)
H: up to 130mph (209k/hr)
V: over 130mph (209k/hr).
Where there is no speed letter, as on some moped tyres, the

speed rating is up to 93mph (150k/hr).

Tyre size markings refer to the width of the tyre – defined as being from one sidewall to the other – and the diameter of the beaded edge – that is, the inner diameter. If a tyre is marked 3.25S18, for instance, this means that the width is 3.25in (90mm) and the inner diameter is 18in (457mm). This means that the tyre will fit an 18in (457mm) wheel, while the 'S' means that it can be fitted to a machine capable of a maximum speed of 112mph (180k/hr).

Sometimes the sidewall width is given in millimetres and another measurement is introduced to denote 'aspect ration.' This is the depth of the

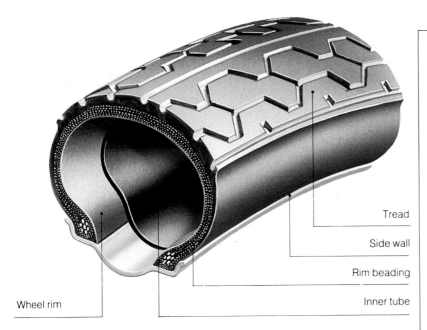

Tread

Side wall

Rim beading

Inner tube

Wheel rim

Modern tyres show major advances in construction and tread design. Wheels have also changed considerably in the last decade, alloy spoked wheels now being common *(left)*. Though these do not possess the same shock absorbing qualities of wire spoked wheels, they require less maintenance.

tyre sidewall expressed as a percentage of the tyre width. For example, a tyre marked 130/80H18 has a sidewall width of 130mm (5.1in) and a sidewall depth that is 80% of that measurement. It will fit an 457mm (18in) wheel and has an H speed rating – that is, it will cope with speeds up to 130mph (209k/hr).

Tubeless tyres
Some machines are now fitted with tubeless tyres as standard. Tubeless tyres are a safety advance, since, if a puncture occurs, a tubeless tyre usually deflates gradually; a punctured inner tube all too frequently suffers from a sudden blow-out. The slower deflation gives the rider more time to bring the

machine to a controlled halt.

A tubeless tyre must be fitted to an air tight wheel. It is important that you check this, since many of the alloy wheels you can buy from accessory shops are not air tight and so cannot be used without an inner tube.

Alloy and spoked wheels
Over recent years, it has become fashionable to fit alloy wheels, which have now replaced the traditional spoked wheel to a large extent. Alloy wheels are maintenance free, but do not have the same ability to absorb road shocks as the spoked varieties. On these, the spokes must be correctly tensioned.

Until recently, spoked wheels have always had to be fitted with a tyre with an inner tube. Now, however, some spoked rims are designed to take tubeless tyres, thus combining traditional looks with safety.

Problem diagnosis

Regular and thorough motorcycle maintenance obviously minimizes the chances of breakdown. If, however, you take a personal interest in your bike's maintenance – rather than leaving it totally to a professional mechanic – you will be better prepared to deal with those unexpected, infuriating and inevitable mechanical disasters that can stop your bike in its tracks.

This involves mental preparation as well as a modicum of mechanical ability. Preparing yourself with a mental toolkit – as well carrying an emergency toolkit under your seat or sidepanel – will help you to avoid the tedium of a long hard push, or dejected hours of waiting for help to arrive.

This chapter is purpose-planned to help you by showing you how to tackle fault finding in a clear, logical order. To get the best out of it, imagine yourself confronted with a problem, think of what you would do to deal with it and then compare your approach with the ones suggested here.

If you can deal with minor problems promptly, you should be able to reach your destination. If the repair is beyond you, at least knowing what is wrong may save you a good deal of worry and expense.

Roadside security
If you have to abandon your bike for any length of time, one of your main worries will be whether or not it will be where you left it when you return to the scene. Motorcycles and scooters are all too easy to steal, because, even if immobilized, they can be manhandled in to the back of a pick-up or truck.

If you are forced to abandon your bike in a built-up area, push it to the nearest house and ask if you can leave the machine in the householder's custody. If you have to leave the machine unguarded, make sure that you lock the steering and put any anti-theft device you may have fitted into action.

Never leave the machine's documents on the machine and make sure that you have a note somewhere at home of engine and frame numbers. In addition, record any specific distinguishing features, such as a small dent in the exhaust pipe, a chipped cylinder fin and so on. If the machine is stolen, the thief may well grind the numbers off the engine and frame, so having a record of other marks and blemishes will not only help the police to recover your bike, but also help you to prove ownership.

Motoring organizations
If you regularly travel long distances, you should consider joining a motoring organization, such as the AA or RAC. Like other similar bodies, both provide on-the-spot assistance and a get-you-home service for an annual fee. Their advantage is that they operate in Europe as well as the UK.

Basic diagnosis
If you are faced with diagnosing a fault, it helps to have a 'clean' patient. By cleaning your machine regularly, you may well detect faults in their early stages before they become real problems. If, for instance, your weekly spring clean reveals a minor oil leak – and you take immediate steps to cure it – you will avoid the risk of engine seizure that otherwise could result.

Let us assume, then, that you clean your bike regularly, the chain is correctly tensioned, the brakes are working effectively, the fluid levels are correct and that the tyres are correctly inflated and in good condition. You know how your bike sounds and feels in this state. If the engine note changes suddenly, or a new noise makes itself heard, you should stop and investigate. It is foolhardy to ride on regardless.

Basically, any bike problems can be split into two main categories – those affecting the engine and those affecting cycle parts. First determine which category the problem falls into and proceed from there. Suppose, for instance, that the engine will not start. Obviously, there is an engine fault. Has the machine started to weave from side to side? Then, there is a cycle part problem.

Check the obvious first. If the engine will not start, see whether or not there is fuel in the tank. If there is, see if there is a spark at the spark plug. If there is no spark, try a new plug. If this fails to solve the problem, check the ignition circuit fuse, the HT (high tension) cap, HT lead, the coil for earthing, the low tension wire to the coil ad so on, working through to the battery in a logical manner.

Think about the circumstances of the breakdown. Has the machine been left outside in the rain all night, for instance? If so, it could be that the HT current is finding its way to earth via moisture on the leads or cap. Wipe both dry, spray with a dewatering fluid and try again. By using logic and common sense, it should prove possible to isolate – or at least to narrow down – the problem to one component, or a small group of components.

If there is fuel in the tank and a spark at the plug, but the engine refuses to fire, examine the plug for fuel wetting. If the plug is dry, the fault lies elsewhere in the fuel system – the tank tap may be blocked by debris, for instance. Remove the fuel pipe from the carburettor and see if the fuel flows when you switch on the tap (you may have to suck on the tap if your bike is fitted with a vacuum model). If the fuel flows freely, your next logical step is to check the carburettor for blockages.

Follow the same logical approach when diagnosing cycle part problems. If the bike breaks into a weave, for instance, look for obvious causes first, such as a deflated tyre, or loose or broken spokes.

If you cannot detect an obvious physical fault, again think of the circumstances. Are you carrying heavy luggage on the rear rack for the first time? This can upset weight distribution, since the bike's front end will be unusually light and the handlebars will wiggle from side to side as a result. Or perhaps you have just had new tyres fitted that are not a particularly successful front and rear match. As a result, the machine may try to break into a gentle weave at a certain speed, or to react in a more sudden manner when crossing raised white lines or tarmac strips on the road surface. In such a case, you either adapt to the new characteristics, or change the tyres, if you are really unhappy with the way the bike is handling.

If the problem persists, you should check the bearing play, or for bearing failure at the headstock, in the wheel hubs and in the swinging arm pivot.

When to consult a professional

You may find some symptoms difficult to track down – if so, consult an expert. If the engine develops a knocking noise, for instance, it may prove difficult to determine whether the main bearings, big ends, or, in the case of a four-stroke, the cam drive mechanism is to blame. An experienced mechanic should be able to pinpoint the problem –

or, at the least deduce the probable causes – and estimate the likely repair costs.

In all events, you should investigate any strange engine noise immediately. If you disregard it, the faulty or worn component could spark off a chain reaction, leading to a major mechanical disaster. To help in this, place the pointed end of a screwdriver on the appropriate part of the engine block and resting your ear against the handle. The screwdriver acts like a stethoscope, so enabling you to locate the source of any strange noise.

The procedure can save you time and worry. If, for instance, your bike is fitted with an overhead cam engine and a distinct knock develops at the top, isolating the knock means that you only have to remove the cam cover to search for the cause, rather than embarking on a total stripdown.

The golden rules

Thus, the golden rules of problem solving are straightforward. By ensuring that your machine is properly serviced and by keeping it clean, you should have sufficient early warning of the majority of problems to be able to do something about them before they become serious. If unexpected problems arise, the thing to do is to use logic to enable you to identify them promptly.

Dealing with a breakdown/1

Breakdowns are an inevitable fact of biking life, as it is often impossible to tell when a particular component will fail. Naturally enough, regular maintenance will decrease this risk, but it is obviously a commonsense precaution to make yourself aware of when this is most likely to occur.

First, think of circumstance. If, for instance, you generally use your bike for short 'stop-go' journeys in heavy town traffic, it should be obvious that the different demands of a long, high speed motorway journey will make different demands may disclose a fault that otherwise would have remained concealed. As the winter nights draw in and you are using your lights more and more, any electrical problems that have not manifested themselves during the summer could now reveal themselves to leave you stranded. Likewise, trying to start your bike on a cold winter morning puts a major strain on the ignition, fuel and electrical systems, the failure of any one of which could leave you immobilised. So the first lesson is preventative; it is to make sure that your bike is well maintained.

Safety first

If a breakdown does occur while you are on the road, the first thing to ensure is your safety and that of other road users. If trouble develops while you are out on the road, move safely and promptly to the verge or nearest lay-by. Do not dither as this can be fatal – especially if you find yourself coasting in the fast lane of a congested motorway with a dead engine.

Once out of the traffic, seek a place where you can investigate the fault and work on your machine safely. Try to avoid working where dust or rain is likely to get into the engine and never work over or close to an open drain. It is amazing just how far loose nuts and bolts can roll.

What tools?

The number of tools you can carry is obviously limited, so you should make a check list of the basic essentials. At the least, you need a spare spark plug, a plug spanner and a set of spare fuses, as well as the tool kit that normally comes with the machine. Whenever you use up one of your spare plugs or fuses, buy replacements at the first opportunity.

Most bikes have tool storage space under the seat or behind a sidepanel. You can also utilize other nooks and crannies to store extra tools and spares. Spare headlight and tail light bulbs, a chain joining link and a puncture repair kit – plus a bicycle pump – should always be carried, if possible. Do not carry screwdrivers, spanners and the like in the pockets of your riding jacket – such tools can turn into lethal weapons if you are involved in an accident. A few nuts and bolts, a roll of insulating tape, a torch, or a bulb which can be easily wired up to the bike's battery are also useful extras.

If you find yourself stranded without the tool you need, this it is not always as disastrous as it might seem. In many cases, you can adapt another tool to serve as a temporary substitute for the missing item, though, inevitably, this will not be as satisfactory as the real thing.

If, for instance, the spanner that fits the nut you have to undo is the one that has been left at home in the garage, it is sometimes possible to wedge the blade of a screwdriver between a larger-sized spanner and one of the flats of the nut. This will enable you to achieve the necessary grip.

One trick that can come in very useful in the garage as well as out on the road is making a makeshift electro-magnet. This may sound far fetched and uneccessary, but the alternative is worse. There is nothing more infuriating than struggling for hours to try to retrieve a nut, screw or washer that has fallen somewhere inaccessible.

Making an electromagnet is simple if your bike has a battery and you have a screwdriver and a good length of fine, insulated wire. Simply coil the wire around the blade of the screwdriver and attach the ends to the battery terminals and the screwdriver's blade will become magnetized as the current flows. The 'magnet' can be switched off while you position the blade and then switched on to pick up the missing nut when the blade makes the necessary contact.

If you have an old inner tube to hand, cut off strips to make thick rubber bands. These versatile aids can be wrapped around many parts of a bike in an emergency. They can be used to hold a loose side panel in place, to hold up a sidestand or mainstand with a missing spring, and to tidy up a wiring loom which has been pulled apart for inspection, for example.

As always, study the professionals and learn from their example. Endurance riders, for instance, often tape spare cables next to those in use, so that, in the event of a cable failure, the ready routed replacement can be fitted quickly and efficiently. The ends of the cable should be taped to keep out dirt. Some riders also carry spare inner tubes in their jacket pockets; if you were to be stranded on a lonely road far from help, you might find this invaluable, always provided that you have remembered to include a tyre pump in your emergency tool kit as well.

Breakdown causes

Common causes of roadside breakdowns include plug failure, engine seizure, a holed piston, a flat battery, a broken cable, a blocked air filter or carburettor jet, short circuits, a broken or thrown drive chain, punctures and simply running out of fuel. Most of them can be prevented by regular maintenance and a little forethought. However, if a problem strikes out of the blue, there are several 'get-you-home' tricks of the trade you can try.

If, say, you have run out of petrol, try laying your bike as far over on its side as possible, so that any fuel in the bottom of the tank will be channelled towards the fuel tap. Try to start the machine and, if it fires, ride off gently. If the engine falters, use your choke. This trick may give you power for a few hundred yards up to a mile. This may be the crucial difference between reaching a filling station – or being stuck by the roadside.

Plug problems

If you are riding a single cylinder machine and the engine stops because of a faulty spark plug, there is no need to despair if you are not carrying a spare. Remove the faulty plug to see if it is oil-fouled or whiskered. If so, clean it and refit it. This may be enough to get you home.

If, however, the plug has failed completely, a replacement is the only answer. If you borrow one, check to see whether it is long reach or short reach. If your engine takes a short reach plug and the only replacement to hand is a long reach one, do not be tempted to fit it unless you can pack the plug with washers. Otherwise the piston or valves may come into contact with the plug – if this happens, serious mechanical damage will result.

Also check the plug's heat range. On Champion plugs – one of the two most popular plugs fitted to bike engines – the lower the plug number, the harder (colder) the plug. NGK plugs, however, are coded the other way around. As a rule of thumb, using a spare one up or one down from the coding of the original is acceptable.

A B8ES NGK plug (equivalent to an N3 Champion) is fitted to many Japanese machines, for example. In this instance, a B9ES or B7ES will get you home. The harder B9ES will not harm your engine however hard you ride, though you may find that your bike is prone to stall at very low speeds.

However, you should take more care with the softer (hotter) B7ES plug, as this will run hotter in the engine than a standard plug. This should not cause problems if you ride gently to help keep the engine cool. If you are forced to fit an even softer plug, ride at no more than half throttle and be prepared to stop to give the engine a chance to cool down if it tends to cut out or fade.

This is particularly important as far as two-stroke machines are concerned. On this type of engine, plug heat is more critical than with a four-stroke, because the operating temperature of the engine is higher in any case. If you use a plug that is too soft for too long a period, the piston can be holed.

With a multi-cylinder bike, you should be able to limp to a garage if just one plug fails. You will probably need to use your gearbox more frequently because of lack of power and you should take care not to over-rev the engine or, on the other hand, let it labour.

Because the live cylinder or cylinders have extra work to do in driving the dead cylinder as well as the bike, there will be a tendency for the engine to over-heat. This is especially true in the case of lightweight twin-cylinder machines. If you feel engine power fading, ease the throttle back, or stop for a few minutes to allow the engine to cool.

If you are riding a water-cooled machine, keep a close eye on the temperature gauge.

Piston emergencies

Two-stroke engines suffer from holed pistons more frequently than four-strokes, because a two-stroke engine fires on every stroke of the piston, rather than every other, and produces more heat as a result. Hence, with two-strokes, ignition timing and carburation are more critical.

If, for instance, you are running a machine where the inlet system has been modified – the air box may have been removed, for example – you should check to see that the carburation has been altered accurately to compensate for the change. If not, a holed piston is a possibility. You can detect warning signs by checking the spark plug; the

Dealing with a breakdown/2

core will be covered by a grey film of alloy filaments eroded from the piston.

If the engine starts to fire on only one cylinder, or, in the case of a single-cylinder machine, it cuts out completely, you can carry out a simple test to check to see whether or not a piston is holed. First, try turning the engine over with the kickstart lever. If this is abnormally easy, then the cause of the lost compression is likely to be a holed piston. To investigate further, remove the plug from the cylinder in question and insert a pencil down the plug orifice.

If the piston is at the top of its stroke, move the pencil over the piston crown. This will enable you to detect a hole or rough area where part of the piston has been eaten away. If the piston is near the bottom of its stroke, remove the pencil, make sure that the gearbox is in neutral and then gently depress the kickstart lever (if the bike is not fitted with kickstart, push it forward gently in gear). Re-insert the pencil and feel for the piston crown as just as you did before.

Never leave the pencil in the cylinder while the engine is being turned over. The pencil can easily become jammed by the piston.

On a multi-cylinder machine, you can still ride on to a garage even if a piston is holed, provided that you ride steadily. If, however, the piston has broken up, rather than just being holed, the machine should not be ridden, since there is likely to be debris in the crankcase. This could cause further expensive engine damage.

Engine seizure
You should have reasonable

warning of an engine seizure, because the engine usually tightens up and the revs die. The couple of seconds notice this gives can be vital. You will just have time to get ready to pull the clutch lever in – should you indeed be faced with this problem – and so prevent the rear wheel from locking.

Seizures on four-strokes are often due to lack of oil, either because the oil level has not been topped up or because of oil loss. The latter can be caused by a holed piston, or, more commonly, broken piston rings. In this case, the gases under pressure in the combustion chamber leak past the piston and into the crankcase because the piston ring or rings can no longer provide an effective seal. The pressure inside the crankcase then blows the oil out through the crankcase breather tube.

Seizures occur in varying degrees of severity. A solid piston seizure means that the piston is locked solid in the bore and the machine cannot be used until the fault has been fixed. A partial seizure means that the piston is nipped momentarily in the bore. There can be various reasons for this, including worn piston rings, gummed-in rings that do not pass heat from the piston to the bore efficiently and inadequate lubrication.

This can be a particular problem on two-strokes fitted with oil reservoirs, since, if such machines are ridden hard for long distances, the oil consumption can be surprisingly high. Watch the oil warning light – most modern machines have this as a standard fitting – as this will tell you if the oil level is running dangerously low. Never allow the reservoir to run dry, as

this makes a piston seizure inevitable. An air lock in a two-stroke oil pump can be another cause of seizures.

Dealing with a seizure
If a piston seizure occurs, pull in the clutch lever in order to stop the back wheel locking and then coast to a halt. Allow the engine to cool, checking the oil level while you wait.

Once the engine has cooled, try to turn it over gently in neutral, using the kickstart. If the engine will not budge, it has seized solid; if it frees, the seizure is only partial. In this case, you may be able to continue your journey, but you must ride slowly and be prepared for the seizure to re-occur. Following a partial seizure, the engine should be inspected at the earliest opportunity to assess the extent of the damage and to establish why the seizure occurred.

Gearbox seizures
Fortunately, gearbox seizures – their commonest cause is lack of lubricant – are rare. If one occurs while the machine is on the move, the rear wheel inevitably locks. Unlike piston seizures, pulling in the clutch lever cannot help, since the gearbox is linked directly to the back wheel.

Well before the seizure occurs, you will find the gears jumping out of selection, while the gearbox itself becomes very noisy. Both these symptoms will give you plenty of warning that something is amiss. Start by re-filling the box with fresh oil. If it is still noisy after that, get a garage to inspect it for wear.

Fuses and battery
If the engine stops because of a

blown fuse, you can use a piece of wire, or silver paper from a cigarette packet, as a temporary resort if you are not carrying a spare. Either will carry the current across the fuse holder terminals. If silver paper is used, wrap it around the blown fuse and refit the fuse.

Any temporary substitute should be replaced by a fuse of the correct rating as soon as possible. While the temporary fuse is in place, you should be on the watch for any electrical malfunction and be ready to stop quickly if one occurs.

If the engine misfires and the lights dim, the likely cause is a flat battery. Switching from high beam to low beam will reduce the load on the battery, as will using the brake light and indicators as sparingly as possible. At the same time, you should keep the engine revs up to help the battery to recharge. This can be done without increasing road speed by using a lower gear.

If the bike comes to a halt, make sure that all its electrical circuits are switched off and allow the battery at least ten minutes to regain some of its charge. When you start up again, use the kickstart, or push start the bike. Once you have the engine running, keep the revs up.

There can be several reasons why a battery constantly becomes flat. If the battery is an old one, it may simply be the case that a new replacement is needed. Otherwise there may be a fault in the charging system, the brake light may be sticking on, or the problem is due to the machine being ridden frequently in slow-moving traffic, with most of its electrical systems in use. If the last is the case – and the

battery is in good condition – it is worthwhile charging it fortnightly or monthly, whichever is necessary.

Air filter problems

If your bike runs for a short period, but then slows down dramatically – possibly even coming to a halt – you should check the condition of the air filter. If the filter has been left unchanged for a long time, it may have become so clogged that, though the engine will start, air flow is so restricted that cruising revolutions cannot be maintained.

If the air filter passes inspection and there is a good spark at the spark plug, check for other possible causes. These include a blocked vent hole in the filler cap, a blocked fuel tap filter, incorrectly set carburettor float height and, if the engine is hot, a faulty ignition coil.

Chain and cable defects

If your chain breaks, first check the machine for damage. Then inspect the chain. If the joining link has failed, replace it. As an emergency measure, you can thread a piece of wire through the chain to take the place of the joining link, but remember that this is only an temporary solution. Much depends on the strength of the wire and how well you do the job. You must ride extremely carefully and slowly until you reach a garage. If the chain breaks anywhere else along its length, you will need a special tool, called a chain breaker, to remove the broken link.

If a cable breaks – whether clutch, throttle or brake – you cannot make an adequate temporary repair. It is thus unsafe to continue riding.

Dealing with punctures

Puncture repair is dealt with in detail elsewhere (see pp 120-1). If your tyres are fitted with inner tubes – always assuming you are carrying the necessary tools and tyre levers in your on-board tool kit – it is fairly easy to carry out a roadside repair. Remember, though, that you will need a pump to inflate the tyre.

In an emergency, you can use a tyre inflator aerosol to get out of trouble. Usually these inflators will seal a puncture, provided that it is not excessively large, so enabling you to ride slowly to the nearest garage. Such inflators are available for both tubed and tubeless tyres.

If you can spot the cause of the puncture – a nail, say – you should remove it carefully from a tubed tyre before applying the aerosol. In the case of a tubeless tyre, leave such an object in place.

In a tubed tyre, the object inevitably moves as the machine is being ridden. This movement tends to tear or chafe the tube and so negates the aerosol's effects. With a tubeless tyre, the reverse is the case.

Tubeless tyres are inherently safer than tubed ones. This is because deflation is more gradual in the event of a puncture.

Looking for help

In the world of motor cycles, mopeds and scooters, there is considerable comradeship between riders. If you are in trouble, you will find that many fellow bikers are only too willing to stop and help you.

Remember one thing. Though it is legal for one motor cycle to tow another, this is both hazardous and unsafe.

Dealing with a breakdown/3

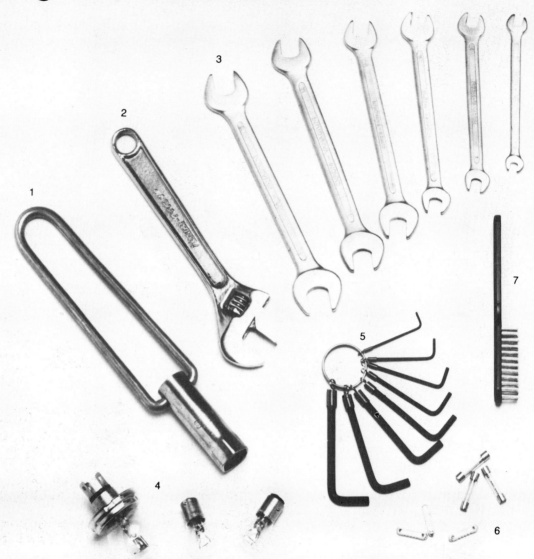

THE EMERGENCY TOOL KIT

When you are out on the road a breakdown can leave you stranded, often miles from the nearest garage. Though space for carrying tools is at a premium on a motor cycle, the equipment illustrated here can be fitted into a fairly small space; it should be enough to tackle most of the minor problems that can affect you.

1 – Spark plug spanner By removing the spark plug and checking the condition of the electrodes, the cause of many engine problems can be diagnosed quickly. In addition, you can check the ignition system by seeing if there is a spark at the plug. **2 – Adjustable spanner** This is when you need to shift the nut that none of your other spanners seem to fit, or when you need two spanners of the same size, one to hold the bolt while the nut is undone with another. **3 – Open ended spanners** These come in metric and imperial sizes, so make sure the set you buy is suitable for your motor cycle. If no spanner fits, try using one of a larger size and wedging the blade of a screwdriver between the flat of the nut and the jaw of the spanner, but this is a last resort. **4 – Bulbs** A spare headlight, brake/tail light and indicator bulb should be carried, wrapped in tissue paper. **5 – Allen keys** Many components on motor cycles are held by studs that can only be turned with an Allen key. **6 – Fuses** A blown fuse can totally cripple a motor cycle, but a new one is easy and quick to fit. Carry several fuses, making sure that they cover the specific types and ratings required for each individual circuit. **7 – Wire brush** Many electrical failures turn out to be caused by nothing more than a dirty contact, which you can easily clean with a wire brush. **8 – Screwdrivers** A flat blade and cross head screwdriver are vital tools when it comes to tackling any roadside repair. If there is enough space, it is worth carrying a set of stubby screwdrivers for use in confined areas. **9 – Knife** An essential tool in practically any roadside emergency. **10 – Pliers** A pair of bull nosed and thin nosed pliers

The puncture repair kit
(below), includes
everything you are likely to
need to repair a puncture
in a tubed or tubeless tyre.
Included are patches and
rubber solution for
repairing an inner tube,
French chalk, tyre levers,
pump hose and mushroom
plugs, which can be used
to repair both tubed and
tubeless tyres, though they
should only be used for
temporary get-you-home
purposes. You will also
need a pump to re-inflate
the repaired tyre.

should be sufficient for any job you might
have to tackle. **11 – Circuit tester** A self
powered circuit tester is probably the
most useful, irrespective of whether your
motor cycle has a batter Not only can it
be used to see if an electrical circuit is
providing power, but also to check
whether a circuit or component has
electrical continuity. **12 – Insulating tape**
Though its main use is for electrical
connections, this strong, waterproof
tape can also be used to temporarily
hold a broken panel or other component.
13 – Torch As many breakdowns occur
at night, a good torch is a vital part of any
survival kit.

Engine starting

**Engine is difficult to start,
or
fails to start**

Fuel fault

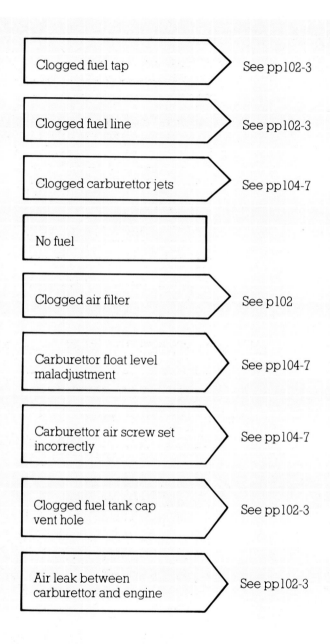

Clogged fuel tap — See pp102-3

Clogged fuel line — See pp102-3

Clogged carburettor jets — See pp104-7

No fuel

Clogged air filter — See p102

Carburettor float level maladjustment — See pp104-7

Carburettor air screw set incorrectly — See pp104-7

Clogged fuel tank cap vent hole — See pp102-3

Air leak between carburettor and engine — See pp102-3

Engine will not start at all

Ignition fault

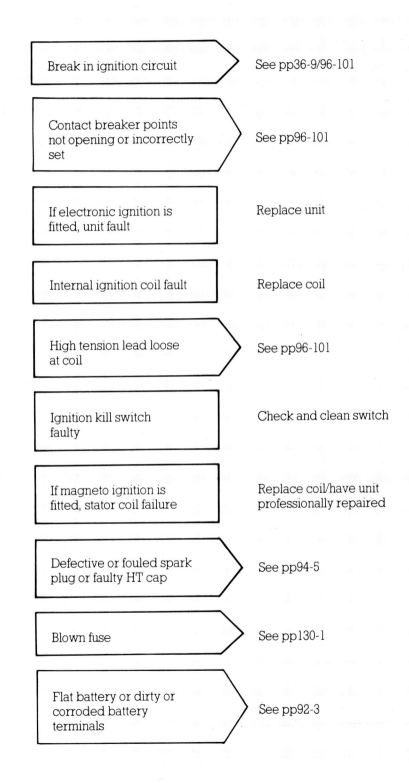

Break in ignition circuit — See pp36-9/96-101

Contact breaker points not opening or incorrectly set — See pp96-101

If electronic ignition is fitted, unit fault — Replace unit

Internal ignition coil fault — Replace coil

High tension lead loose at coil — See pp96-101

Ignition kill switch faulty — Check and clean switch

If magneto ignition is fitted, stator coil failure — Replace coil/have unit professionally repaired

Defective or fouled spark plug or faulty HT cap — See pp94-5

Blown fuse — See pp130-1

Electrical fault

Flat battery or dirty or corroded battery terminals — See pp92-3

Engine starting

Engine difficult to start

Ignition fault

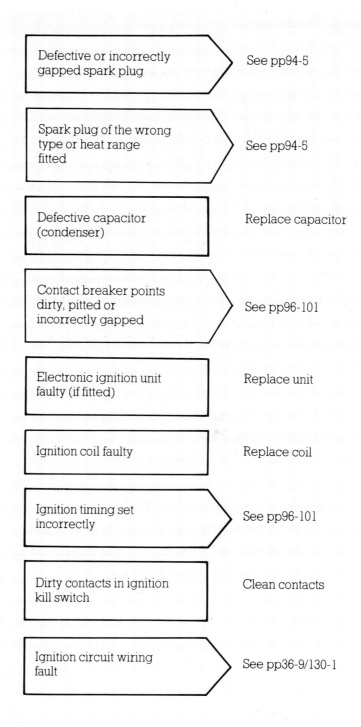

Defective or incorrectly gapped spark plug	See pp94-5
Spark plug of the wrong type or heat range fitted	See pp94-5
Defective capacitor (condenser)	Replace capacitor
Contact breaker points dirty, pitted or incorrectly gapped	See pp96-101
Electronic ignition unit faulty (if fitted)	Replace unit
Ignition coil faulty	Replace coil
Ignition timing set incorrectly	See pp96-101
Dirty contacts in ignition kill switch	Clean contacts
Ignition circuit wiring fault	See pp36-9/130-1

Engine difficult to start

Lack of compression
To check for a lack of compression, a compression tester is needed

| Blown head gasket |

| Excessive bore/piston/ piston ring wear |

| Broken or sticking piston rings |

| Cracked cylinder head |

The following faults can only be checked and rectified by dismantling the engine. If this is beyond your ability, it is best to leave the job to a garage or skilled mechanic

Faults that occur on four- stroke engines only

| Broken valve spring |

| Sticking valve |

| Incorrectly set valve clearance |

| Inadequate valve seating |

Note: Unusually high compression pressure may be due to excessive carbon build-up on piston crown and in combustion chamber. Warm the engine to operating temperature, switch off the ignition and set the throttle wide open before carrying out a compression check.

Engine performance

Engine runs for a short distance and then slows down or stops

Fuel fault

| Clogged air filter | See pp102-3 |

| Carburettor dirty or float height set incorrectly | See pp104-7 |

| Fuel starvation – clogged fuel tap or line | See pp102-3 |

Erratic low speed operation

Fuel fault

| Air leak between the carburettor and engine | See pp102-3 |

| Carburettor air screw set incorrectly | See pp104-7 |

| Clogged fuel line or tap | See pp102-3 |

Erratic high speed operation

Fuel fault

| Carburettor float height set incorrectly | See pp104-7 |

| Carburettor air screw set incorrectly | See pp104-7 |

| Clogged air filter | See pp102-3 |

| Air leak between carburettor and engine | See pp102-3 |

Erratic running

Ignition fault

| Wiring fault causing inconsistent current | See pp130-1 |

| Faulty coil | Replace coil |

| Defective capacitor (condenser) | Replace capacitor |

| Ignition timing incorrectly set | See pp96-101 |

| Contact breaker points gap set incorrectly | See pp96-101 |

| Contact breaker points dirty or pitted | See pp96-101 |

| Spark plug fouled or of the wrong type | See pp94-5 |

General loss of power

Fuel fault

| Carburettor float height set incorrectly | See pp104-7 |

| Carburettor air screw set incorrectly | See pp104-7 |

| Clogged air filter | See pp102-3 |

Engine noises

Metallic 'pinging' especially during acceleration. This is known as 'pinking'

Ignition timing too far advanced

See pp96-101

Excessive carbon build-up, causing random ignition

See pp94-5

High spot on cylinder bore, caused by partial seizure

'Slapping' noise from piston

Excessive piston to cylinder bore wear

The following faults can only be checked and rectified by dismantling the engine. If this is beyond your ability, it is best to leave the job to a garage or skilled mechanic

Small end bearing wear

Piston to gudgeon pin wear

'Knocking' noise from crankshaft, especially when the engine is under load

Big end or main bearing wear

Connecting rod or crankpin wear

Regular 'tapping' noise

Loose cam chain (four stroke only)

Excessive valve clearance (four stroke only)

Transmission/Clutch

Clutch slip

Incorrect clutch lever adjustment/no free play

See pp110-11

Friction plates are worn or distorted

The following faults can only be checked and rectified by dismantling the engine. If this is beyond your ability, it is best to leave the job to a garage or skilled mechanic

Weak clutch springs/springs unevenly tightened

Clutch pressure plate worn or distorted

Incorrect oil grade or level

Clutch drag

Incorrect lever adjustment

See pp110-11

Clutch plates stuck together

Clutch plates distorted

Clutch push rod bent

On a wet-type clutch – oil of too heavy a grade has been used

Transmission/gearbox

Difficult or impossible to engage gear

Clutch unit not functioning correctly

See pp110-11

Bent or worn selector drum stopper

The following faults can only be checked and rectified by dismantling the engine. If this is beyond your ability, it is best to leave the job to a garage or to a skilled mechanic.

Broken selector spring

Worn selector forks

Bike slips out of gear

Worn selector forks

Weak selector drum stopper spring

Gear pedal does not return

Broken return spring

Selector spindle binding

Abnormal noise

Worn or broken teeth on the gear wheels

Lack of lubrication

See pp124-5

Transmission/drive chain

Roughness and noise

| Lack of lubrication | See pp112-5 |

| Chain adjusted too tightly | See pp112-5 |

| Dirt or grit on chain | See pp112-5 |

| Excessive wear in the chain or sprockets | See pp112-5 |

Chain snatches or slips

| Loose chain | See pp112-5 |

| Sprocket teeth worn or worn down | See pp112-5 |

| Drive rubbers in rear wheel split |

Tight spot

| Uneven wear | See pp112-5 |

| Sprocket not perfectly circular | See pp112-5 |

Chain becomes excessively hot

| Lack of lubrication | See pp112-5 |

| Chain too tight | See pp112-5 |

Starting

Kick starter lever slips

Lever and spindle splines worn

Ratchet worn

The following faults can only be checked and rectified by dismantling the engine. If this is beyond your ability, it is best to leave the job to a garage or to a skilled mechanic

Kick starter lever does not return

Broken or weak return spring

Spindle bent or too tight in engine case

Electric starter motor does not work

Flat battery

See pp92-3

Circuit fault in wiring

Dirty commutator

Worn brushes

Solenoid switch faulty

The following faults can only be checked and rectified by dismantling the engine. If this is beyond your ability, it is best to leave the job to a garage or to a skilled mechanic

Starter motor rotates, but engine does not start

Clutch not engaging

Starter idler gear slipping on shaft

Cooling

Engine overheats

Lubrication fault (oil level/oil supply inadequate because of these faults)

| Oil filter clogged | See pp124-5 |

The following faults can only be checked and rectified by dismantling the engine. If this is beyond your ability, it is best to leave the job to a garage or to a skilled mechanic

Oil passages blocked

Oil pump malfunction

Air lock or incorrectly adjusted oil pump (two strokes only)

Engine overheats

| Air leak between carburettor and engine | See pp104-7 |

| High speed mixture too weak | See pp104-7 |

| Wrong type or grade of spark plug fitted | See pp94-5 |

| Ignition timing incorrectly set | See pp96-101 |

Engine overheats

Air cooled engines

| Cooling fins clogged | See pp128-9 |

Note: If the mixture is too weak, high speed running on a two-stroke often results in a holed piston. Increase size of main jet to compensate. When mixture is too rich, the engine will tend to hesitate under acceleration

Cooling

Engine overheats

Water cooled engines

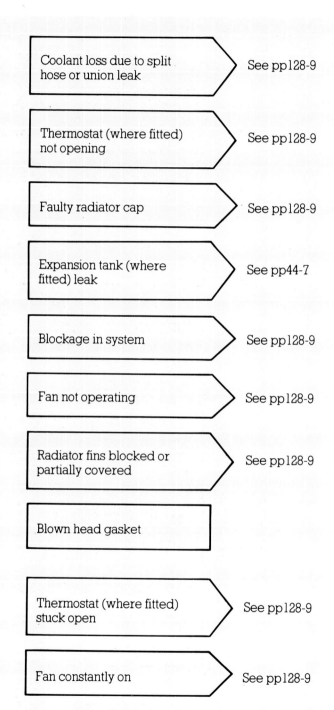

Coolant loss due to split hose or union leak — See pp128-9

Thermostat (where fitted) not opening — See pp128-9

Faulty radiator cap — See pp128-9

Expansion tank (where fitted) leak — See pp44-7

Blockage in system — See pp128-9

Fan not operating — See pp128-9

Radiator fins blocked or partially covered — See pp128-9

Blown head gasket

Engine runs too cool

Water cooled engines

Thermostat (where fitted) stuck open — See pp128-9

Fan constantly on — See pp128-9

Note: In extremely cold weather, lack of a thermostat may cause plug fouling. If a thermostat conversion cannot be fitted, blank off part of the radiator.

Cooling/Electrics

Cooling – abnormal noise

Coolant pump (where fitted) bearings worn

Note: Most liquid cooled motor cycle engines need a 50/50 mix of coolant and distilled water. This provides efficient cooling and prevents internal corrosion of alloy engine parts. Check the coolant specification in your manual.

Electrical faults

Battery discharges

Old, weak battery   See pp128-9

Wiring fault   See pp92-3

Faulty rectifier   See pp130-1

Stator coil faulty   See pp92-3

Battery overcharges

Defective current limiter

Defective battery   See pp130-1

Lights dim

Wiring corrosion

Dirt or corrosion in connector blocks/switch

Electrics

Lights do not work at all

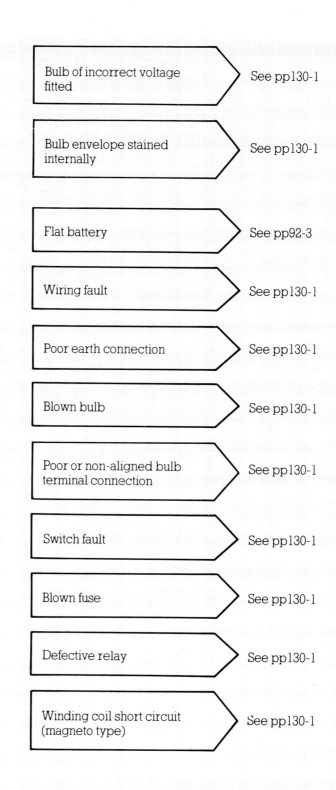

Bulb of incorrect voltage fitted — See pp130-1

Bulb envelope stained internally — See pp130-1

Flat battery — See pp92-3

Wiring fault — See pp130-1

Poor earth connection — See pp130-1

Blown bulb — See pp130-1

Poor or non-aligned bulb terminal connection — See pp130-1

Switch fault — See pp130-1

Blown fuse — See pp130-1

Defective relay — See pp130-1

Winding coil short circuit (magneto type) — See pp130-1

Steering

Heavy or stiff steering

Steering head bearings too tight — See pp116-9

Steering head bearings need lubrication — See pp116-9

Steering head bearings broken — See pp116-9

Steering stem bent — See pp116-9

Front tyre pressure excessively low — See pp116-9

Steering damper (if fitted) adjusted too hard — See pp116-9

Badly routed cables or wires interfering with steering

Loose steering

Head bearings too loose — See pp116-9

Steering head bearings badly worn or broken — See pp116-9

Handling

Bike wanders

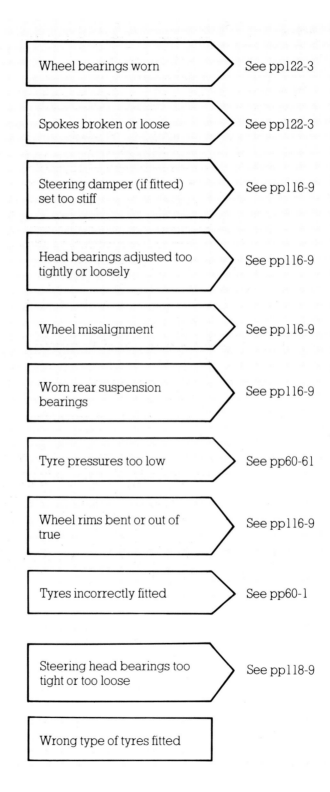

Wheel bearings worn
See pp122-3

Spokes broken or loose
See pp122-3

Steering damper (if fitted) set too stiff
See pp116-9

Head bearings adjusted too tightly or loosely
See pp116-9

Wheel misalignment
See pp116-9

Worn rear suspension bearings
See pp116-9

Tyre pressures too low
See pp60-61

Wheel rims bent or out of true
See pp116-9

Tyres incorrectly fitted
See pp60-1

Bike wobbles or weaves

Steering head bearings too tight or too loose
See pp118-9

Wrong type of tyres fitted

Bike wobbles or weaves

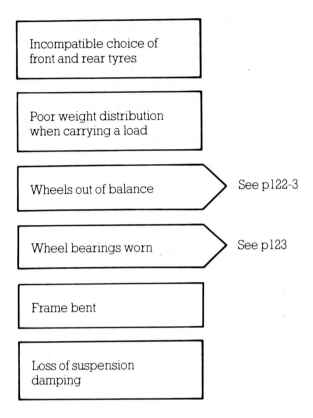

Incompatible choice of
front and rear tyres

Poor weight distribution
when carrying a load

Wheels out of balance — See p122-3

Wheel bearings worn — See p123

Frame bent

Loss of suspension
damping

Note: A few machines – usually those of large displacement – show a tendency to break into a weave at high speed from new. This can often be cured by tyre replacement; consult your dealer for advice. Correct tyre pressures and maintenance of steering components, especially head bearings, is essential.

Tyre testers, too, have found that rider weight has a bearing on high speed weave. A machine with this tendency is inclined to weave earlier with a lightweight rider on board. Usually, leaning forward and easing off the throttle gradually will bring the machine out of the weave

Brakes

Brakes do not work

Drum brakes

Not properly adjusted	See pp52-9
Seized or frayed cable or bent rod	See pp52-9
Seized cam pivot on foot lever pivot	See pp52-9
Worn brake shoes or drum	See pp52-9
Oil on brake shoes	See pp52-9

Brakes do not work

Disc brakes

Loss of brake fluid	See pp52-9
Air in system	See pp52-9
Brake lever incorrectly adjusted	See pp52-9
Oil on disc or pads	See pp52-9
Pads excessively worn	See pp52-9
Piston seized/pins or pivot (sliding type) seized	See pp52-9

Brakes drag

Drum brakes

Brake adjusted too tightly

See pp52-9

Seized cam pivots not allowing shoes to free

See pp52-9

Seized cable or fouled brake rod

See pp52-9

Brake drum unevenly worn

Dirt trapped between brake lining and shoe

The following faults can only be checked and rectified by dismantling the brakes. If this is beyond your ability, it is best to leave the job to a garage or to a skilled mechanic

Brakes drag

Disc brakes

Pad, piston, or pivot seized

Disc out of true

Lever over-adjusted

See pp52-9

Instruments

Cable loose, or inner broken

See pp52-9

Speedometer and tachometer do not work

Circuit fault (electronic type)

Basic repairs and checks

Most bikers soon find that it becomes second nature to take good care of their machines. The instant throttle response and the fact that bike and rider crank through corners in unison are just two of the factors that contribute to the affection a bike owner develops for his or her bike – and to the desire to keep it in top condition.

Carrying out routine checks and servicing and taking care of basic repairs are essential to keep that bike and rider relationship running smoothly. Indeed, bikers often derive a deep sense of satisfaction through being able to care for their machines competently and diagnose problems.

This section of You and Your Bike will help both the newcomer to two wheels and the seasoned biker to tackle basic servicing and checks and to diagnose faults logically. It will not only make riding more enjoyable – it will make it safer, too.

Basic essentials

Start by arming yourself with a good workshop manual, covering your model, plus a good d-i-y tool kit.

Obviously, a manual is essential to check such things as the correct spark plug type and gap, the ignition setting, carburettor jetting and so on. And it is even more essential if you are buying a second-hand machine, when you simply may not know what the previous owner may have done – or left undone.

In fact, it is not uncommon to find that a machine has been put up for sale because it is running slightly sick after the owner has worked on it without really knowing what he or she was doing. Without a manual, you will not be able to see whether or not the components match the ones recommended by the manufacturer and that they are fitted correctly.

It is all too easy, for instance, to fit a carburettor slide back to front. This means that, though the bike will start and run, it will not rev up properly. This could be a tricky problem for a newcomer to biking to solve, but, with a little informed thought, it should be possible to detect the incorrectly fitted component.

Your basic tool kit

To carry out repairs, a good tool kit is essential. Though it is only natural to want to limit the amount you spend, it can be a false economy to buy the cheapest tools available. It is a far better plan to build up your kit as you go along, buying the best quality tools you can afford as and when you need them.

High quality tools can make all the difference when it comes to servicing many of today's machines. Most are powered by lightweight alloy engines, held together by screws and bolts. These can be easily rounded off and damaged by tools lacking in precision and hardness.

If you are trying to remove a clutch cover with a weak or poorly fitting screwdriver, for instance, you might spoil the edges of a crosshead screw. To get it out means using a drill, which, if not handled carefully, can easily damage the alloy casing, while, obviously enough, a new screw will also be needed. From this, you can see that it is quicker and less expensive to buy the right good quality tool for the job in the first place.

Most manufacturers list their own tools, which are available through dealers. They are specifically designed to suit the bike and are often far less expensive than you might expect. As well as a socket set, spanners and screwdrivers, buy a torque wrench, if you can afford it. This will soon repay the investment.

With all tools, you must beware of over-tightening engine and other alloy components. You can crack an alloy crankcase, for instance, by using too much leverage when refitting the oil drain plug.

On board tools

What about the bike's tool kit? In the main, the tools that you will find supplied with your bike are intended only for emergency use. Particularly on lightweight machines, they are spartan in number and of dubious quality. When servicing and carrying out repairs at home, use the better quality kit you are building up.

The importance of maintenance

Prevention is better than cure, so adequate maintenance is an absolute priority. Oil and coolant levels should be checked frequently to prevent the possibility of seizures. So, too, should tyre pressures to lessen the risk of punctures.

This seems simple common sense, but it is surprising how frequently it is ignored. Biker surveys show, for instance, that the most common problem to affect Honda four-stroke 50cc machines is engine seizure, simply because some owners ride their bikes month in month out without ever checking the oil level.

Oil changes should also be carried out at the intervals recommended by the manufacturer. Many four-stroke motorcycles, for instance, feature small bore oilways to lubricate overhead camshafts. Old oil, heavy with impurities, can all too easily partially or completely clog these oilways and so starve the camshaft of its essential lubrication.

Frequent checks and frequent cleaning will reveal many potential problems which should be tackled immediately, thus preventing them from becoming significant. If your machine suddenly feels different, or begins to make a strange noise, always dismount and investigate. There must be a reason.

Never take a bike for granted and always check brakes, tyres, chain and oil. Remember that, though looking after your machine may cost you money, not looking after it could cost you your life.

Essential spares

Of course, no preventative precautions programme can cover the inevitable component failure. You must anticipate and allow for these by carrying a few essential spares. This way, roadside halts for repairs will take up the minimum possible time.

A spare headlight and tail light bulb, wrapped in protective foam, a spare spark plug and chain joining link with circlip should be carried as a minimum emergency parts kit, along with the bike's standard tool kit. More cautious owners sometimes tape spare cables to those in use, while, if your bike is fitted with tubed tyres, it is a good idea to carry a puncture repair outfit and tyre levers.

Punctured tubeless tyres cannot be repaired by the roadside. To beat the puncture problem, carry a small bicycle pump with an adaptor on the machine and an aerosol inflater. Though most tyre companies do not recommend such aerosols, they will get you home, or to the nearest garage, providing you ride slowly. The tyre should then be professionally repaired, or replaced.

Roadside logic

Should your engine cut out, search for the cause in logical steps.
*Make sure that you have not run out of fuel.
Check that there is a spark at the plug, or plugs, by removing the plug, reconnecting it to the HT (high tension) cap, resting it against the cylinder to earth it and then turning the engine over with the ignition switched on.
*If there is no spark at the electrodes, try your spare plug. If this does not work, check that the HT cap is connected tightly to the HT lead and that the lead is similarly securely connected to the coil.
*Where points are fitted on a battery-fed ignition system, check that current is reaching the points by gently levering them open with a screwdriver while the ignition is switched on. If current is reaching them, there should be a spark at the screwdriver's tip.
*In the case of electronic ignition, all you can do is to check for loose, damp or corroded wiring and to make sure that the battery is in good condition.
*If the ignition is working, check the carburettor.
*If the spark plug(s) remains dry despite turning the engine over rapidly, it is logical to suspect a clogged carburettor jet or jets. Remove the float bowl, clean out any sediment and blow through the main jet to clear it of any impurities.

Further checks are detailed later in this section. By putting all of them into practice, you will keep your bike in top working condition.

Battery maintenance

You should check your battery at least once a week as a matter of routine. Make sure that the electrolyte level is between the lower and upper level marks on the side of the battery and use only distilled water for topping up, if this is necessary. Tap water shortens battery life, because 'fur' forms inside the battery.

Keep electrodes free from corrosion by smearing them with petroleum jelly. Make sure that the connections are tight and that the pad fitted to the bottom of the housing is present and preventing vibration.

Check that the overflow pipe is not clogged or kinked and that it is correctly routed, usually to below the level of the bottom frame tubes. Route it away from the final drive chain. This is important, because, if battery acid gets on to a chain, it can cause links to become brittle and possibly snap. Check that the seat or sidepanels do not crush the pipe when you replace them.

Make sure that the battery casing is free from cracks and dry. Water is a good conductor of electricity and will short the battery out if the two electrodes are linked by it.

Battery condition

If your battery is old or its condition suspect, check it with a hydrometer. This measures the specific gravity (density) of the electrolyte.

You can buy a hydrometer from your dealer, or an auto accessory store. Buy the smallest type available, especially if you are dealing with a small six-volt battery, which will have only a limited electrolyte capacity per cell.

The float reading in the hydrometer should be 1.26. If all

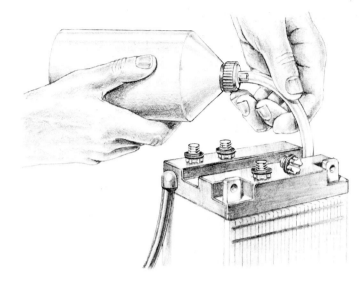

Check the electrolyte level once a week, topping up if necessary. Use distilled water, not tap water.

readings are lower than this, recharging is necessary.

Reasons for replacement

If one cell is faulty, it will be discoloured and may get very hot during the charging process. The battery will not be able to provide full voltage and eventually will need to be replaced by a new one.

On a 12-volt machine with an electric start, an effective way of telling if a fully-charged battery is in good condition is to remove the high tension leads from the spark plugs, connect a voltmeter across the battery terminals, switch the ignition on and the kill button off and press the starter button. If the voltage drops below nine volts while the engine is being cranked, the battery should be replaced.

On a six-volt machine without electric start, put the voltmeter across the battery terminals, switch on the ignition, the

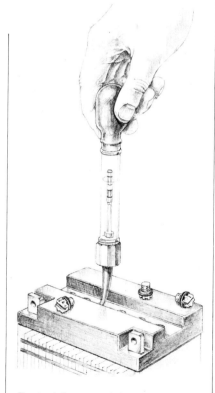

To check the state of charge, draw up a little electrolyte from a cell with a hydrometer. If the float reading is under 1.26, recharge the battery.

indicators and all the lights. Hold the brake light on. If the voltage across the terminals falls below five volts, the battery should be replaced.

If a battery requires frequent topping up and has a tendency to 'boil', it is likely to have suffered serious internal damage and so should be replaced.

Charging the battery

However, the most common causes of battery performance loss are failure to keep the battery topped up and failure to keep the battery charged when not in use. In the latter case, the battery should be trickle charged once a fortnight. If this is not done, sulphuration occurs. The plates erodes and sediment collects at the bottom of the cells, causing an internal short circuit. Eroded plates and sediment can be seen through the transparent casings on the batteries fitted to most bikes and scooters.

Before charging a battery, take it off the machine. Make sure that the battery is topped up and the vent tube clear. Set the charger to six or 12 volts, depending on the battery type. Connect the charger's red lead to the battery's positive terminal and the black one to the negative terminal and then switch on the charger.

Strictly speaking, a battery should be charged at one-tenth of what is termed the amp-hour rating. For example, a 14Ah battery from a large bike should be charged at 1.4amps.

Ensuring this means purchasing a special trickle charger purpose designed for motorcycles, but a general-purpose charger with, for example, an 0-6 amp scale, which progressively increases

Use two spanners to release the terminal bolts. Remove bolts, washers and cable.

Clean corrosion off battery posts with a stiff wire brush and smear them with petroleum jelly to protect them.

When recharging, make sure that the charger is set to the correct voltage and the leads are running to the right terminals before switching on the power. If the cells have individual caps, remove these before charging.

the charging rate as the battery accepts a charge, can be safely used in practice, provided that the battery is checked every 15 to 20 minutes. However, garage-type high amperage boost chargers should be used only as a last resort. The danger is that too powerful a charge can buckle the battery plates.

Bear in mind that battery electrolyte is dilute sulphuric acid. So charging should be carried out in a well-ventilated atmosphere and keep naked flames away from the battery. Always switch the charger off at the mains before disconnecting leads to prevent sparks. If you spill acid on your skin, bathe the affected area copiously with plenty of cold water.

Checking spark plugs

In a medium performance four-stroke bike engine, the maximum lifespan of a spark plug is generally considered to be 10,000 miles (16,000km). If you own a high performance two-stroke machine, you should halve this figure; a turbocharged engine may need new plugs every 2,000 miles (3200km). Thus, a spark plug is the first component that should be inspected if a problem occurs.

Fitting a spark plug

To remove a spark plug, first detach the HT (high tension) lead, clean the area around the plug. Then, using a spark plug socket, or box spanner, unscrew the plug.

If the plug will not budge, do not use undue force. Spray the base of the plug with penetrating fluid and try again. Threads in alloy cylinder heads are easily stripped if excessive force is used to try to free a seized plug.

Before fitting a new plug, check the coding on its side to make sure that it suits your machine. Lightly coat the plug threads with copper anti-seizure compound. Screw the plug in finger tight until it seats and then tighten it one-quarter turn with a spanner. Where a screw-on terminal is required to mate with the HT cap, make sure that this is firmly in place.

Checking for a spark

To check for a spark at the plug electrodes, remove the plug from the engine, insert the plug back into the HT cap and allow the plug to rest against a metallic part of the engine, such as the cylinder. This will provide an earthing point. Then turn the engine over either by electric or kick start with the ignition on.

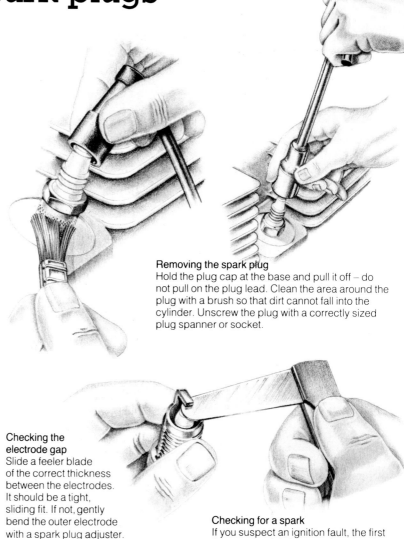

Removing the spark plug
Hold the plug cap at the base and pull it off – do not pull on the plug lead. Clean the area around the plug with a brush so that dirt cannot fall into the cylinder. Unscrew the plug with a correctly sized plug spanner or socket.

Checking the electrode gap
Slide a feeler blade of the correct thickness between the electrodes. It should be a tight, sliding fit. If not, gently bend the outer electrode with a spark plug adjuster.

Checking for a spark
If you suspect an ignition fault, the first thing to check is for a spark at the plug. Rest the plug, with HT cap attached, against the cylinder. Turn the ignition on and turn the engine over; there should be a strong, blue spark between the electrodes.

A strong blue spark should be observed at the plug electrodes. If not, try a new plug. If this fails, look for reasons for the failure. These may include a loose HT lead, a faulty HT cap, or, if fitted, the points may not be opening.

Diagnosing faults

Checking the condition of a spark plug often provides a good indication of how well or efficiently your engine is running. The key part of the plug is the porcelain area around the centre

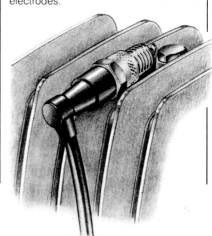

electrode. Basically a light tan colour indicates that the engine is in good running order, pure white is a sign that the mixture is too weak and black that it is too rich. If the plug has a wet oily look, this is a sign that there is excessive piston-to-bore or valve-to-guide clearance and oil is entering the combustion chamber. Rectifying this is a garage job.

The electrodes should be checked for signs of wear. If they have rounded, rather than squared, ends, then they are worn. If this wear is excessive, replace the plug.

If the engine misfires, change the plug, or plugs, as a matter of course. If this cures the problem, but only for a short period, look elsewhere for its cause.

Plug problems

One of the commonest causes of misfires on modern four-stroke engines is lead fouling. This occurs usually because fuel of too high a grade is being used in the mistaken belief that this will improve performance.

The lead content in the higher octane fuel leaves deposits on the core nose of the insulator. These deposits, which are yellow in colour, allow the current that should be supplying the spark to earth, rather than jumping the gap to the outer electrode.

Another common error is the use of plugs one grade harder (colder) than those recommended by the manufacturer – again in the belief that their use will make the engine run more efficiently. In fact, the plugs will be too cold and will be prone to fouling at low speeds since they will conduct heat away from the combustion chamber too quickly.

In consequence, the burning of the mixture is incomplete and deposits form on the insulator nose. These again allow the current to earth, rather than jump the plug gap.

Dirt or moisture on a plug's outside can allow the current to earth, causing misfires. This is 'flashover'. Keep the outside of the insulator clean to prevent this.

Beware of resistor-type plugs. These usually have the letter 'R' in their coding and are common on Japanese machines. They usually work well, but if they do become faulty and cause misfiring, they can fool the rider because they may still spark and

look perfect. Checking them out involves the use of an ohm meter; the resistance should read 5000 ohms.

Loose plugs cause their own problems, too. They are prone to over-heating because they cannot pass combustion heat to the cylinder head effectively.

Too wide a gap between the electrodes can damage the ignition. So, too, can the fitting of an HT cap with too high a resistance. In both cases, the current, which always looks for the path to earth with the least resistance, may find that burning through the ignition coil insulation is easier than jumping the electrode gap.

PLUG PROBLEMS

If the plug electrodes have worn as much as this, the plug will not produce a good, strong spark and engine performance will suffer as a result. The plug should be replaced.

Because the electrodes of this plug are oiled up, it cannot produce a good spark. Continual oiling up is a sign that wear within the engine is allowing oil into the combustion chamber.

If the plug electrodes are covered with a black, sooty deposit, the fuel/air mixture is too rich. The electrodes can be cleaned, but the carburation should also be checked.

If the central electrode has a hard white deposit on it, then the plug has overheated while the engine has been running. This is often caused by an excessively weak fuel/air mixture.

Ignition checks/1

Whatever make or model of bike you possess, accurate ignition timing is vital. Without it, both engine performance and reliability will suffer.

If the engine hesitates momentarily when the throttle is opened, or knocks when the throttle is opened wide from low revs, this is a sign that the ignition timing may be too advanced – that is, occuring too early. On the other hand, loss of power and a tendency for the engine to overheat may indicate that the ignition timing is retarded – in other words, occuring too late.

Normal timing
Normally, the spark is timed to occur at a set distance just before the piston reaches top dead centre, the uppermost point in its travel. The exact point will be given in your manual as a distance – 0.0787in (2mm), for instance – or in degrees – 20° BTDC (before top dead centre).

If a spark occurs before this timing point, the ignition is advanced. A spark after the timing point means the ignition is retarded.

Checking timing
The only way of checking the timing on an engine with points ignition means setting the points gap first. You must then check the spark timing with the engine running. With electronic ignition, you check timing with a stroboscopic timing light. With such a system, this is the only way in which to determine that the spark is occuring at the correct time in relation to piston travel.

To check the points, start by examining their contact faces. If these are badly pitted, replace the points. If pitting is combined

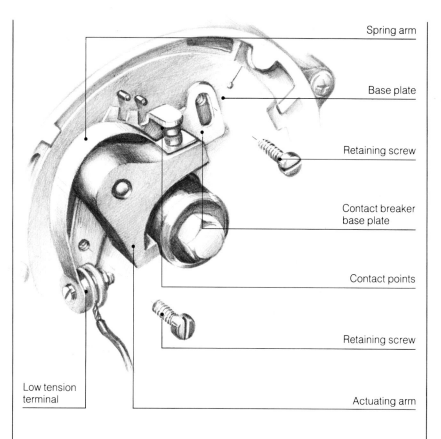

Spring arm

Base plate

Retaining screw

Contact breaker base plate

Contact points

Retaining screw

Low tension terminal

Actuating arm

with a misfiring engine, this indicates that the condensor is faulty. This, too, should be replaced.

An engine that tends to 'pull back' intermittently under acceleration may simply be suffering from dirty point faces. If this is the case, you can clean them with a points file. Wipe the faces with methylated spirit and then re-set the points gap, as specified in your workshop manual.

In some cases, it may prove impossible to clean the points without removing them. If this is the case, make a note of the order in which you remove the various components to ensure that you replace them correctly. It is all too easy – especially with fibre washers – to inadvertently

reassemble the components in the wrong order and find, as a result, that there is no spark because the points have been earthed permanently.

Preserving the points
With the cleaned, or new, points fitted, lightly grease the cam that bears against the heel of the points, or oil the felt pad (if fitted). This prevents premature wear of the points heel. This is important, since, as the heel wears, the gap between the points closes up, so retarding the ignition timing.

Setting the points gap
Set the points gap with the heel of the points against the highest point of the points cam. The can can be rotated via the nut on the

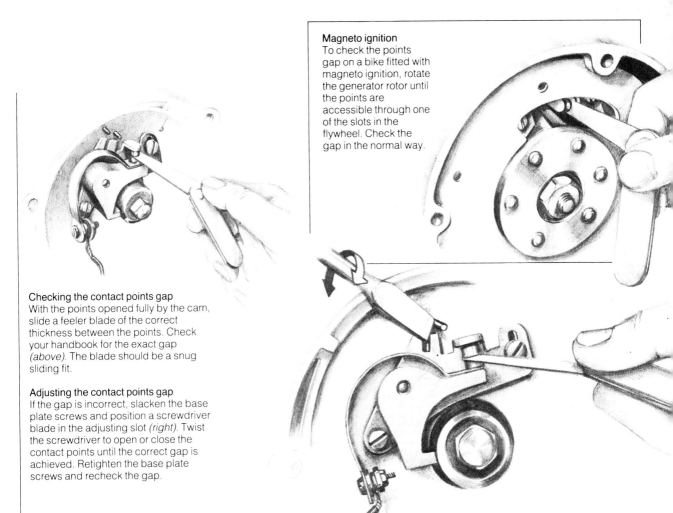

Magneto ignition
To check the points gap on a bike fitted with magneto ignition, rotate the generator rotor until the points are accessible through one of the slots in the flywheel. Check the gap in the normal way.

Checking the contact points gap
With the points opened fully by the cam, slide a feeler blade of the correct thickness between the points. Check your handbook for the exact gap *(above)*. The blade should be a snug sliding fit.

Adjusting the contact points gap
If the gap is incorrect, slacken the base plate screws and position a screwdriver blade in the adjusting slot *(right)*. Twist the screwdriver to open or close the contact points until the correct gap is achieved. Retighten the base plate screws and recheck the gap.

end of the crankshaft, with the engine in neutral. Points adjustment is made via the adjustable points arm.

Use the appropriate feeler gauge to set the width of the gap to the figure quoted in your workshop manual. The gauge should be a snug fit. The setting can be double checked by a method known as 'go - no go'. For example, if the points gap is specified as 0.015in (0.3mm), set the gap using a 0.015in feeler blade. Then try a 0.016in blade – it should not fit ('no go'). But a 0.014in blade should slide between the faces with no appreciable resistance ('go').

By setting the points gap you also set the 'dwell' period, which is often referred to in degrees of rotation. This is the time the

REMOVING THE FLYWHEEL

If you need to adjust the contact breaker points gap on a motor cycle fitted with magneto ignition, you may have to remove the generator rotor in order to get to the points assembly. Ideally, you should use a special tool to lock the rotor in place while you loosen the locking nut *(left)*. Hold the locknut with a spanner and use a rotor puller to remove the rotor *(right)*.

Ignition checks/2

points are closed and is the main object of the points setting exercise.

While the points are closed (dwell) current is passed to the coil in which a magnetic field builds up so that a healthy spark can be produced for efficient ignition. The dwell can be checked using a dwell meter, or a multi-function meter that has this facility built into it. This is the most accurate method of achieving the correct points gap, especially if the points are worn and the faces are out of parallel.

The meter terminals are connected to the low tension terminal at the points and a convenient earth. With the engine running, the meter will register the dwell angle – the correct figure should be specified in your handbook. If the dwell is not correct, stop the engine and readjust the points until the meter reading is correct.

With the points gap set to give the correct dwell period, the next job is the timing of the ignition. This involves adjusting

the ignition so that the spark occurs at the right time in relation to the position of the piston.

Timing the spark
A timing figure should be quoted in your handbook, expressed as degrees before top dead centre – in other words, just before the piston reaches the top of its stroke. In the case of a two-stroke single, firing occurs each time the piston approaches TDC. In the case of a four-stroke single, this occurs every other stroke, the points cam being driven at half the number of crankshaft revolutions to take this into account.

With a multi-cylinder four-stroke, make sure that the piston is approaching TDC on its firing stroke – not the exhaust stroke – in the cylinder for which the timing is being set. To ensure this, check that the inlet and exhaust valves are firmly closed to seal the cylinder during ignition. At this point there will be free play in the mechanisms that operate both inlet and

TIMING MARKS

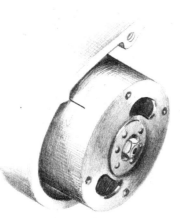

On motor cycles with magneto ignition, the timing marks are often stamped on the generator rotor and line up with a static mark on the crankcase *(above)*. Some motor cycles have a window in the crankcase that enables you to see the marks without removing the crankcase side cover *(below)*.

Four-stroke motor cycles usually have the timing marks stamped on the rotor of the generator *(above)*, with the static mark on one of the fixed magnets, or on the generator casing *(below)*.

On twin cylinder machines with two sets of contact breaker points, there should be two sets of timing marks. One set for the left hand cylinder has the prefix L before the F and T marks.

exhaust valves. For this, rocker or cam covers will have to be removed, unless the manufacturer has specified another way of checking piston position.

Static timing

The information in your handbook is given so that you are able to carry out a 'static' timing check – that is, with the engine not running. In most cases this involves aligning a mark on the flywheel with a fixed 'index' mark. You will find this stamped on the engine casing.

The flywheel mark to be aligned is usually denoted by the letter 'F' for firing. As the flywheel is turned in the normal direction of rotation, the contact breaker points should just begin to open as the marks align. The easiest way to check this is with a circuit tester, a screwdriver with a bulb inside it and a lead with a crocodile clip attached.

In the case of a bike without a battery, the circuit tester must have its own, built-in battery. To check this system, first disconnect the low tension lead from the points to cut off the path to earth. Connect the tester between the low tension terminal and a convenient earthing point. When the points are closed, the bulb in the tester will light. The instant the points open, the bulb will go out. When this happens the F mark should align with the fixed index mark. If this is not the case, adjustment is necessary.

On a system which uses a battery to provide the primary current, you can use a circuit tester without its own power supply or just a bulb with two connector leads. The tester should be connected to the low tension terminal and a

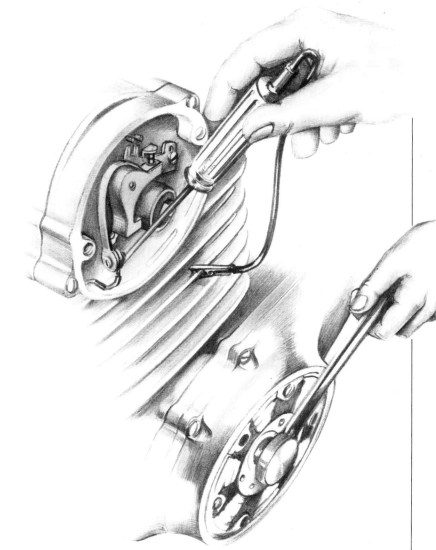

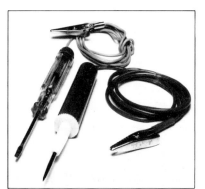

A circuit test screwdriver is an inexpensive and handy tool. If your bike does not have a battery, use a self-powered test screwdriver *(right)*; otherwise you can use the type with just a bulb in it *(left)*.

Timing the ignition
Statically timing the ignition involves ensuring that the points are just opening when the F mark on the rotor is in line with the fixed timing mark. This can be checked accurately with a circuit test screwdriver. If the motor cycle has a battery, connect the earth terminal to thé metal of the engine and touch the blade to the low tension terminal on the points assembly. Rotate the flywheel until the timing marks align, at which point the bulb in the screwdriver should light. If it does not light at this point, then the timing is out and will need to be adjusted. If the motor cycle does not have a battery, use a circuit test screwdriver with a built-in power source. Follow the same procedure; in this case, the bulb will go out when the points open.

Ignition checks/3

convenient earth as before.

Switch the ignition on. As soon as the points open, the test light will shine because the current is flowing through the tester, while the F mark should align with the fixed index mark. If the mark does not align, then timing adjustment is necessary.

Adjusting the timing

The usual method of adjustment is by moving the backplate to which the points are attached. The plate is usually held in place by two or three pinch screws. When they are slackened, the plate can be carefully moved clockwise or anti-clockwise as appropriate in order to establish the correct timing.

On some small low output engines, backplate adjustment may not be provided. Instead a tolerance for the points gap may be quoted as 0.012 to 0.016in (0.3 to 0.4mm); the timing can be altered by varying the gap within this range. Widening the gap will have the effect of advancing the ignition, while narrowing it will retard the ignition. If correct timing cannot be achieved within the specified tolerance, then the points set is worn and should be replaced.

On high power two–stroke engines, accurate ignition timing is crucial. For this reason, most modern high performance two-strokes have pointless electronic ignition, which does away with the need for this kind of adjustment. On older high performance two-stroke bikes, however, conventional points ignition is standard and this must be checked in the usual way at the usual intervals.

If no index marks are provided to enable you to check the timing, it is necessary to use a

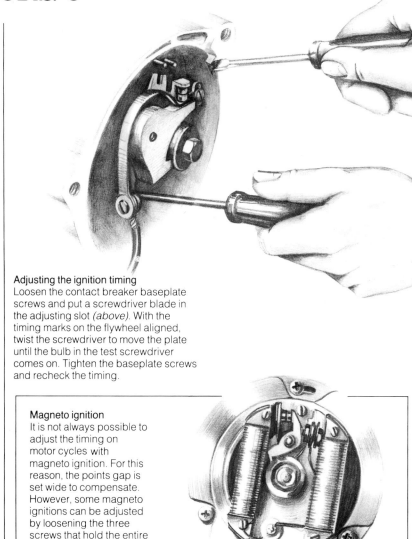

Adjusting the ignition timing
Loosen the contact breaker baseplate screws and put a screwdriver blade in the adjusting slot *(above)*. With the timing marks on the flywheel aligned, twist the screwdriver to move the plate until the bulb in the test screwdriver comes on. Tighten the baseplate screws and recheck the timing.

Magneto ignition
It is not always possible to adjust the timing on motor cycles with magneto ignition. For this reason, the points gap is set wide to compensate. However, some magneto ignitions can be adjusted by loosening the three screws that hold the entire assembly and rotating this until the timing is accurately set.

dial gauge to determine piston position. As this can be a complex job, it is best left to a professional.

Stroboscopic checking

With some engines, you can check the timing while the engine is running. This involves the use of a stroboscopic timing light. Such a light, when connected between the spark plug and HT lead, emits a beam of light when the spark jumps the gap between the plug's electrodes.

By pointing the light at the 'F' mark on the flywheel, the instrument 'freezes' the mark, so making it look as if it were static. Thus it can easily be checked in relation to the fixed index mark.

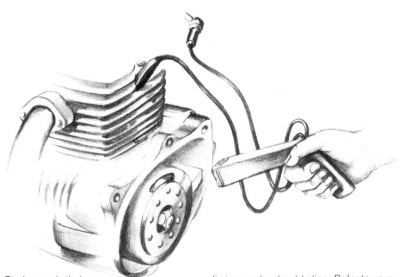

Stroboscopic timing
Often, it is necessary to check the ignition timing (especially ignition advance) with the engine running. This can be done with a timing light, wired into the spark plug cap and the spark plug (above). The light will flash every time the plug fires – at this point the timing marks should align. Refer to your handbook for exact details. The flashing of the light will 'freeze' the timing marks, allowing you to check their position in relation to the fixed timing mark. It helps to see the marks if they are given a dab of white paint.

Further adjustments

Your workshop manual should give you the details of the timing checks that should be made at tickover speed and higher rpm. The manual may state, for instance, that the 'F' mark should align with the index mark at an engine speed of 1200rpm.

If such an adjustment is necessary, stop the engine, loosen the screws holding the back (stator) plate in position and move the plate carefully in the direction required for correct alignment. Then, after tightening the stator screws, double check by running the engine again.

On some engines, you will find it necessary to remove the flywheel to get to the securing screws. Special tools will be required, so if you do not possess these or feel confident using them, the job is best left to a garage, or a competent mechanic.

In addition to a low rpm timing check, a check at high rpm – 6,000 rpm, say – may be specified. In such a case, the 'F' mark is not involved. Instead, look for two (or sometimes three) closely-spaced marks further along the flywheel circumference. The area between them should align with the fixed index mark at the specified rpm.

If the information for this check is available, it should be carried out with a strobe light, as this is without question the most accurate way of going about the job. Incorrect ignition timing at higher rpm – where the engine develops the bulk of its power – is more likely to cause serious mechanical damage, such as overheating and holed pistons, in the long run.

Ignition advance

Most four-stroke and some two-stroke engines feature some form of ignition advance. This is necessary since, though, with any rise in revs, the piston naturally reaches the top of its stroke sooner, the mixture still takes the same time to ignite. Thus, a method of advancing the spark automatically is required.

You can check visually to see whether or not the advance system is operating correctly with the aid of a strobe light. This enables you to see the 'F' mark moving away from the fixed index mark as the engine revs increase. As you allow the revs to drop, the 'F' mark should move closer towards alignment with the fixed index.

On engines with mechanical advance/retard units, the unit should be stripped and lubricated if this movement is jerky. This can be a complex job and so is best left to a qualified mechanic.

At a certain point up the rev scale, maximum advance will be reached. This figure is usually specified by the bike's manufacturer – it is normally between 3,000 rpm and 6,000 rpm. At this point, the closely aligned marks on the flywheel should align with the fixed index.

Where a machine with electronic ignition is not working correctly, inspect wiring and switches for corrosion and breaks in the insulation. The most common problem is corrosion of the contacts in the handlebar 'kill' switch. If there are no such outward indications as to the source of the problem, consult a professional mechanic, or your dealer. Do not meedle with the system, as it is all too easy to make matters worse.

Fuel system maintenance/1

The key operating part of any air filter is its foam or paper element. It is essential that such elements are cleaned or replaced, according to the manufacturer's instructions.

Foam elements can be washed in a solvent, such as paraffin, squeezed dry and re-oiled. The last stage is essential, since the oil traps particles of dust and dirt, hence protecting the inlet system. Paper elements are impossible to clean, so new ones must be fitted at the specified service intervals.

Detecting filter wear

Since filters only become contaminated gradually, you may not realize that your machine's performance is being impaired until the problem becomes obvious. Remember, too, that the power output of some engines can be partially restricted by the standard air filtration system. Usually, this is because there is insufficient space for an adequately sized filter; in such instances, regular attention is even more important.

Tell-tale signs of possible heavy filter contamination include the darkened appearance of the filter, the refusal of the engine to take full throttle and sooty black deposits around the spark plug's central electrode. Strangely, the engine will often start readily from cold. This is because the clogged filter has the same effect as a choke. Once warm, however, though the engine may run happily at low throttle openings, it will refuse to produce power when the throttle is opened more fully.

Replacing a filter

Fitting a filter is normally straightforward. Make sure that

Air filters Most motor cycles are fitted with a paper element cartridge filter or a sponge filter. A paper filter should be replaced when it becomes clogged with dirt, whereas a sponge filter can usually be cleaned with solvent.

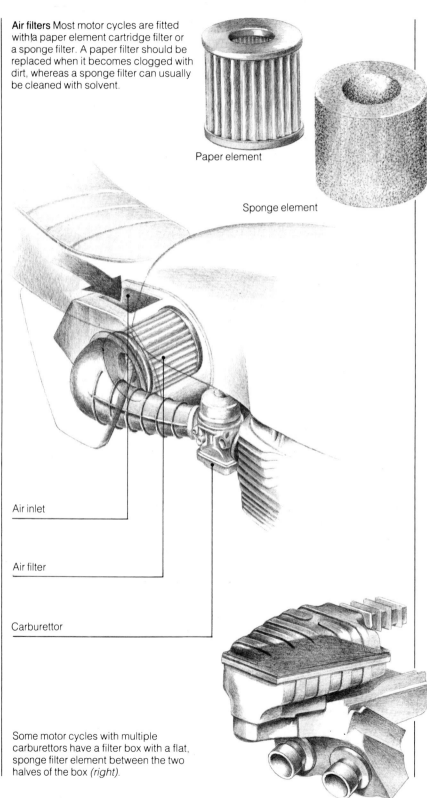

Paper element

Sponge element

Air inlet

Air filter

Carburettor

Some motor cycles with multiple carburettors have a filter box with a flat, sponge filter element between the two halves of the box (right).

the air passage leading to the airbox is not covered – it has been known for underseat inlets to be blocked inadvertently with cleaning rags, for instance.

With the filter in place, make sure that there are no gaps between any mating surfaces, as such gaps could allow unfiltered air to reach the carburettor. If you are fitting a foam filter, one simple and effective way of avoiding the problem is to smear a light coating of grease around the edge of the filter to seal it where it butts against the inner face of the airbox.

Checking the breather tube
Many large four-stroke engines are fitted with a breather tube, which runs from the engine to the airbox. This tube is often referred to as ' PCV (positive crankcase vent); its job is to vent the combustion gases that have been blown by the pistons into the crankcase back into the airbox. If such a tube is fitted, you should check it at regular intervals to ensure that it is not kinked or clogged.

Checking fuel flow
If the engine simply refuses to run, first make sure that there is fuel in the tank. To check this, remove the fuel pipe from the carburettor, hold the end over an empty jar and switch on the fuel.

The next step depends on what sort of fuel tap is fitted. If no fuel flows through a non-vacuum tap, remove the tank's filler cap and see what happens. If fuel starts to flow, the problem may be caused by a blockage in the cap's vent hole. Any such blockage should be cleared.

Where a vacuum tap is fitted, you will have to suck carefully on the petrol pipe to check for fuel

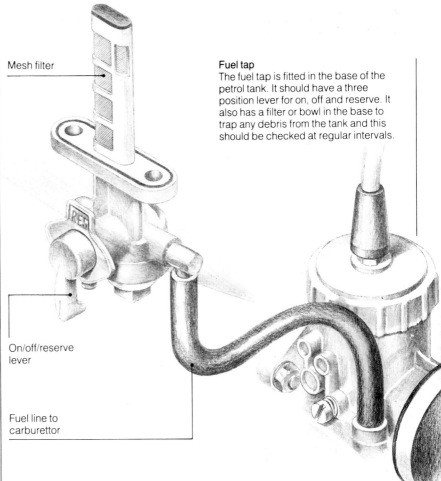

Mesh filter

Fuel tap
The fuel tap is fitted in the base of the petrol tank. It should have a three position lever for on, off and reserve. It also has a filter or bowl in the base to trap any debris from the tank and this should be checked at regular intervals.

On/off/reserve lever

Fuel line to carburettor

flow. If this does not work, the filter in the tap may be blocked. Remove the tap and clean or replace the filter, plus any damaged gaskets or rubber O-rings, if either are fitted.

In the event of an actual carburettor blockage, you may be able to carry out an emergency roadside repair by undoing the float bowl drain screw. Unscrew this with the fuel switched off and inspect the fuel residue as it escapes, checking for the presence of sediment.

This may be sufficient to allow you to finish your journey. However, like all emergency repairs, it is only a temporary measure. Evidence of dirt or rust particles means that the fuel tank line and carburettor should be cleaned as soon as possible.

Removing fuel tank dirt
One way of removing the worst deposits of rust and sediment from the fuel tank is to drop half a dozen smooth stones, or large ball bearings, into the tank. Shake the tank so that the loose stones or bearings can dislodge the sediment and then empty the tank via the filler neck. Finally, flush out the tank with fresh fuel.

Carburettor checks
Though carburettors are precision instruments, the alloy used to make them is usually surprisingly soft. This means that they can be damaged easily, stripped threads being the

Fuel system maintenance/2

commonest problem. For this reason, any maintenance work you undertake should be carried out with care, patience and avoiding the use of undue force.

The key to seeing whether or not a carburettor is working efficiently means making sure that the carburettor is clean, does not leak, that its moving parts function correctly and that they are adjusted properly. If more than one carburettor is fitted, both units must be synchronized to make sure that they work in unison.

You should always make sure that the engine's ignition system is functioning correctly before you start to check the carburettor itself *(see pp116-7)*. Many bikers, when faced with a misfiring engine or one that is running erratically, tend to think that the carburettor must be at fault, when, more often that not, it is the ignition that is causing the problem.

Before removing a carburettor from the body of the engine, check to see that the union between carburettor and airbox is secure and that there are no gaps through which contaminated air could pass.

Checking idle mixture and speed

If your bike refuses to tick over reliably, or pick up smoothly as you open up the throttle, the idle fuel/air mixture should be checked.

On a single cylinder machine, you must first locate the idle mixture screw (also known as the pilot screw). Start by screwing the mixture screw clockwise, until it is seated lightly. Then, unscrew it the number of turns specified in the manufacturer's manual, taking care not to damage the screw's fine threads as you do so. In most cases, you will need to loosen the screw by between one to two-and-a-half

turns; a safe average is one-and-a-half turns.

Start the engine and allow it to warm up to its normal operating temperature. Then adjust the idle speed screw to set the machine on a fast tickover speed of around 1,500rpm. Make quarter turn adjustments to the idle mixture screw to make the engine revolutions rise or fall. You can check what you are doing by the machine's tachometer (if fitted), or by ear.

The highest rpm level is the optimum mixture setting – this should be very close to the one-and-a-half turn original setting. Once the mixture has been set, you should bring the rpm down to the speed recommended in

CHECKING THE FLOAT CHAMBER

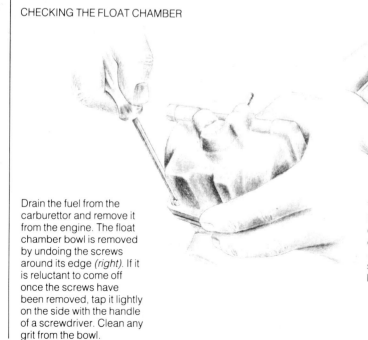

Drain the fuel from the carburettor and remove it from the engine. The float chamber bowl is removed by undoing the screws around its edge *(right)*. If it is reluctant to come off once the screws have been removed, tap it lightly on the side with the handle of a screwdriver. Clean any grit from the bowl.

With the carburettor inverted, check the height of the floats above the edge of the chamber *(above)*. The correct height should be stated in the handbook.

Adjust float height by carefully bending the float tab that controls the needle valve.

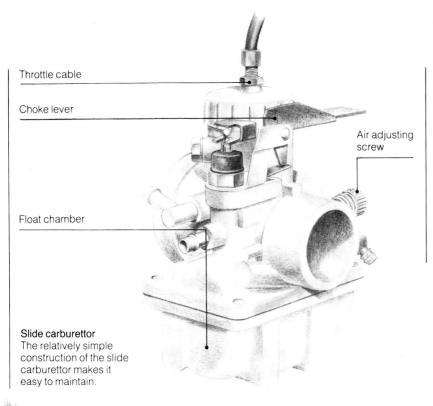

Throttle cable

Choke lever

Air adjusting screw

Float chamber

Slide carburettor
The relatively simple construction of the slide carburettor makes it easy to maintain.

your manual. Do this by adjusting the idle speed screw.

If you decide to remove the idle mixture screw completely to check that it is not bent, make sure that any O-ring – if fitted – is not lost or squashed in the housing when the screw is replaced in position.

If a reliable tickover speed cannot be obtained, check the pilot and main jets for blockages. Also check the float height and float needle condition.

CHECKING THE NEEDLE VALVE AND MAIN JET

Pull out the retaining pin holding the float assembly *(left)* and remove the floats. Use a ring spanner to remove the needle valve *(below)* and check the needle point is sharp and does not have a ridge worn into it. If it has, the valve should be replaced. Unscrew the main jet and the pilot jet *(right)* and check that the jet holes are clear and free from dirt. If the jet is clogged, do not attempt to clear it with anything hard or sharp – it is best to blow through it with compressed air.

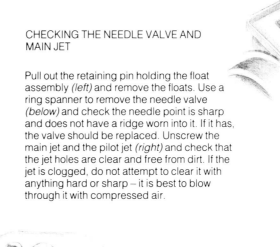

On some carburettors, you may find the assembly includes the main jet, the emulsion tube and needle jet *(above)*. Others have a separate main jet.

Fuel system maintenance/3

Checking the float mechanism

To check the carburettor's float mechanism, first remove the float bowl from the carburettor.

You should clean the float bowl at the recommended service intervals – your handbook will specify what these are – because sediment, dirt and water accumulate gradually in the bottom of the bowl. Otherwise the carburettor jets may eventually be blocked, leading to fuel starvation, or the float needle may jam open, with flooding as the result.

Where a hollow-type float is fitted, check to see if it is punctured by seeing if it sinks in a bowl of water. Next, see whether or not the float pivots freely. To see whether or not the float needle valve is sealing properly, support the float gently with a finger and lift it to close the needle. Then switch on the fuel. If the valve is working properly, no fuel should pass the needle.

To double-check this, lower the float so that the needle moves off its seat. Then, lift the float to see whether or not the valve cuts off the fuel supply.

If fuel escapes via the overflow when the bike is parked and the fuel switched on, this could indicate that the valve is not sealing properly. This may well be caused by dirt.

Sometimes tapping the side of the carburettor lightly will seat the valve. If this fails, a jammed float pivot, an incorrect float height setting, or a punctured float could be other causes.

Checking float height

You should check the float height regularly. As a rule, this involves removing the carburettor from the machine, turning the carburettor upside down and

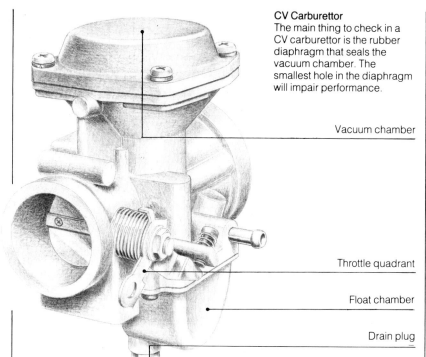

CV Carburettor
The main thing to check in a CV carburettor is the rubber diaphragm that seals the vacuum chamber. The smallest hole in the diaphragm will impair performance.

Vacuum chamber

Throttle quadrant

Float chamber

Drain plug

measuring the distance from the gasket face to the base of the float. Any necessary adjustment can be made by bending the tang that bears against the float valve.

If the tang closes the valve too quickly, the engine will probably start easily enough, but will then falter and die because the float bowl has been drained. After a few minutes or so, the bowl will fill sufficiently to allow you to carry on for a short distance.

The engine may fail in the same way for another reason. When a machine has covered over 10,000 miles (16,000km), wear at the valve may mean that the mixture is too rich. The physical sign of this is a sooted spark plug. If adjusting the float height does not solve the problem, you must fit a new valve. Where a non-adjustable float is fitted, a new valve and float will both be required.

Checking the jets

While the float bowl is removed, take the opportunity to inspect the main carburettor jet. If this is clogged, blow the jet clear. Do not attempt to clean it with a thin piece of wire, as this may damage the jet hole, the size of which is crucial for correct carburation. Other jets should be similarly checked and cleaned.

If your bike is fitted with a slide carburettor, the needle that controls quarter to three-quarter throttle performance can be checked for trueness by removing it and rolling it across a piece of glass, or a similar flat surface. If it is even slightly bent, it is best to replace the old needle with a new one.

Checking slide travel

The slide should be checked for smooth travel up and down the carburettor bore. If dirt has penetrated the carburettor –

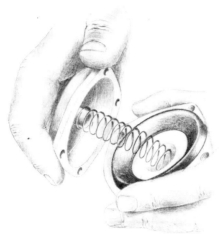

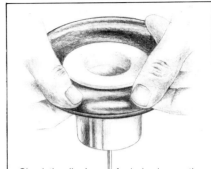

Check the diaphragm for holes by gently pulling it taught and holding it up to the light. If any holes are found, the diaphragm must be replaced.

Check the diaphragm and needle
Unscrew the retaining screws on the top cover *(above)*. Remove the cover, noting the position of the spring underneath *(right)*. Lift the piston and needle with the diaphragm attached. Then check that the needle is straight, not scored *(right)*. If the latter, replace.

either through the mouth or the top – the slide can jam. This can be particularly dangerous, as, if the slide does not drop down the bore when the throttle is closed, the throttle will fail to act and the bike will end up out of control.

Checking a CD carburettor
Where a CD (constant depression) – also known as a CV (constant vacuum) – carburettor is fitted, remove the top and check that the diaphragm membrane is in good condition. If it is a piston slide type, check that the piston is not scored or corroded.

You should also check that the throttle butterfly shaft is operating smoothly. If not, the shaft should be removed, carefully cleaned and lightly greased. When replacing the shaft, make sure that the retaining nut is not overtightened.

Synchronization
If your bike is fitted with more than one carburettor, the units, as already stated, must be synchronized to act together. Engine rattles at idling speed on twin- and multi-cylinder machines are often caused by the two carburettors being out of tune with one another.

On many modern two-stroke twins with slide carburettors, a small circular window is fitted at the top of the carburettor body to make it easier to achieve the necessary synchronization. As the twistgrip is opened, indents in the slides should both be clearly visible through the windows at the same time. If not, the throttle cables should be adjusted accordingly.

On a multi-cylinder engine – particularly one fitted with CD carburettors – it is best to get a professional to check the synchronization, using vacuum gauges. These are attached to the stubs or blanked-off drillings that are an integral part of the

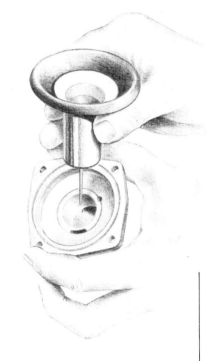

majority of carburettors now fitted to modern machines.

Basically, one carburettor is the master and the other has to be synchronized to match it. The vacuum gauges allow a mechanic to run the engine, observe readings on both of the carburettors and alter the synchronizing screws that act on the butterflies or slides (depending on carburettor type) until they match the master.

Throttle cable maintenance

Without an effective twistgrip throttle, any bike is inadequate at the least and positively dangerous at the worst. Efficient and effective throttle operation not only makes riding more of a pleasure, but is also essential for safety. A stiff, neglected throttle is potentially dangerous, since it makes a bike more difficult to control and may tire the rider's hand prematurely. A well set-up throttle should be as light as possible in operation, should snap shut when released and should have at least 2mm (0.1in) free cable play, so that the throttle is not too sensitive for road use.

Cables showing any signs of fraying should be replaced at once. Frequent lubrication with light oil is similarly essential. However, you should never grease exposed wire sections of the cable, because the grease will attract and hold grit. This may become lodged between the inner and outer sections of the cable and so cause premature wear. Instead, you should make sure that the cable ends are covered by protectors and lightly oiled to prevent rusting. Follow the same guidelines for routing as with a choke cable.

Both ends of the cable usually have a threaded section, plus a lock nut, for adjustment, though some machines feature what is termed a push-pull throttle, with a second cable to positively close the carburettor. Check your handbook to see which type is fitted to your machine.

Once the cable has been set – as previously stated, some free play is desirable – move the handlebars from lock to lock, checking the throttle cable to make sure that it is not pulled

Some motor cycles have a double cable on the throttle twistgrip. One cable opens the carburettor, while the other closes it. Lubricate both of them regularly.

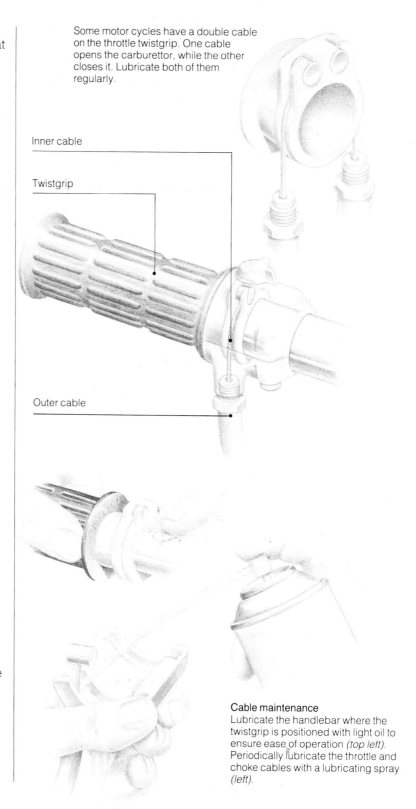

Inner cable

Twistgrip

Outer cable

Cable maintenance
Lubricate the handlebar where the twistgrip is positioned with light oil to ensure ease of operation *(top left)*. Periodically lubricate the throttle and choke cables with a lubricating spray *(left)*.

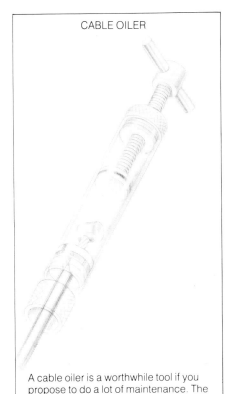

CABLE OILER

A cable oiler is a worthwhile tool if you propose to do a lot of maintenance. The cables to be lubricated are held within a cylinder, which is filled with lubricant. A piston is screwed down, forcing the lubricant along the cable.

tight. If this happens, you must adjust the cable, as otherwise there is the risk of the throttle slide or butterfly being pulled open. If this happens, it can be extremely dangerous.

The twistgrip itself should fit snugly over the handlebar and be tightened just enough to allow the grip to revolve freely. Where the inner face of the twistgrip revolves against the handlebar, polish the bar and, if desired, apply a light coating of oil to keep the action smooth.

If throttle cable adjustment affects two-stroke oil pump adjustment or carburettor synchronization – as on a two-stroke twin, for instance – the adjustment should be checked at the carburettors.

Checking a choke cable

Check any choke cable fitted to your bike at regular intervals. If such a check is not made on a regular basis, the cable may either seize, because of lack of lubricant, or loosen, so failing to act on the choke butterfly. This will make the engine difficult to start. Alternatively, if the cable seizes and the choke butterfly is permanently engaged as a result, the engine will start easily from cold, but will falter under load because the fuel mixture is too rich.

Such cables should be lubricated frequently and also checked for frayed strands. The easiest way of lubricating such a cable is to use a cable oiler, a purpose designed tool which makes it easy to do the job with the cable in place on the bike. If the cable is difficult to reach, however, it should be removed for attention.

Whenever you remove the cable, pay close attention to the way it is routed before you take it off the machine. Make a sketch if you have to, so that you can replace the cable exactly as it was before you removed it. This is important with modern machines, as their cables are tailored to suit fixed design requirements, with no margin for routing error.

While the cable is disengaged from the choke butterfly shaft, you should close the butterfly and then let go of the shaft. The butterfly should spring open. If the action of the butterfly is notchy, remove both the shaft and the housing and clean them carefully, lightly greasing the bearing surfaces.

If your bike is fitted with a cold start lever – this is attached to the carburettor body – you will usually find it trouble-free. Simply oil the pivot from time to time for smooth operation.

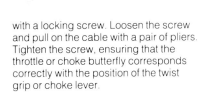

Adjustment at the carburettor

On a slide carburettor *(left)*, adjust the throttle cable by releasing the locknut on top of the carburettor barrel and turning the knurled cap. Retighten the locknut. On a CV carburettor *(right)*, the throttle and choke cables are held in a collar with a locking screw. Loosen the screw and pull on the cable with a pair of pliers. Tighten the screw, ensuring that the throttle or choke butterfly corresponds correctly with the position of the twist grip or choke lever.

Clutch maintenance

By adjusting the clutch mechanism, you can compensate for the wear that inevitably occurs in the conventional clutches fitted to most bikes. This is particularly important if you spend the majority of your time battling with slow-moving traffic in town riding conditions, which demands constant use of the clutch. Riders who face such conditions should check the mechanism for adequate free play more often than riders living in sparsely populated areas.

Adjusting free play

The free play at the end of the clutch lever on the handlebar should usually be between 0.4in (10mm) and 0.8in (20mm). Basic adjustment should be carried out at the engine end of the clutch cable; final adjustment should be made via the cable adjuster fitted on the handlebar.

Start by screwing the adjuster at the hand lever all the way home to give the maximum amount of free play. This should produce a very loose feel at the handlebar lever. Then consult your manual to check the specific adjustment procedure.

Three stage adjustment

Normally, adjustment involves three separate stages. In the first, you will have to loosen a locknut and tighten an adjuster screw, which controls clutch engagement and disengagement. This mechanism is usually protected by a rubber grommet or engine sidecover.

The second step involves loosening another locknut and taking up the adjustment at the cable adjuster. This is usually located in the engine casing, near the clutch actuating arm.

Finally, you must take up the fine adjustment at the handlebar lever adjuster. Here, you can make allowances for your own preferences, providing you

remain within the range of tolerances specified in your handbook.

Clutch problems

If the gearbox tends to 'crunch' when put into gear, or if the machine tries to creep forward when revved at a standstill with the lever pulled in, then the clutch is dragging. This means it needs adjustment to take up excessive free play.

In bikes where the gearbox

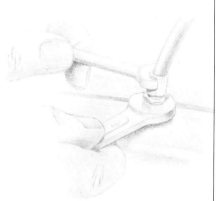

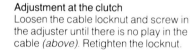

Adjustment at the clutch
Loosen the cable locknut and screw in the adjuster until there is no play in the cable *(above)*. Retighten the locknut.

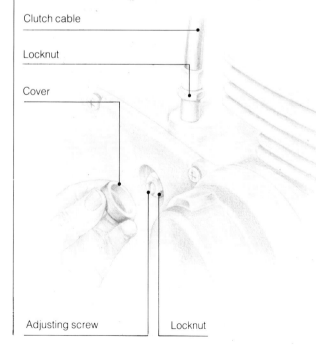

Clutch cable

Locknut

Cover

Adjusting screw   Locknut

Remove the cap covering the clutch adjustment screw. Loosen the locknut and turn the adjusting screw in or out *(above)* until there is the correct amount of play at the handlebar lever. Tighten the locknut and replace cover.

and clutch share the same oil supply, the problem can also be caused by using oil which is too thick, instead of the lighter oil usually recommended for motorcycle engines. The thicker oil tends to make the clutch plates stick together slightly, so that they are reluctant to free themselves when the clutch is engaged. As a result, the clutch tends to drag and gear-changing is slowed down. The latter is usually accompanied by the crunching noise from the gearbox described above.

The opposite complaint to clutch drag is clutch 'slip'. This occurs when the clutch is not engaged fully. As you open the throttle to accelerate, the revs will rise, but there will be very little increase in acceleration, if any. Free play should then be increased in an attempt to cure the slip.

If, in either case, you find that the adjustment you are making is outside the manufacturer's specifications, or a cure cannot be affected, then the clutch must be stripped for inspection.

Clutch adjustment should be checked every 2000 miles (3000km) and the clutch cable kept lubricated and free from

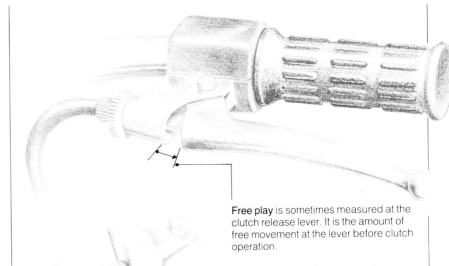

Free play is sometimes measured at the clutch release lever. It is the amount of free movement at the lever before clutch operation.

Adjustment at the lever
Fine clutch adjustment is made at the lever. Check for the allowable amount of freeplay in your handbook. If adjustment is needed, turn the cable adjuster until there is the correct amount of freeplay. Then tighten the locknut. Check clutch operation by starting the engine and engaging first gear. If the bike stalls or creeps forward, the clutch is not fully disengaged; if it slips, it is not fully engaged. Re-adjust accordingly.

excessively tight turns in its routing. Always change the lubricating oil at the recommended service intervals and, in addition, change it when any clutch components have been replaced. The oil gradually becomes contaminated as material is worn off the clutch friction plates and new parts will last longer if treated to fresh oil.

Changing the clutch cable
If either end of the clutch cable is frayed, or if it tends to stick and will not free itself when oiled, the cable must be replaced.

Before removing the cable, note how it is routed. Then slacken all adjusters to make removal easier. Fit the new cable starting from the engine. If you find it difficult to fit the cable to the handlebar lever, try removing the lever from its bracket, inserting the cable nipple into the lever's nipple recess and then 'levering' the lever into its normal position.

Adjust the clutch. When you have finished, make sure that all locknuts are tight and all protectors, such as grommets and sleeves are in place.

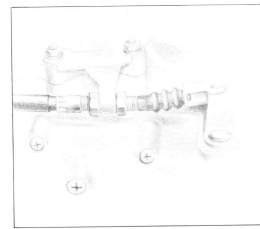

Some motor cycles allow you to make adjustments at the clutch end of the cable. The cable is held in a bracket, with a locknut and adjusting nut *(left)*. To make an adjustment, the locknut is released and the adjusting nut tightened or loosened. Once adjustment has been made, retighten the locknut.

Chain maintenance/1

Chain life depends on owner maintenance. A neglected chain will suffer from premature wear, as will its sprockets. As a consequence, the transmission will become harsh and noisy, so reducing riding pleasure.

The final drive chain should be inspected to check play and lubrication on a daily basis. Both jobs are swiftly done, provided you understand what to check. By establishing a routine, you will extend chain life and so save money in the long run. Also, you will reduce the likelihood of chain breakage, which could cause an accident or expensive bike damage, such as a holed engine crankcase. This is a common problem when a broken chain jams itself between the drive sprocket and the engine case.

Checking for wear

Simple visual checks should tell you whether your chain is in need of closer, more detailed inspection. If the chain is rusty, for instance, it obviously has not been receiving enough attention and is likely to be worn. See if you can pull the chain off the rear sprocket. If the chain is in good condition, it will be difficult to lift it off the teeth, but a well-worn chain will move away readily, exposing the wells between the teeth.

If the chain adjusters have very little adjustment left, this is another sign that the chain may soon have to be replaced. If all the available adjustment has been used up, then the chain is worn out.

Inspect the rear wheel sprocket for 'hooked' teeth. If they are excessively worn on one side – giving them a hooked appearance – then both the

chain and the sprockets are worn and should be replaced as a set.

Next, position the machine on the main stand, so that the rear wheel is off the ground. Make sure that the gearbox is in neutral and turn the wheel by hand. A well oiled chain in good condition should allow the wheel to spin fairly freely, accompanied by a subdued whirring noise. If the chain is worn, the wheel will be reluctant to spin. The chain's sideplates and rollers may rattle and it may grate and crack as it engages with the sprockets.

If the wheel suddenly tightens up while you are turning it, then the chain has a tight spot, usually caused by uneven wear. The tight spot will show itself up along the top run of the chain and should always be engaged when the rear wheel's chain tension is being adjusted.

As you turn the wheel, watch to see how the chain engages with the rear sprocket. A badly rusted chain may be kinked and will not engage smoothly and progressively. It may also tend to ride over the sprocket teeth.

The final test

If your chain displays some or all of the above symptoms, the final test for wear is to remove the chain from the machine, wash it thoroughly in paraffin and allow it to dry.

Pull the chain to full extension and measure the overall length. Next, take up all the play in the links carefully by pushing them together and measure again. If the difference is three per cent or more, the chain should be replaced.

Lubrication

To lubricate a chain really thoroughly you must take it off the

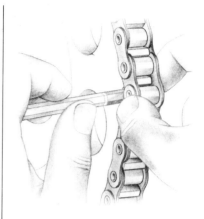

Check for wear in the chain. If there is enough play for you to push a pencil between the chain and the rear sprocket, replace the chain.

machine. Wash the chain in paraffin – a paintbrush is useful here to flick out dirt jammed between the chain's side plates – and leave it to dry. Then soak the chain in a chain grease bath warmed over an oven hotplate, or similar. This allows the melted grease to penetrate to the pins and bushes, which wear rapidly if not cushioned on a protective layer of lubricant.

After the links have been saturated thoroughly with grease, remove the chain from the bath and hang it up to dry. Once the grease has solidified, wipe off the excess with a rag and refit the chain to the machine. When you do this, check to see whether a joining link is fitted and, if so, make sure that the closed end of the circlip always faces the direction of chain travel. This is to prevent the circlip being forced off should the chain become so slack that it strikes another part of the motorcycle, such as the chainguard.

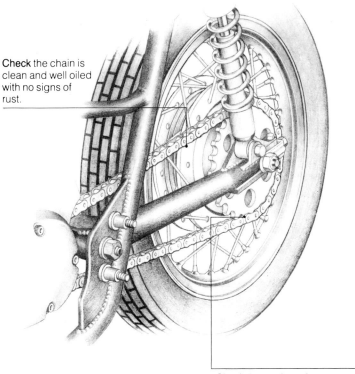

Check the chain is clean and well oiled with no signs of rust.

Check the teeth on the rear sprocket for wear. If the chain has worn the teeth into a half-moon shape, then the sprocket and chain should be replaced.

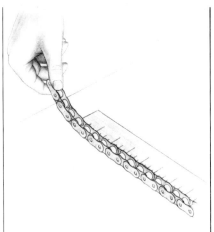

Check the chain for 'stretch'. Lay it on a flat surface against a ruler, links compressed. Pull the chain to extend the links and measure the difference. Check this against the handbook figure.

Using an aerosol

You can use an aerosol lubricant as a supplement to the grease bath. The best way to apply an aerosol is to stand the machine on the mainstand and to turn the rear wheel by hand. Turn the wheel forward and direct the spray to meet the chain where it meets the rear wheel sprocket. Make sure that the spray penetrates between the sideplates and down into the pins and bushes.

Protect the rear tyre from overspray with a piece of cardboard, or something similar. Once the grease has penetrated and dried on the chain, wipe off any excess to prevent it being thrown over the machine – and your clothing – while you are on the road.

O-ring chains

An O-ring chain can be identified by the rubber O-rings which are clearly visible between the inner and outer link plates.

REMOVING A CHAIN

If the chain has a removeable link with a circlip, it is a fairly simple matter to prise off the link with a pair of pliers *(right)*. When you reassemble the chain, ensure the circlip has the closed end facing in the direction of rotation. If the chain has no removeable link, you will have to use a chain splitter *(below)* and fit a link with a circlip for reassembly.

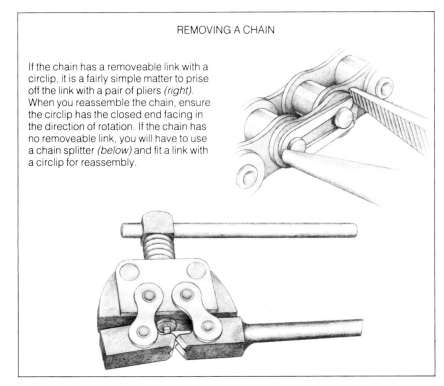

Chain maintenance/2

With an O-ring chain, often termed a 'self-lubricating chain', lubrication should be carried out by applying a heavyweight gear oil, such as EP90, with a paintbrush, or by using a lubricant specifically made for O-ring chains. Such chains generally enjoy long life because the lubricant is sealed in by the O-rings. But, after a time, the O-ring seals tend to perish, so allowing the lubricant to escape and dry up. If this happens, you must follow the conventional lubrication routine.

Avoid the use of aerosols in this instance, as most spray-on lubricants contain solvent, which can be harmful to the rubber O-rings.

Cleaning O-ring chains
Before cleaning such chains, consult your dealer or the chain manufacturer. Some recommend that the chain should not be cleaned at all. Others say 'light cleaning' with paraffin should be carried out periodically. If you can find no specific guidance, the best thing to do is to clean the chain and the sprockets carefully with a rag to remove grit.

O-ring chains are endless – that is to say they have no joining link. So, too, are many non O-ring chains. Since a joining link is in effect a weaker link than the rest, manufacturers tend to fit endless chains on the more powerful machines. This means that O-ring chains are usually found only on what are popularly termed 'superbikes'; in whatever case, they should never be modified to accept a split link.

Fitting a joining link
Removing an endless chain, either for cleaning or replacement usually involves

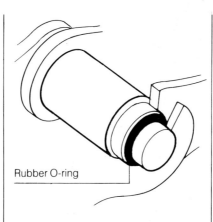

Rubber O-ring

An O-ring chain has its lubricant sealed within each link by a rubber ring. For this reason such chains generally last longer than standard ones. If you are not sure if such a chain is fitted to your bike, check the links to see if they have rubber rings between them. If they do and the rings look perished, you can maintain the chain as you would do normally, or fit a new one

removing the swinging arm fork. Check your workshop manual for the proper procedure. Because this can be complex, many owners may consider fitting a joining link. For safety reasons, it is very important that you consult your dealer or the chain manufacturer before carrying out any such modification.

If you find that it is safe to go ahead, you will need a link extractor tool, sometimes called a chain-breaker. If the chain is a heavy duty type, it may be necessary to file or grind away a rivet head on one of the links in order to make the job easier for the tool. Since a complete link has to be removed, two pins have to be pushed out by the link extractor. Double check that the joining link is of the correct dimensions and that you fit the spring clip with its closed face in the direction of travel.

When a new chain is fitted, always check sprocket alignment as well as chain tension. Sprocket misalignment will cause rapid chain and sprocket wear.

Chain adjustment
Unless your workshop manual states otherwise, for correct chain adjustment it is essential to ensure that the centre points of the drive sprocket, swinging arm pivot point and rear wheel spindle are in a straight line. In this position, the chain is at its tightest. Often, the easiest method of ensuring this is to ask a helper to sit on the machine and adjust his or her weight until all three points are aligned.

On a typical lightweight machine, free play, using this method, will usually be between 10mm (½in) and 50mm (2in) halfway along the chain's bottom run. But you should always refer to your workshop manual to find out exactly how much play is allowed, where it should be measured and the exact details of the adjustment procedure. For example, Honda quote free play with the machine on the main stand.

Before any adjustment is carried out, the chain should be cleaned and lubricated. The normal way of making the adjustment is to search for a tight spot on the chain and, if present, to keep it engaged. Remove the rear wheel spindle split pin, slacken the spindle nut, loosen the locknut on each of the two chain adjusters and take up free play by equal amounts on both sides of the swinging arm unit. Graduated marks should be stamped on the swinging arms and a single reference mark on each adjuster to make uniform

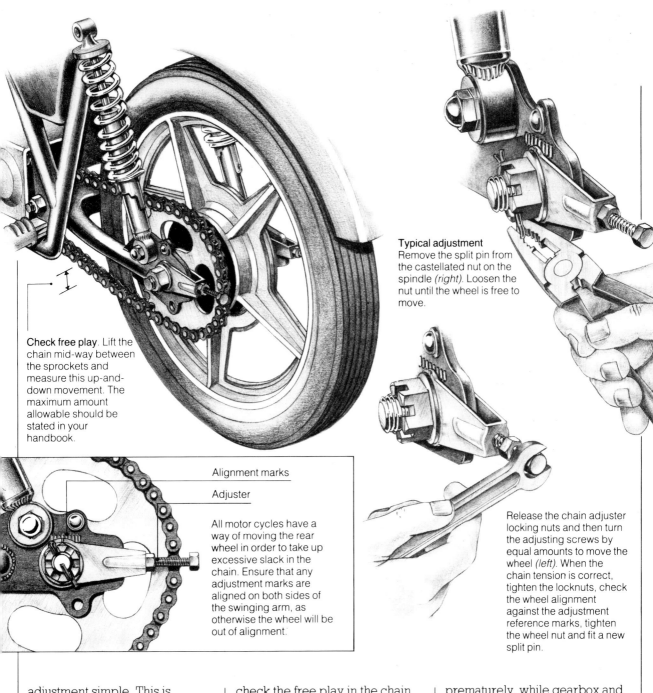

Check free play. Lift the chain mid-way between the sprockets and measure this up-and-down movement. The maximum amount allowable should be stated in your handbook.

Alignment marks

Adjuster

All motor cycles have a way of moving the rear wheel in order to take up excessive slack in the chain. Ensure that any adjustment marks are aligned on both sides of the swinging arm, as otherwise the wheel will be out of alignment.

Typical adjustment
Remove the split pin from the castellated nut on the spindle *(right)*. Loosen the nut until the wheel is free to move.

Release the chain adjuster locking nuts and then turn the adjusting screws by equal amounts to move the wheel *(left)*. When the chain tension is correct, tighten the locknuts, check the wheel alignment against the adjustment reference marks, tighten the wheel nut and fit a new split pin.

adjustment simple. This is important, as otherwise the rear wheel will be twisted out of alignment.

Once the correct adjustment has been made, tighten the locknuts and rear wheel spindle. Check the condition of the split pin – if there is any doubt about this, a new one should be fitted. Go for a short test ride and re-

check the free play in the chain on your return home. Make a further adjustment, if necessary.

Take care not to over-tighten the chain. If this happens, the chain will be prone to breakage because there is no free play to act as a transmission shock absorber. In addition, the excess friction will create heat, which will dry out the lubricant

prematurely, while gearbox and wheel bearings will also suffer. An excessively loose chain, on the other hand, may fail to engage with the rear wheel sprocket.

In either case, a chain that breaks, or is thrown off, could cause the back wheel to lock, if the chain becomes entangled with wheel or sprocket.

Suspension checks/1

By checking the condition of your suspension by eye, you should normally be able to detect the first symptoms of any problem that is affecting the system and take steps to deal with it before it becomes serious.

Fork problems

The most common suspension problem is oil seal failure, which is indicated by oil smears on the fork legs. If this is not dealt with promptly, the oil, which is the all-important damping medium, will escape and so the spring rebound energy will not be absorbed properly.

In extreme cases, this can lead to fork bounce and potential loss of control. The cure is to remove the forks and have new oil seals fitted. Make sure that you fill each leg with the quantity and grade of oil specified in your workshop manual.

If the fork legs are pitted with rust, however, the rust will tear any new seal and oil will quickly leak again. The only lasting cure in this case is to fit a new fork leg.

Checking rear suspension

Rear suspension units should also be checked for oil loss and pitting of the exposed section of the damper rod. If faulty units do not have the facility for oil seal renewal, they should be replaced with new ones.

Physical checks

In addition to the visual checks described above, both the front and rear suspension can be checked physically. With the machine off the mainstand, push the handlebars down hard in order to compress the forks. These should return smoothly to their normal position as soon as the pressure is released.

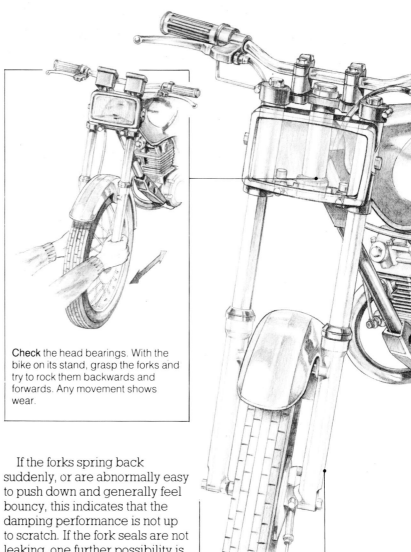

Check the head bearings. With the bike on its stand, grasp the forks and try to rock them backwards and forwards. Any movement shows wear.

If the forks spring back suddenly, or are abnormally easy to push down and generally feel bouncy, this indicates that the damping performance is not up to scratch. If the fork seals are not leaking, one further possibility is that the damping fluid is old and contaminated and needs to be changed. If your forks are not fitted with a drain plug at the bottom of each leg (slider), the fork must be removed from the machine and turned upside down in order to be drained.

Check your manual for the correct way to remove the forks. When removing the top cap, the fork should be at full extension. Having drained the old oil, pour fresh oil of the correct grade slowly and carefully into the fork

Some motor cycles have a drain plug at the base of the fork, making it simpler to change the damping oil.

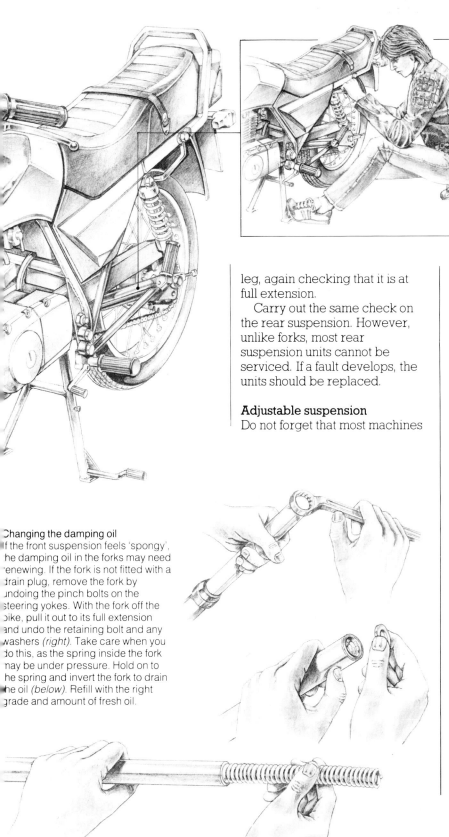

Check the swinging arm. With the bike on its main stand, put one foot on the stand and hold the frame to keep it steady. Grasp the rear wheel and try to move it from side to side. Any movement is a sign of wear in the swinging arm bearings, though you must ensure that you do not confuse this with movement of the whole bike.

leg, again checking that it is at full extension.

Carry out the same check on the rear suspension. However, unlike forks, most rear suspension units cannot be serviced. If a fault develops, the units should be replaced.

Adjustable suspension
Do not forget that most machines feature adjustable suspension for varying loads. The rear suspension, for instance, can usually be adjusted by turning a ring on the suspension unit. For high performance riding or when carrying a pillion passenger, the adjuster should be turned to compress the spring. This will increase ground clearance.

The amount the suspension can be adjusted from bike to bike. Some bikes allow extensive adjustments to be made; the facilities enabling you to do this include fork preload, air assistance for both the forks and rear suspension units and, insofar as the rear suspension is concerned, damping adjustment to compensate for bumps, rebounds or both. Check in your manual for full details.

Take great care when making any adjustment on suspension units that feature air pressure. These usually have very small air chambers, which are easy to over-inflate. For this reason, never use an air line to make the adjustment. Use a handpump or footpump instead.

Checking the steering for wear
Wear or play in the headstock bearings – their job is to allow

Changing the damping oil
If the front suspension feels 'spongy', the damping oil in the forks may need renewing. If the fork is not fitted with a drain plug, remove the fork by undoing the pinch bolts on the steering yokes. With the fork off the bike, pull it out to its full extension and undo the retaining bolt and any washers *(right)*. Take care when you do this, as the spring inside the fork may be under pressure. Hold on to the spring and invert the fork to drain the oil *(below)*. Refill with the right grade and amount of fresh oil.

Suspension checks/2

the front fork assembly to pivot smoothly from lock to lock – will cause imprecise handling. This can be extremely dangerous in cases of extreme wear and maladjustment. Head bearing play is the commonest cause of bike weave.

To check the head bearings, the front wheel of the machine must be off the ground. On most bikes, this can be done simply by putting the machine on its mainstand. Then grasp the bottoms of the fork legs with either hand and try to rock the forks backwards and forwards in a horizontal plane. Any detectable play, especially if accompanied by a knocking noise, indicates that the bearings need to be adjusted.

Adjusting the bearings

Slacken the fork leg pinch bolts on the top yoke and the top yoke main nut. Then loosen or tighten the adjuster nut as required, using a C-spanner, or a large screwdriver. Cover the tip of the screwdriver with a rag, place it in one of the indents in the nut and tap the handle gently with a hammer to move the ring. Tighten the top yoke nut with a torque wrench in order to obtain the correct tension. Finally tighten the fork leg pinch bolts on the top yoke.

You must also take care not to over-tighten the steering head bearings. With the front wheel still off the ground, turn the handlebars slowly from lock to lock. If they are stiff, the bearings either need greasing, or are too tight. Before making any necessary adjustment, however, it will pay you to check that the stiffness is not being caused by a tight headlight cable, as the symptoms are the same.

ADJUSTING THE HEAD BEARINGS

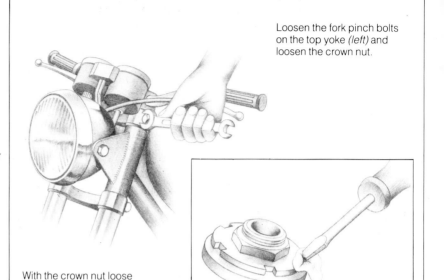

Loosen the fork pinch bolts on the top yoke *(left)* and loosen the crown nut.

With the crown nut loose enough to allow movement in the adjusting nut, tighten or loosen the nut as necessary. Ideally, use a C spanner to do this *(right)*, but, alternatively, you can tap the adjusting nut round with a screwdriver in one of the slots on the bolt *(inset)*. Wrap the end of the screwdriver with a piece of cloth to protect the slots in the nut.

Greasing steering head bearings

Regular greasing is also important, but, because it is quite complex, you are best advised to leave it to a professional. If neglected, the grease lubricating the bearings will dry up, with rapid bearing wear as the result. After greasing and adjustment, recheck the tension of the bearings after 200 miles (300km) and adjust if necessary.

You can tell when greasing is required, because the steering becomes 'notchy'. Often, you can feel this as the front wheel passes through the straight ahead position when when turning the handlebars from lock to lock.

Fitting new bearings

If greasing and proper adjustment does not cure this problem, new bearings and races should be fitted to both upper and lower yokes. This job is best left to a mechanic.

To check that the job has been done properly, raise the bike, so that the front wheel is off the ground and all resistance to the forks removed. Turn the forks slightly to one side of the straight ahead position and see whether or not the fork assembly drops gently on to full lock. If the forks stick, the bearings are too tight. If the steering flops freely, they are too loose.

Checking rear shock absorbers

To check for play on twin shock absorber systems – these are more common than single systems – make sure that the rear wheel is clear of the ground, grasp the rear tyre and try to rock the swinging arm/wheel assembly from side to side, taking care not to twist the machine on its mainstand.

There should be no perceptible play at the end of the swinging arm fork. If there is, the swinging arm bearings should be serviced and, if necessary, replaced. Also, check your service manual to see if your bike has grease points for lubrication. If so, lubricate at the recommended intervals.

On machines fitted with single shock absorber systems featuring linkages, you should carry out an additional test to establish whether or not there is wear in the linkage bearings. With the rear wheel off the ground, gently lift the wheel a fraction of an inch, feeling for free play.

If the system is in good condition, you will be unable to feel any free play. In a worn system, however, there will be a noticeable amount of free play before the suspension unit becomes engaged effectively.

Checking wheel alignment

Before you check wheel alignment, the bike's steering head and rear suspension bearings should be checked to see that they are correctly adjusted.

Most modern bikes have indented marks stamped on the swing fork legs, above the slots for the wheel spindle (see chain wear). The chain adjusters feature a mark stamped at twelve

You can roughly check alignment by putting the bike on its stand, with the front wheel on the ground. Look along the centre line of the rear wheel *(above)*, the centre of the front wheel should align with this. To check this more accurately, place a plank, parallel to the bike, just below the level of the hubs *(right)*. While the plank is pressed against the rear tyre, it is unlikely that it will touch the front one, since this tyre is usually narrower. The gap between the the plank and the two points where it would otherwise touch the front tyre should be of equal measurement.

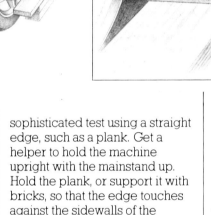

o'clock. When the chain is adjusted correctly, the swinging arm and the adjuster marks should correspond on both sides of the swinging arm. Though this is usually accurate enough for correct wheel alignment, it is well worth double-checking, as all this involves is a simple visual test procedure.

Put the machine on its mainstand, or get a friend to hold the bike upright. Make sure that the front wheel is pointing straight ahead and that the machine is on level ground.

Walk 30ft (10m) or so behind the machine and lay down on the ground. Then sight the wheels as if you were looking down a gunsight. With the rear tyre just off the ground, the front tyre should appear to be dead in line with it. If it does not – and the bearings are correctly adjusted – then check for other causes, such as incorrectly positioned wheel spindle spacers.

You can make a more

sophisticated test using a straight edge, such as a plank. Get a helper to hold the machine upright with the mainstand up. Hold the plank, or support it with bricks, so that the edge touches against the sidewalls of the bike's rear tyre.

Since the rear tyre is almost always wider than the front tyre, there should be a gap between the straight edge and the front tyre – and this gap should be the same at the two points where the plank would otherwise touch the tyre. Any variation indicates that the front and rear wheel are not aligned correctly.

Carry out the same procedure on the other side of the machine. When you have completed this, you will have established four measurements at the front wheel. These should all be the same. If two on one side are identical, but differ from those on the other, this tells you that both wheels are pointing straight ahead, but are offset for another reason.

Repairing a puncture

Look at the palm of your hand. Each of your tyres has only about that much area in contact with the road. For safety's sake, check tyre condition frequently. Damaged tyres, or ones whose treads are worn to or below the 1mm legal tread limit, should be replaced quickly.

Repairing punctures
It is impossible to repair a tubeless tyre permanently at home. With tubed tyres, you can fix a minor puncture yourself, though, if the inner tube has been punctured before, it pays to replace it with a new one.

Remove the wheel from the machine and, working in a clean area, remove the nurled nut of the valve stem and press the tyre bead from its seat. If security bolts are fitted, these must be loosened first.

Refitting the tyre
Before refitting the tyre, check to see if you can find a physical

reason for the puncture. If, for instance, you find a nail or a piece of glass in the tyre, remove it.

You can use a spray-on rubber lubricant or soapy water, to make refitment easier. If possible, the tyre should be refitted without the use of tyre levers, as it is all too easy to nip the tube with them, so causing another puncture. Place the wheel on a sheet of cardboard to prevent

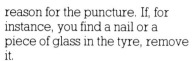

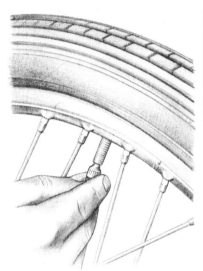

1. Unless the puncture is obvious, check the valve. If you suspect it is at fault, it is simple to replace it.

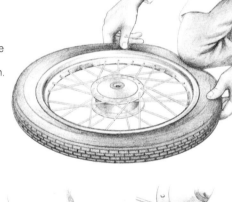

2. With the tyre deflated, ease the edge of the tyre away from the rim.

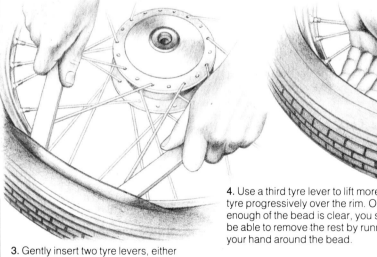

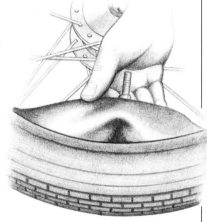

3. Gently insert two tyre levers, either side of the valve and lift the bead of the tyre over the rim.

4. Use a third tyre lever to lift more of the tyre progressively over the rim. Once enough of the bead is clear, you should be able to remove the rest by running your hand around the bead.

5. With the one edge of the tyre free of the rim, undo the valve locknut and

gently pull out the inner tube. With the tube removed, you can find the puncture by partially inflating the inner tube, immersing it in water and looking for the telltale bubbles.

REPAIRING THE INNER TUBE

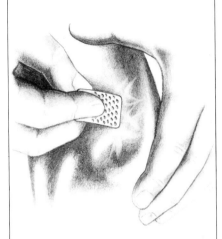

With the puncture located, make sure that the tube is clean and dry and roughen the area to be repaired.

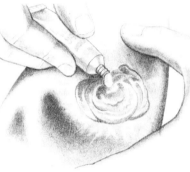

Apply a coat of rubber solution to this area and allow to dry. Apply a second coat and wait until it becomes tacky. Peel the backing off the repair patch and burnish it down. Remove the top protective layer.

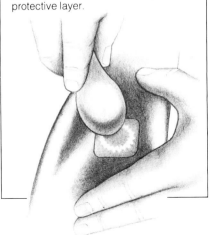

damage to the wheel and its components, such as a brake disc.

With the tyre on the rim, inflate it to the recommended pressure and examine its sidewalls carefully to make sure that the tyre is seated properly. Correct seating is essential for safety and overall wheel/tyre balance.

If an area of the tyre is 'tucked in', deflate the inner tube, spray that area with rubber lubricant and pump the tube up again, checking once more to see that the tyre wall seats itself properly. If necessary, repeat the process.

Where a tyre has a heavy or light mark indicated – these are usually marked with white spots – the heavy spot should be opposite the valve and the light spot should be at the valve.

With the tyre fitted and reinflated to the recommended pressure, leave the bike for half an hour or so and then re-check to make sure that no air pressure has been lost before putting the wheel back on the machine. Always fit a valve cap to prevent dirt and dust getting in to the valve core.

6. Once the puncture is repaired, carefully feed the inner tube back into the tyre and over the rim. Slot the valve through the rim and replace the locknut. Partially inflate the inner-tube. Start fitting the bead of the tyre back over the rim, working outwards from opposite the valve making sure that the inner tube is not trapped between rim and tyre. To seat the last part of the tyre over the rim, you can either use two tyre levers or you may find it easier to push the bead over the rim with the heel of your shoe, steadying the rest of the tyre. Inflate the tyre fully.

Wheel checks

Correct wheel balance is essential for smooth bike riding and safe road handling.

An out-of-balance front wheel can be particularly risky and uncomfortable. In extreme cases, the absence of balance can cause handlebars to judder like a pneumatic drill and compromise road grip. This is because the unequal weight distribution will effect the smooth revolution of the wheel. The balance of the back wheel, whether chain or shaft driven, is less critical, because any weight bias tends to be dampened out by the transmission.

Balancing a wheel

The most effective way of balancing the wheels is by machine, with the wheels on the bike, but few garages cater for this. The more usual method involves taking each wheel off the bike and spinning it at road speed on a special machine called a dynamic balancer.

This device will reveal and measure a weight bias at one particular part of the wheel/tyre combination. The mechanic deals with this by adding weights to the opposite side of the wheel until the bias is cancelled.

In the absence of a dynamic balancer, dealers use a jig and spin the wheel by hand, noting where it stops. Though this method is slower and not as up-to-date as the dynamic balancer method, it is still reliable. When the jig is spun, an out-of-balance wheel will stop in the same place each time – that is, with the heaviest part coming to rest at six o' clock.

Weights are then added at the opposite side of the wheel, the wheel being re-spun after each addition, until the wheel finally

Checking balance and true
Place the wheel on a pair of stands *(left)*. Gently spin the wheel several times and mark each time the point on the rim at which it stops. If it continually stops at one point – the heavy spot –weight should be added opposite the heavy spot to compensate. To check that the wheel is true, hold a pencil against the rim and spin the wheel. The rim should remain in constant contact with the pencil *(above)*.

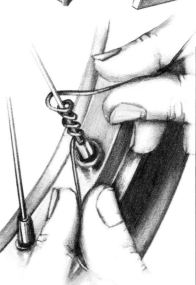

Adding weight
To add weight for wheel balance, wrap thin wire around a spoke. On cast alloy wheels, use a clip-on or adhesive weight.

stops at random. When this occurs, it indicated that no one spot on the wheel is heavier than the rest of it.

Home balancing

By following these principles, you can balance a wheel effectively at home. The easiest way to do this is to remove the wheel from the machine. Then insert the wheel spindle, supporting either end of the spindle on axle stands, or similar supports, so that the wheel is vertical. If you want to balance a wheel on the machine, you will have to remove all the components that cause drag first. These include the chain, brake pads or shoes, speedometer cable, drive gear and even the valve dust cap.

Spin the wheel several times and mark the tyre with chalk at the position at which it comes to rest. This determines the heavy spot.

On a wire spoked wheel, balancing can be carried out by twisting lead wire around the spoke diametrically opposite the heavy spot. With a cast alloy wheel, you should use press-fit weights. These are specifically designed for balancing purposes and are available from tyre fitting bays and accessory stores. Make sure that any such weights are fitted securely.

Checking bearings

The wheel bearings should be checked at least as often as a tyre is changed. The simplest way of doing this is to take the wheel off the machine. With the wheel spindle removed, place a finger on either side of the hub and lift the wheel by the inner bearing races. Any roughness can be detected by feel.

If lubricating the bearing with engine oil makes the roughness disappear, then packing it with high melting point grease may effect a cure for a few thousand miles more. It is better, however, to replace the bearing, plus its rubber seal (where fitted).

Fitting a new bearing

It may prove possible to tap the old bearing out, but gentle heating of the hub may be required in order to create sufficient expansion for you to do this. To make it easier to fit a new bearing, wrap it in polythene and freeze it in a refrigerator for an hour or so first.

Fit the bearing while the hub is still warm, if necessary. Make sure that the replacement is seated correctly and that the long spacer usually fitted between the wheel bearings is in place.

If a bearing has to be pressed or lightly tapped into position, always press the bearing by the outer race. Pressing the inner race can damage the ball bearings. Use a socket of the same diameter as the outer race to push the bearing home. It is always worth fitting new oil seals when replacing the bearings.

Always refer to your manual to check procedure.

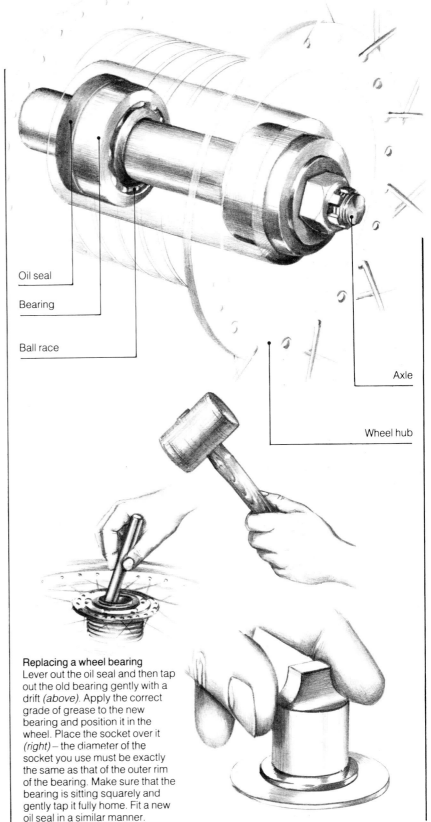

Oil seal

Bearing

Ball race

Axle

Wheel hub

Replacing a wheel bearing
Lever out the oil seal and then tap out the old bearing gently with a drift *(above)*. Apply the correct grade of grease to the new bearing and position it in the wheel. Place the socket over it *(right)* – the diameter of the socket you use must be exactly the same as that of the outer rim of the bearing. Make sure that the bearing is sitting squarely and gently tap it fully home. Fit a new oil seal in a similar manner.

Changing the oil

Checking the oil level

Ideally, you should check the oil level on a daily basis – and certainly before starting out on any long journey.

How you do this varies from bike to bike. On some bikes, you check the level with a conventional dip stick; with others, you need to locate the level plug on the side of the crankcase. Check the location in your handbook and what grade of oil you should use. The checking method can also vary from bike to bike. On most Honda four-strokes, for instance, the dipstick must be unscrewed and rested on top of the crankcase threads to get an accurate measurement.

Whenever you check oil levels, make sure that the machine is standing upright and that you allow the existing oil time to settle. Never over-fill.

Four-strokes and two-strokes

If, on a four-stroke, gearbox and sump are separate, oil levels in both should be checked. However, unit construction engines, where the same oil lubricates crankshaft, valve train and gears, are now more common.

On a two-stroke, check the gearbox oil level, plus the level of two-stroke oil in the reservoir on a machine with automatic lubrication. Checking the gearbox level is important, since, if the crankshaft oil seals fail, gearbox oil will seep into the crankcase to be burnt in the combustion chamber.

Why change the oil?

Oil stops the load-bearing parts of the engine coming into metal-to-metal contact with each other. It also keeps the tiny bits of dirt

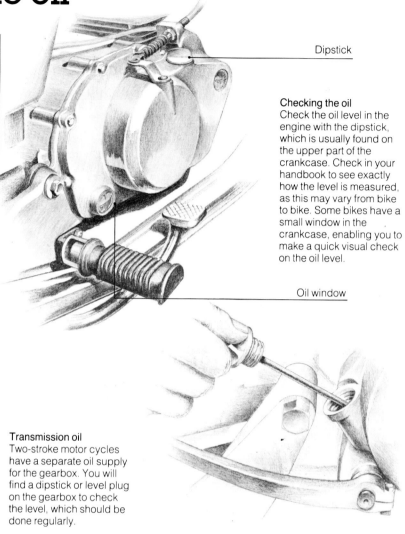

Dipstick

Checking the oil
Check the oil level in the engine with the dipstick, which is usually found on the upper part of the crankcase. Check in your handbook to see exactly how the level is measured, as this may vary from bike to bike. Some bikes have a small window in the crankcase, enabling you to make a quick visual check on the oil level.

Oil window

Transmission oil
Two-stroke motor cycles have a separate oil supply for the gearbox. You will find a dipstick or level plug on the gearbox to check the level, which should be done regularly.

that accumulate inside the engine in suspension.

This is why oil turns black with age. Unchanged, it can become so heavily contaminated that it can no longer support impurities. As a result, the oilways clog. Such clogging can have serious results, if the situation becomes so extreme that the engine's moving parts are starved of their essential lubrication.

Changing the oil

Before changing the oil, run the engine until it reaches its normal operating temperature. By doing this, you help to drain the engine thoroughly, since warm oil flows more freely. Then switch off.

Make sure that the container you stand under the bike to catch the oil is large enough to take all of it. While the oil drains, replace the oil filter or clean it.

Replacing an oil filter

When replacing a filter, always use the one recommended by the bike's manufacturer. Where possible, prime the filter by partially filling it with the

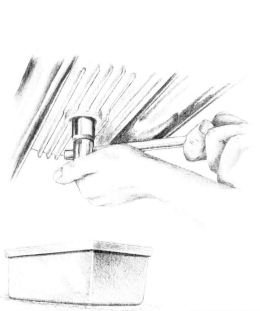

Changing the oil

Run the engine to normal working temperature and place a container under the engine, making sure that it will take the full capacity. Remove the drain plug *(left)*. Allow all the oil to drain, clean and replace the plug and fill up the sump with the correct grade and amount of fresh oil *(right)*.

recommended grade and type of oil. Fit a new gasket or O-ring as required; in the case of a new O-ring, lightly smear the ring with oil to prevent it snagging and to aid removal.

Where a centrifugal oil filter is fitted, this should be removed and scraped clean at 10,000 mile (16,000km) intervals. Though some bikers steer clear of this job, it is well within the scope of a competent amateur mechanic, but you will need a special tool to carry it out.

When you refill the engine, make sure that you use the correct grade of oil. Though most modern four-strokes require only 10W40 oil, for instance, some owners use 20W50, thinking that the heavier grade will provide better protection. This is not the case.

With a four-stroke, build up oil pressure before starting the engine. Crank the bike via the electric start with the kill button off for a few seconds, or, on a non-electric start model, kick the engine over. Always check the oil level again after going for your first ride.

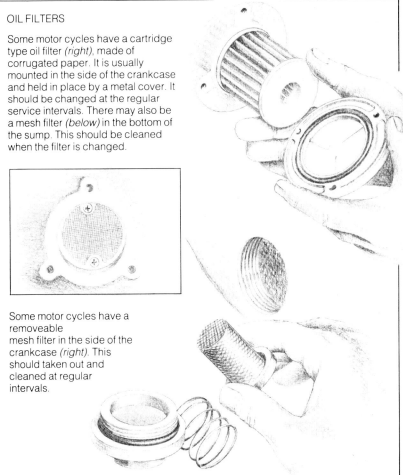

OIL FILTERS

Some motor cycles have a cartridge type oil filter *(right)*, made of corrugated paper. It is usually mounted in the side of the crankcase and held in place by a metal cover. It should be changed at the regular service intervals. There may also be a mesh filter *(below)* in the bottom of the sump. This should be cleaned when the filter is changed.

Some motor cycles have a removeable mesh filter in the side of the crankcase *(right)*. This should taken out and cleaned at regular intervals.

Replacing gaskets

For obvious engineering reasons, it is essential to create and maintain gas-tight, oil-tight and water-tight seals wherever engine components are bolted together. This is achived by inserting a device called a gasket between the adjacent mating surfaces. These gaskets are made from a variety of materials, depending on their position in the engine and the particular job they are intended to fulfill.

If you find that your engine is leaking oil, water or compressed gas from the combustion chamber, you must fit a new gasket to seal the leak. This must be tough enough to resist pressure and heat.

On two-strokes fitting a new cylinder head gasket is not a difficult job, but you must ensure that the replacement maintains the specified head-to-cylinder clearance. Changing a head gasket on a four-stroke is more complicated and the job is best left to a dealer. Check that the new gasket fits correctly and make sure that all the stamped-out holes in the gasket are clear of any obstruction.

How you tighten the cylinder head is important, both for proper sealing and to avoid the risk of warping the head. The job should be done in stages – check these in your handbook – using a torque wrench to ensure that the correct amount of leverage is applied. After finishing the job, go for a short test ride and inspect the gasket and re-check the head studs for tightness after it. Retighten the head studs if this proves necessary.

Sealing a gasket

Wherever a gasket of any type is fitted, the mating surfaces should

There are several types of gasket sealer on the market, though basically they come in three different forms. Hard setting compound should be used between surfaces that you want to permanently bond; on components that have to be separated at major services for example, it is better to use a semi-rigid compound. Silicon-type instant gasket can be used instead of a paper gasket on components such as contact points covers, where the clearance is not an important factor.

be clean and smooth. Badly-pitted surfaces are almost impossible to seal.

One point is worth noting. Most modern engines use jointing compound, rather than gaskets, to mate the two halves of the crankcase together. So always check which is the case.

Use jointing compound sparingly. Any excess will be squeezed out of the joint when the components are tightened together and may clog oilways.

Silicon-type 'instant' gasket can be used on some outer components, such as points covers, and in circumstances where clearance is not an important factor. However, it is not fuel-proof and so should not be used to seal components within the fuel system.

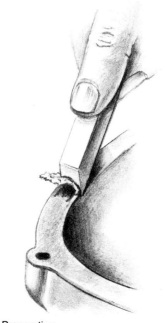

Preparation
Scrape off the old gasket with gasket remover spray, a sharp piece of wood, or a screwdriver. Take care not to score the metal.

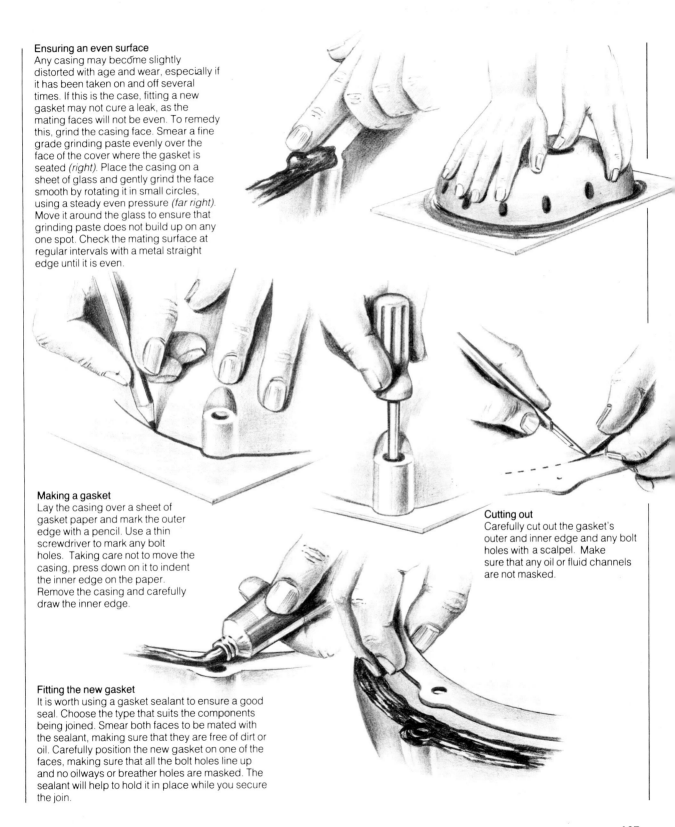

Ensuring an even surface

Any casing may become slightly distorted with age and wear, especially if it has been taken on and off several times. If this is the case, fitting a new gasket may not cure a leak, as the mating faces will not be even. To remedy this, grind the casing face. Smear a fine grade grinding paste evenly over the face of the cover where the gasket is seated *(right)*. Place the casing on a sheet of glass and gently grind the face smooth by rotating it in small circles, using a steady even pressure *(far right)*. Move it around the glass to ensure that grinding paste does not build up on any one spot. Check the mating surface at regular intervals with a metal straight edge until it is even.

Making a gasket

Lay the casing over a sheet of gasket paper and mark the outer edge with a pencil. Use a thin screwdriver to mark any bolt holes. Taking care not to move the casing, press down on it to indent the inner edge on the paper. Remove the casing and carefully draw the inner edge.

Cutting out

Carefully cut out the gasket's outer and inner edge and any bolt holes with a scalpel. Make sure that any oil or fluid channels are not masked.

Fitting the new gasket

It is worth using a gasket sealant to ensure a good seal. Choose the type that suits the components being joined. Smear both faces to be mated with the sealant, making sure that they are free of dirt or oil. Carefully position the new gasket on one of the faces, making sure that all the bolt holes line up and no oilways or breather holes are masked. The sealant will help to hold it in place while you secure the join.

Cooling system maintenance

Air cooled engines are almost maintenance free. However, you must keep the cooling fins, cast into the piston bores and cylinder head, clean, since, if they become clogged, heat loss will be impaired. Use a stiff brush and a degreasant on them when you clean your bike.

Checking the radiator

A liquid-cooled system needs more attention and maintenance, however. Most liquid-cooled bikes carry only a small amount of coolant, so it is essential to check the coolant level at least once a week.

Ideally, you should carry out this check before starting the engine. If the level has to be checked when the engine is hot, cover the filler cap with a rag and ease it undone gently, allowing the hot air and water under pressure inside the radiator to escape gradually.

Checking for leaks

If the system needs to be constantly topped up, the probability is that there is a leak somewhere in it. Any such leakage must be repaired. Start the engine and check the coolant hoses for splits and leaks, especially where they are clamped to unions and spigots. Also check the cylinder head and water pump housing for possible leaks. Where an expansion tank is fitted, make sure that this is not leaking and that the level of the coolant with which the tank is filled is between the upper and lower level marks.

Checking the water pump

If you suspect that your water pump is excessively worn, check it thoroughly. If a water or oil seal

is worn – most pumps have both – they should be renewed. The tell-tale sign of this is a leakage of either water or oil from the bleed hole below the pump housing.

Checking the cap and fan

Check the radiator cap rubber at regular intervals for tears or signs of perishing. Also check for a weak spring, especially if there are signs of overheating.

Where a fan controlled by a temperature switch is fitted, check that the switch is working by allowing the engine to idle. The fan should start working

before the temperature gauge's needle reaches the red zone. If not, switch the ignition off and check the temperature switch circuit and fuse.

Draining the system

All cooling systems should be drained at least once every two years. Draining points are usually found at the base of the cylinders and at the water pump. Remove the radiator cap to speed up the process.

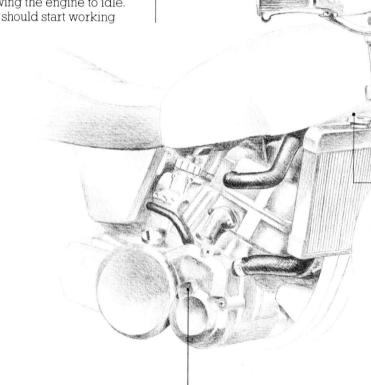

Water pump
The water pump is usually situated in the base of the crankcase. It takes the form of an impeller, which is driven by the engine to circulate the coolant. Though the pump is mostly maintenance free, you can check it by trying to rock it in its mounting. Any movement usually indicates that the bearings are worn.

Flush the system thoroughly with tap water. This should normally be enough to clean out the system, unless the radiator is clogged. If you suspect this, remove the radiator from the machine and reverse flush it.

Replace all suspect components and fill the radiator with a 50/50 mix of water and

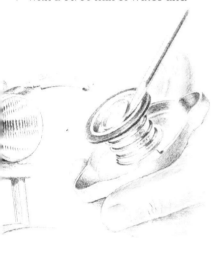

Radiator cap
The spring and rubber seal on the radiator cap regulate the pressure of the coolant in the system. Check that the spring is operating and that the seal is not perished. The pressure rating should be stamped on the cap. If you need to replace it, make sure the rating is correct.

anti-freeze. Ethylene Glycol based anti-freeze is best for bike engines because of its anti-corrosive properties. Use distilled water if you possibly can, though boiled or tap water can substitute. Do not use hard tap water, because the mineral deposits it will leave in the cooling system could cause blockages as well as corrosion.

Refill the system, topping up the radiator until the coolant reaches its neck – if the bike is fitted with an expansion tank, top this up to the lower mark – thus allowing for water expansion. Start the engine with the radiator cap off. This will allow any air trapped in the system to escape (a few bikes have an air bleed nipple fitted on the thermostat housing to assist in this). Top up again, if necessary. Replace the cap and rev the engine slightly, checking for possible leaks .

If all seems well, take the machine for a ten minute ride. This should give the coolant time to reach normal working temperature. Check once again

for leaks. Give the engine time to cool down and then re-check radiator level.

Thermostat maintenance
If your bike is fitted with a thermostat – in many cases this is a standard fitting – and if the needle on the temperature gauge tends to stay in or near the red zone, the thermostat should always be checked. If it is faulty and is not opening, it will stop the coolant reaching the radiator.

To check this, remove the thermostat. Place it in a pan of water and heat the water to the temperature at which the thermostat should open. The exact figure should be given in your manual.

Conversely, if the engine seems to take a long time to warm up, the thermostat may have stuck open. You can check this visually. In either case, the thermostat should be replaced.

Always fit new gaskets and O-rings where necessary. Should coolant be spilt on paintwork, wash it off immediately.

Check the hoses
Check coolant hoses for cracks or weak spots by gently squeezing them. A faulty hose should be replaced.

Replacing a hose
Undo the circlip holding the hose in place and gently ease it off the stub. Replace it with a hose of the same diameter and length.

Problem hoses
If you have difficulty removing an old hose, carefully cut it off the stub with a sharp knife. Replace it with a new hose of the correct size.

Electrical checks

If any electrical component fails, check the appropriate fuse first. Usually, the fuse, or fuse block, is located behind a side panel, or under the seat. Check your handbook for the exact location.

Always carry a variety of spare fuses, making sure that their amp ratings are matched to all of the existing fuses in the fuse block. Fitting a wrongly rated fuse is useless, since it will either blow immediately or allow circuits to be overloaded.

Checking circuits

If a correctly rated fuses blows frequently, there must be an underlying reason for the fault and this must be established. The most common cause is damaged wiring, one particular trouble spot being at the headstock, where cables tend to chafe with the turning of the handlebars. Other cause include excessive machine vibration, which can fret a fuse element until it breaks and excessive current from the generator, due to a regulator fault.

If you think that a wire has broken, or is corroded internally, it is relatively simple to check this. Simply fit a wire the same length of the suspect wire as a temporary replacement. If the component involved works, the original wire is obviously faulty and should be permanently replaced. Alternatively, you can use a bulb and a dry cell battery. Connect the two with the wire you are checking. If the bulb lights, the wire is passing current to it.

When replacing wiring, always use wire of the same type. Wire that is too fine for the demands being made on it could overheat and its plastic insulation could burn through as a result.

A multimeter *(left)* is a useful piece of equipment to have when checking electrical circuits and components. It can also be used when checking the ignition timing on engines with contact points.

Fuses Motor cycle fuses are either of the glass or ceramic type *(above)*. Both types are usually held in a fuse box, *(left)* by contact clips, which should be clean and grip the fuses tightly. The box's cover often shows which circuits the fuses control.

Some circuits are protected by a line fuse *(above)* – a standard fuse held in a plastic case, joining two wires.

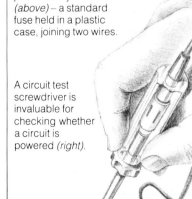

A circuit test screwdriver is invaluable for checking whether a circuit is powered *(right)*.

Wire of slightly too great a thickness can be used – but only as a temporary measure.

Using a multimeter

A multimeter with an ohms (electrical resistance) scale is a most useful tool for checking circuit continuity. It can also tell you whether components are functioning correctly.

You can use a multimeter instead of a bulb and dry cell battery, for instance. Having linked the multimeter into the circuit, set the meter on the ohms scale. If the circuit is good, the needle will deflect across the scale.

The same scale can also be used to measure the resistance of the high tension (HT) cap. Remove the HT lead from the cap and connect the meter to either end of the cap. This check should always be carried out if the engine misfires or refuses to run. In addition, make sure that the HT lead is a tight fit with coil cap and that the cap is not cracked.

Checking the HT cap

If you suspect that your HT cap is faulty – and you do not own a multimeter – you can still check to see if the coil and HT lead are functioning.

Disconnect the HT lead from the cap and hold the end of the lead against the cylinder, using a pair of pliers with insulated handles for safety. Switch on the ignition and turn the engine over. You should see a spark flash between the HT lead and the cylinder.

Testing the points

To check whether contact breaker points are in good condition, you can use a voltmeter to carry out a voltage, or pressure, drop test. Connect the voltmeter across the battery terminals and see what the reading is. If, for example, your bike is fitted with a six-volt battery in good condition, the meter should read six volts.

Next connect the voltmeter across the contact breaker with the points closed. Switch on the ignition. If the reading is more than half a volt, the faces of the points should be cleaned with a points file. If the reading does not improve, the points should be replaced.

Bulbs

Most motor cycles, especially lightweights, are fitted with separate headlight bulbs and reflectors. Some fast or large capacity machines have high intensity quartz-halogen bulbs. while a few have car-type sealed beam headlight units.

In the case of the high intensity quartz-halogen bulb, the quartz 'envelope' must be kept free from dampness and grease and should be handled only by its metal base. Something as tiny as a bead of sweat on the quartz envelope can change the surface temperature enough to cause a crack. The unit's construction means that dirt, dust and moisture problems are eliminated, protecting the reflector from deterioration. The disadvantage is the unit's size, which makes it difficult to carry a spare on most bikes.

Bulb checks

The approximate life of a headlight bulb is only 100 hours. Likely causes of bulb failure are excessive vibration, the erosion caused by normal wear and tear – this is usually accompanied by staining of the glass – bad connections or a bad earth and excessive voltage, possibly due to a faulty voltage regulator.

A blown bulb is normally easy to detect, since the filament is usually broken, with the fragments clearly visible at the bottom of the glass casing. If there is no such debris, the filament may simply have snapped in two. This is quickly detected by visual examination.

If a new bulb of the correct type does not light up, first check the relevant fuse, since this may have blown at the same time as the failed bulb. If the fuse has not blown, check for a bad contact. In a bayonet-type bulb, this may be caused by a mismatch between the contact points on the bulb holder and those on the bulb. Switch the light on and twist the bulb in its holder. If the light flashes when the bulb is twisted either side of its proper position, the bulb holder contacts should be re-aligned carefully to ensure a secure contact.

Next check for a bad earth and for corrosion in switches and wiring block connectors. Both are common problems – check for them in particular if lights work, but seem to be unusually dim. Excessive corrosion in wiring and switches or a bad earth connection all lead to a voltage drop.

Clean any mould off the components and coat them in silicon grease – or use an electrical spray – to help prevent further corrosion. Also check the condition of the headlight reflector. This may be rusty or dulled with age. If bulbs blow frequently, have the voltage regulator checked by a garage or an electrician.

No matter whether bulbs are bayonet or push-in, clean and tight connections are essential. Bulb connections are designed to ensure that the bulb can only be inserted the right way around, so never try to force a bulb into a socket. If it will not fit, you are either trying to fit it incorrectly, or a component has been bent out of shape or otherwise damaged.

Checking a flasher unit

If the indicators do not work, check that the connections are secure. If the indicator lights come on, but refuse to flash, the likely cause is a flat battery. If the bulbs, contacts, wiring and fuse are all in good condition – and the flasher still will not work – it is cheaper to fit a new unit than go to the trouble and expense of repairing the existing one.

The keys to survival

Experienced motor cyclists will tell you that motor cycling is one of the most exhilarating forms of road travel ever devised. On a warm day, there is little to compare with the thrill of riding a good machine competently along a winding road into the hills.

Attractive though this sounds, there is more to motor cycling than this, as most young novice riders soon discover. For them, that first road-going bike is their introduction to the harsh realities of the world they are about to discover. To survive in it, you need to know the basic survival rules.

This chapter sets out to provide you with specific information on the keys to survival on two wheels. It covers rider training, what to wear, coping with adverse weather conditions and much more. It is your passport to full riding pleasure and fulfilment.

Survival basics

In motor cycling, there are two main keys to survival. The first is the awareness and observance of legal rules and regulations, in all their complex forms. The second is to obey the simple, rules of good roadcraft and show commonsense riding skills. This means, for instance, that you should learn how to ride your bike properly – to do this, you should have professional tuition – have an idea of at least the basics involved in adequate machine maintenance, wear the right clothing, observe good road manners and much more.

Think of this another way. If you fail to take advantage of professional tuition you stand a poor chance of passing the Part One test (see p135). If you ride a badly maintained bike, it is almost certain to let you down at some stage – as well as attracting police attention. Inadequate riding gear increases the risk of injury in an accident and will make your life a misery in cold weather. And bad road manners, such as aggressive overtaking, will understandably antagonize motorists, who may take retaliatory action.

So the first rule of motor cycling is to obey the law and show commonsense on the road. If other road users think you are incompetent or inconsiderate, then you are probably both and may be treated accordingly.

Defensive riding

Contradictory though it may sound, the second thing to remember is that there are no legal 'rights' when it comes to survival, as far as motor cyclists are concerned. Any motor cyclist who relies on his or her 'rights' on the road is simply asking for trouble, because, unlike bigger vehicles, there is simply no way of enforcing natural justice. A good many road users respect only size and power – think of how large trucks can literally force their way into traffic streams and think how the majority of drivers react to such behaviour from a motor cyclist.

Rights are an abstract. They do not glow and are not shock-absorbing. The fact that you may be well within them is no guarantee that you will avoid a collision with the car whose driver fails to 'see' you as the vehicle pulls out from a side turning across your path. Thus, always drive defensively and take nothing for granted.

Cornering can kill

Your motor cycle has one unique characteristic. It can bank around corners. For many motor cyclists, this is the focus of interest – so much so that their efforts to find the 'perfect' corner approximates to the dedication of the committed surfer, who will occasionally sacrifice everything in the search for the perfect wave. Here, however, the parallel ends. Unlike surfers, who pursue their goal individually, young motor cyclists tend to ride in groups, with the result that cornering has a competitive edge.

This is extremely dangerous. It is all too easy for the aggressive competitive urge to replace a rider's vital survival instincts and, without them, safety depends almost solely on luck. To count on this is to court disaster –

remember that you are almost totally vulnerable and protect by little more than your wits.

If you question this, look at the official statistics. These show that the majority of serious motor cycling injuries – and 50% of the fatalities – are not caused by other road users. They are the sole result of a misjudgement by the rider involved

So never race, particularly around corners. Though you may get away with this for a few months, one day it will either maim or kill you.

Coping with acceleration

You also have to come to terms with your machine's other unique attribute – its extraordinary acceleration. In general terms, the average motor cycle can accelerate from 0-60mph in half the time it takes the average car. This, though a source of immense satisfaction to many motor cyclists, frequently comes as a shock to car drivers.

If you combine this with the extreme agility of a motor cycle at low speeds, it should come as

no surprise to you that, in the event of an accident, many car drivers will claim that they simply did not see you. Even though this is no excuse, drivers find it relatively easy to overlook a motor cycle's small profile, because it has appeared unexpectedly in an entirely unanticipated position on the road. Keep this in mind and try to be in the right place at the right time and at the right speed.

Brake power

No experienced motor cyclist relies on the brakes to get out of trouble, largely because it requires considerable skill to brake hard and safely. In wet weather especially, panic braking will lock the wheels and put the machine into an uncontrollable skid. This is the single biggest contributor to motor cycle accidents, since skidding on locked wheels inevitably means a crash.

If you want to survive, never treat your brakes as trouble shooters. Ride so that you never have to use their full power.

Rider training/1

When you decide to take up motor cycling, it is simple common sense to learn the basics of machine control before venturing out on to a public highway. Even this requires some pre-planning, since anyone who imagines that they are free to ride without a licence and without insurance anywhere off the road should think again. If you do, you may be breaking the law.

Whatever their age, riders without licences may only ride powered two-wheelers on private land to which the public has no general access. In addition, the landowner's written permission must be obtained. This means that, while it may be legal to ride in a farmer's field or wood – provided you fulfill the above stipulations – it is illegal to ride along footpaths and green lanes (unsurfaced old roads), over commons and through disused quarries, open woods and parkland and along beaches.

Proper insurance cover is equally vital. Riding without insurance is a serious legal offence. If you are riding uninsured and are involved in an accident, you will be personally liable to make good any damage or compensate for any injury, whether or not you caused the accident in the first place.

Age limits

It is legal for a 16-year-old to ride a moped on a public road – a moped is officially defined as having an engine of no more than 500cc and a top speed no greater than 30mph – while a 17-year-old can ride a motor cycle. You apply for a provisional licence in the first instance; a full licence is only granted when you have passed the government test. A full moped licence is only valid as a provisional motor cycle licence; a car licence can also be used in the same way. Anyone wanting to ride off-road before they are of licencing age should consult their local bike dealer, police station or local authority safety officer about suitable land and clubs.

Once a provisional motor cycle licence has been granted, the holder has two years in which to pass his or her motor cycle test. If, by this time, no full licence has been granted, you will be refused a further provisional licence for 12 months. This may seem harsh, but it is the law for general purposes.

There are exceptions to this rule. If you can show that you were ill, or abroad, for a specific period, the time involved will be added on to the statutory two years. If you hold a full moped or car licence, your provisional motor cycling is not governed by the two-year stipulation.

Riding tuition

Experts all agree that the route to passing the test lies in professional tuition. This is not compulsory, but the chances of success without it are low.

All good motor cycle dealers will be able to advise you how best to go about finding suitable riding tuition. The best will be prepared to deliver the machine they are selling you to a special instruction area and will ensure that novice customers are fully conversant with the principles of safe riding before allowing them to take to the road. Others will put their customers in touch with local riding instruction schemes.

If you are buying a bike privately, consult your local authority road safety officer, the police, or a motor cycle dealer. All of them will be able to offer advice.

Training schemes

There are three national training schemes in current operation. These are the National Rider Training Scheme, which operates the 'Star Rider' training programme; the RoSPA (Royal Society for Prevention of Accidents) scheme, associated with the AA; and, finally, the BMF (British Motorcyclists' Federation) scheme. All three operate locally organized schools, run by highly skilled practising motor cycle tutors who themselves have been specially trained.

All three schemes are government authorized. In each case, they cover all aspects of moped and bike training, from pre-riding classroom theory through both parts of the driving test and further into advanced motor cycling. The cost of a full Part One instruction course – that is, the basic course including the first part of the driving test – is between £20 and £35.

Other purely local 'safe riding' courses are operated by local authorities and commercial concerns, such as the British School of Motoring. Some of these have an extremely wide range of training facilities, including trail parks.

Assessing a scheme

To establish whether or not a training scheme is up to standard, you should check to see whether it meets the following standards.

The instructors should hold advanced riding certificates issued by any of the three main national schemes, or by the IAM

(Institute of Advanced Motorists, Motorcycle Division). Full theoretical classes on roadcraft theory should be available. A large area of 'private' ground is essential. On-the-road instruction should be given in company with at least two instructors to four novice riders.

These tips will help you to distinguish between a good and a bad riding school. The latter can be recognized by their scarcity of staff, their lack of adequate training facilities and, most importantly of all, their inability to offer more than basic tuition. Any scheme that offers nothing more than quick success at the basics should be avoided at all costs.

All the national schools and the better local ones guide pupils through the complete safe riding system. They all carry out their own tests prior to the official ones to ensure that you stand the best possible chance of a first-time pass. This is done by educating pupils to considerably beyond the official standards.

Naturally enough, official examiners will be strongly inclined to favour test pupils who they know have been instructed fully and correctly and who display machine control and road-craft skills superior to those of the obvious novice.

As already stated, the cost of a basic training programme should be between £20 and £30. More advanced pupils should expect to pay a further £40 for further training.

In addition, it may pay you to hire a bike from the training course – the charge is usually nominal. New, or nearly new, machinery is extremely vulnerable in unskilled hands and repair costs are high.

Test contents

In many respects, the Part One test is more demanding than its successor because it must be taken so early in a new rider's career. It also demands what may seem to the novice to be a surprisingly high degree of machine skill, but this is precisely the intention. The sheer volume and speed of modern traffic simply does not give the average novice the chance to learn machine control and roadcraft simultaneously.

Anyone who wobbles off into busy traffic, or even along an apparently deserted road, without proper experience of a motor cycle's controls stands a 50/50 chance of the ride ending in tragedy. It takes a lot of skill to simultaneously balance, change gear, be aware of the traffic ahead, keep an eye on the rear mirrors, signal and accelerate into another traffic lane to overtake, for instance. It may well prove necessary to carry out all these operations simultaneously every few minutes during an ordinary ride across town.

This is why official thinking now places a great deal of stress on basic machine control as the first step on the road to competent motor cycling. The result is that the learner riders of today should only have to concentrate on roadcraft when they first hit the highway.

The Part One test

Although it is not a legal requirement to pass the Part One machine control test before riding on a public road, common sense should tell you that it is sensible to undertake some form of basic training before you do so. It is equally sensible to

undertake this tuition and ride the test as soon as you have the confidence to do so.

The test itself involves seven separate manoeuvres within an area of 12.4sq m x 5.5sq m (133 x 60sq ft), the area being marked out carefully with large orange plastic cones. Though the layout may appear confusing initially, the cones indicate the various routes involved.

Each of these routes is explained by an examiner until he or she is satisfied that the candidate understands the instructions fully. Thus, you only have to remember one set of instructions per manoeuvre. It is also important that you only agree to start each manoeuvre when you are fully confident about the particular route involved.

The only practical roadcraft involved is the requirement for all candidates to glance over their shoulder before they move off. This should be simple common sense, but, to reinforce the point, riders who fail to do this are penalised from the start.

Examiners award candidates penalty points according to a clearly defined table. A score of eight is a fail. You will score this automatically if you fall off your bike, crash, take the wrong course, or go outside a marker cone. If you touch a marker cone, you score two points. You score one point for each of the following: starting, or trying to start in gear, whether or not the clutch is lifted; stalling the engine; putting your foot down on the ground; going outside the prescribed test area; or wobbling noticeably. Thus, if you start in gear, realize what you have done, brake in a panic, stall the engine and steady yourself

Rider training/2

by putting your feet down on the ground, you may lose at least three points before you even start the test proper.

Test manoeuvres

The examiners term each of the seven manoeuvres exercises. In the first, you have to ride anti-clockwise between a set of three cones set 1.2m (4ft) apart on each of the four corners of a 20m (100ft) by 10m (50ft) rectangle. A fifth pair of cones set 6m (20ft) beyond the third turn are spaced at only 99cm (3ft 3in); they are followed immediately by a sixth pair 1.2m (4ft) apart. The second exercise is identical to the first one, but you ride it clockwise as opposed to anti-clockwise.

The third exercise is the same as the second one, but involves a compulsory stop at the start of the second corner. Although this is supposed to resemble a junction stop and start, the close proximity of the cones makes it one of the trickiest test manoeuvres and therefore it needs a good deal of practice. Try it out at home, with markers only 107cm (3ft 6in) apart.

The fourth exercise is almost as tricky. You must accelerate to 15mph (40k/hr) between cones spaced 24m (80ft) apart and stop in full control. The front wheel's spindle must also project right into a square marked by four cones, the nearest pair of which are 1.2m (4ft) apart and the further ones spaced at 99cm (3ft 3in). The examiner will be checking to see that both brakes are used correctly – 75% of the braking force should come from the front brake – and that you do not stall your engine.

The fifth exercise involves riding a figure-of-eight slalom course between five cones, set apart at 1½ times the length of your motorcycle. Two boundary markers set 2.7m (9ft) out from the centre add to the problems. You are asked to carry out this manoeuvre only once; it starts and ends at the same cone. The next exercise is similar, but it involves two cones slightly further apart, with boundary markers on both. You are required to complete three circuits. It is easy to fall into the trap of over-confidence and speed excessively towards the end. If you do, you may well feel giddy and control will suffer as a result.

The seventh exercise is a simple slow riding test. You will be expected to ride alongside the examiner as he walks along an 24m (80ft) straight line course, matching your speed to his occasional changes of pace. If you wobble excessively, you will be penalised.

The final stage involves answering half a dozen simple questions on various aspects of machine control and general motor cycling hazards. None of these relate to the Highway Code, or the law.

The Part Two test

Because this test is totally devoted to roadcraft, it is impossible to describe in detail, since its pattern obviously depends on road and traffic conditions at the time. To pass, you must convince your examiner that you possess road commonsense as well as road skill. It is pointless, for instance, to display good machine control and to emergency brake to perfection if you demonstrate clear ignorance of road positioning, or of the Highway Code.

Other demands, however, can be less stringent. A stalled engine, for example, will be overlooked, if you can show you can deal competently with the problem if it arises and can go on to manoeuvre safely and fluidly through traffic streams.

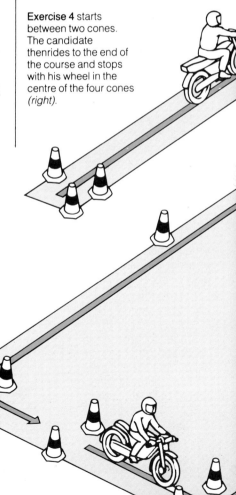

Exercise 4 starts between two cones. The candidate then rides to the end of the course and stops with his wheel in the centre of the four cones *(right)*.

Exercises 1, 2 and 3 are ridden on the same course in left and right hand circuits *(right)*.

The test itself normally lasts for about 20 minutes. Before you start off, the examiner will first ask to see your provisional licence and will then test your eyesight by asking you to read a car number plate at a distance of around 25yd. He or she will then check the motor cycle to make sure that the controls are in good order, the tyres satisfy legal requirements, the lights work properly and so on. Such things

as a rusty, loose chain and worn chain sprockets may cause test cancellation.

The normal procedure is for you to be told the route to take for the first part of the test. This is usually little more than a round-the-block circuit. It will include an assortment of traffic hazards, such as road junctions, pedestrian crossings, traffic lights and parked cars; it will also normally include a right turn against oncoming traffic.

It is vital that you understand which route you are supposed to

take fully. If in doubt, ask. Examiners are familiar with test nerves and far prefer explaining things a few times, rather than having to deal with a hopelessly lost candidate.

The examiner positions himself close to these hazards – he or she will normally try to

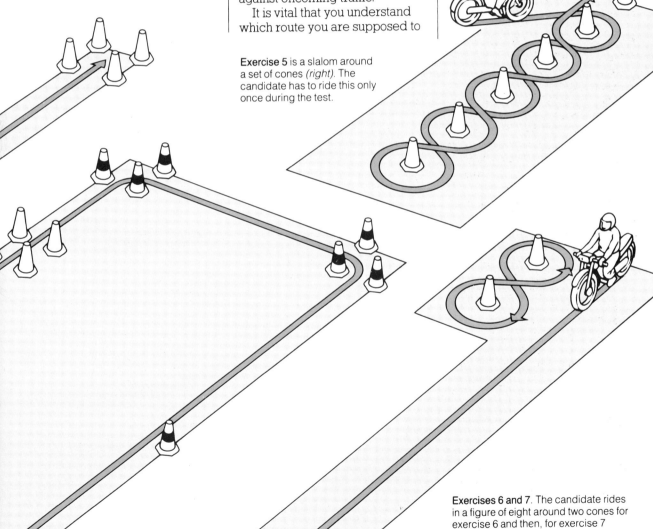

Exercise 5 is a slalom around a set of cones *(right)*. The candidate has to ride this only once during the test.

Exercises 6 and 7. The candidate rides in a figure of eight around two cones for exercise 6 and then, for exercise 7 *(above)*, rides slowly between two points, keeping pace with an examiner.

Rider training/3

remain unseen – to ascertain how well you cope with them. This means you must demonstrate your ability to cope with them extremely clearly. It is a good idea, for instance, to slightly exaggerate rearward glances and hand signals, while, rather than just glancing into your rear mirrors, it will pay you to move your head slightly as well. Remember that you are penalised heavily for fierce acceleration, late braking, overtaking traffic moving at normal town pace, cutting corners, inadequate signalling and for failing to react sufficiently to such hazards as pedestrian crossings, parked cars in shopping areas, school, hospital and factory entrances, loose dogs, children at play and cyclists.

Relying on indicators alone is insufficient. Examiners expect to see the full range of your signalling proficiency

demonstrated – this involves you using your hands even if there is no other traffic in close proximity.

Your attitude to the test is all-important. You should not be excessively bold or too timid. You will probably fail if you ride your motor cycle as though it was a bicycle – too slowly and in the gutter. Over cautiousness gives a strong impression of inexperience and so should be avoided.

The emergency stop is usually the last part of the test. It involved nothing more than coming to a smooth halt without stalling the engine in response to a pre-arranged signal from your examiner. Nothing unexpected or unsafe will be asked of you, so you should simply rely on your front brake to provide 75% of the stopping power – as you would do normally – and lift the clutch. Pay no attention to gear changing.

As with the Part One test, you

will be asked questions on the Highway Code and roadcraft. Approximately six questions on each is normal.

After the test

If you fail the test, arrange to see your instructor and discuss what went wrong. Make another application to take the test immediately and start corrective instruction.

If you pass, you should realize that you have not won an expert rider award. All you have achieved is the officially recognized minimum riding standard. At this point, the real training starts, particularly insofar as self-discipline is concerned. It will pay you to enter an advanced training course to achieve an even higher standard. Your motor cycling responsibilities now include not only the safety of other road users, but also of your pillion passengers.

WHERE YOU CAN TRAIN

The most popular rider training scheme is 'Star Rider', run by the National Motorcycling Training Scheme. The NTS is the biggest motor cycling training organization in Britain, with 508 Star Rider training centres and 367 locations where you can take the Part One test.

Within the scheme, various courses are operated. The most basic is the Bronze Course. This costs £12 and is intended for the first time rider, who has never ridden a powered two-wheeler before and may not even known how the controls operate.

The course is held off the public road – in school

playgrounds and the like. It is supporter by many dealers, who, as part of the deal, will deliver the machine you buy from them to the training site, so that you can learn how to handle it there, rather than on the road.

The next course is the Silver Course. This costs around £29.50 and involves a total of 12 hours of tuition, usually split into two-hour sessions on consecutive Sundays mornings. If you complete it successfully, you are considered up to the Part One test standard and so will be given an automatic pass. However, you still have to pay the official test fee.

If you achieve Silver standard

you will also possess the neccessary skills to pass the Part Two test. This, however, is independent of the scheme; you have to ride it and will be judged by the riding skills you demonstrate on the day. The fee is £14.40.

For riders who want to improve their riding skills further, the NTS scheme offers a Gold Standard course. The course itself costs £27.50, while the optional NTS test at the end costs a further £13.50. You can save money by enrolling for the two together from the start – this costs £26.50.

Department of Transport
ROAD TRAFFIC ACT 1972

Statement of Failure to Pass Test of Competence to Drive

Test Centre:

Name ....

has this day been examined and has failed to pass the test of competence to drive prescribed for the purposes of section 85 of the Road Traffic Act 1972.

Date ....

Authorised by the Minister of Transport to conduct tests

Examiners have regard to the items listed below in deciding whether a candidate is competent to drive. The matters needing special attention are marked for your information and assistance and should be studied in detail. (See Note 1 overleaf)

1. ☐ Comply with the requirements of the eyesight test.
2. ☐ Know the Highway Code.
3. ☐ Take proper precautions before starting the engine.
4. ☐ Make proper use of/accelerator/clutch/gears/footbrake/handbrake/steering.
5. ☐ Move away/safely/under control.
6. ☐ Stop the vehicle in an emergency/promptly/under control/making proper use of front brake.
7. ☐ Reverse into a limited opening either to the right or left/under control/with due regard for other road users.
8. ☐ Turn round by means of forward and reverse gears/under control/with due regard for other road users.
9. ☐ Make effective use of mirror(s) well before ⎫
    Take effective rear observation well before ⎬ signalling/changing direction/slowing down or stopping.
10. ☐ Give signals/where necessary/correctly/in good time.
11. ☐ Take prompt and appropriate action on all/traffic signs/road markings/traffic lights/signals given by traffic controllers/other road users.
12. ☐ Exercise proper care in the use of speed.
13. ☐ Make progress by/driving at a speed appropriate to the road and traffic conditions/avoiding undue hesitancy.
14. ☐ Act properly at road junctions:-

    — regulate speed correctly on approach;
    — take effective observation before emerging;
    — position the vehicle correctly/before turning right/before turning left;
    — avoid cutting right hand corners.

15. ☐ Overtake/meet/cross the path of/other vehicles safely.
16. ☐ Position the vehicle correctly during normal driving.
17. ☐ Allow adequate clearance to stationary vehicles.
18. ☐ Take appropriate action at pedestrian crossings.
19. ☐ Select a safe position for normal stops.
20. ☐ Show awareness and anticipation of the actions of/pedestrians/cyclists/drivers.

DRIVING EXAMINERS ARE NOT PERMITTED TO DISCUSS DETAILS OF THE TEST

51-2988 1/83 GBR LTD

SEE GUIDANCE NOTES OVERLEAF

DL 24
6/80

Nobody wants to recieve this form after a test; however, it does give an indication of the areas of your riding ability that must be improved in order for you to pass it. This preview will help you to ensure that you are adequately prepared.

Survival on the road/1

Whatever the road or traffic conditions, whatever the season of the year, you will not go far wrong if you abide by the basic rules of motor cycling whenever you take to the road. According to official statistics, only a comparatively few accidents can be blamed on a particular road feature, or bike defect; in nine out of ten cases, it is an unfortunate fact that the root cause can be traced back to human error.

Think once, think twice...

A motor cycle can be a lethal weapon – and, in ignorant hands, may well turn out to be one. Any machine must be treated with respect and handled with care. This is why developing road knowledge and road sense is so vitally important. The more of the two you have at your disposal, the more confidently you will ride and the greater will be your riding pleasure.

What you should be aiming for is the calm efficiency that is the hallmark of any expert rider. You need to be able to combine the necessary alertness to any potential hazard with a confident, relaxed riding style. And, above all, you must be in control of any given situation. If you can achieve this, you will have also achieved one of the basic essentials of safe motor cycling – the ability to react to any unexpected road hazard or emergency swiftly, so giving yourself time to spare for the appropriate response.

Full control

To establish full motor cycle control, what you need to do is to develop a systematic way of thinking, so that you can apply certain basic rules when you approach any road hazard. Such hazards fall into three main categories. The first are physical features, such as road junctions, roundabouts, bends and hill crests. The second are hazards caused by other road users, while the third are created by variations in the road surface, or by weather conditions.

Whenever you see any hazard, decide on your intended course of action according to the following rules. Though not all of these will necessarily apply to each and every hazard, enough will to make the effort worthwhile. Remember, too, that you must apply them in sequence if you are to use them to the best advantage.

When you first see the hazard, decide on the correct way to approach it. Look in your mirrors and check the rear view over your shoulder. If you need to change your road position, think whether you to signal your intentions to other road users. Check the rear view again and then start to reduce speed if necessary, giving a slowing down signal, if appropriate.

Select the gear best suited to the speed of your machine. Though changing down through the gears will reduce your speed, do not rely on this to slow down – you must use your brakes where necessary. Check the view behind you again and decide whether it is necessary to signal your intentions – either for the first time, or to reinforce a signal you have made already. Sound your horn, if necessary.

Take a last look behind you before altering course. This could be a lifesaver – always expect the unexpected. Then apply the correct amount of acceleration to pass the hazard.

The golden rules

Safe motor cycling has additional golden rules, all of which can be life savers. Follow them religiously whenever you are out on the road whatever the situation, or, as happens all too frequently with other road users, whatever the provocation.

Perfect your roadcraft. Good roadcraft will enable you to avoid awkward and potentially dangerous situations. Ride thoughtfully, planning what you are going to do. When you overtake, do so as quickly as possible, bearing in mind the demands of safety.

Develop the ability to get the most out of your machine, but, at the same time, get to know its capabilities and its limitations. Give proper signals and use horn and headlights thoughtfully. Concentrate on the road and think before you act, exercising restraint and holding back when necessary. Use speed intelligently, especially when cornering, and ride fast only on suitable stretches of road. Above all, obey the rules of the road and show courtesy to all other road users.

Riding in winter

For obvious reasons, the rules of winter riding are simple and strict. Winter riding conditions are harsh and uncompromising, and anyone who takes chances may well be risking his or her life – and the lives of others.

Even the cleanest road loses 50% adhesion when wet; ordinary oil and rubber deposits may raise this figure to 80%. Bear this in mind when riding in these conditions, since a motor cycle loses almost all its advantages of agility, acceleration and cornering ability in the rain.

Experienced riders adopt a super-smooth, gentle riding rhythm that makes no demand on manoeuvrability, avoiding the risks inherent in fierce acceleration or hard braking. They ride with their headlight dipped, at double the the normal braking distance. They indicate changes of direction earlier and pay even more attention than usual to the traffic they see behind them in their mirrors.

Remember that panic braking is a sure way to skid and watching the brake lights of other vehicles immediately in front of you is less of a safety guarantee than observing general traffic flow further ahead. This helps you to develop the trick of anticipating vehicle movements before they occur.

Well-used wheel tracks in traffic lanes are less slippery than central strips, while manhole covers and some white lines are slippery too. Bus and truck depot exits can be like ice in wet weather, because they are saturated with spilled diesel fuel.

Machine tips

Good tyres are important to ensure maximum road grip. Though modern disc brakes are reliable in the wet, you can better their performance by having improved pads fitted. The electrical system should be checked for reliability, all terminals and connections being inspected for corrosion and breakage. This applies especially to fuse and junction boxes, batteries and earthing points. Give them a protective coating of silicon grease.

Lights, too, should be checked. If bulbs appear misty or dark, renew them. Do not wait for them to fail.

What to wear

You are foolhardy if you motor cycle in winter without wearing warm, waterproof clothing. The only suits worth buying are those with written waterproofing guarantees and an insulated lining. Waterproof boots are better all round than leather ones in wet weather – they are also cheaper in any case – while, in heavy rain, it will pay you to cover your gloves with a waterproof overmitt.

Terylene towelling makes the best scarf. It absorbs water well and does not chafe. Denim, however, offers practically no warmth. If worn, long johns and a heavy vest should be worn underneath it.

Mist and fog

Mist and fog can both be killers – particular if you ride into an sudden fog patch at speed. Dip your headlight and ride close to the centre of the traffic lane; gutter creeping is dangerous because of the risk of suddenly coming across parked vehicles. Do not be tempted to speed up and follow a fast-moving car or truck; any motor cyclist who does this can expect a collision sooner or later.

If the fog is really thick, adjust the rear brake light so that it is on permanently. Ride at a speed that will allow you to stop well within the actual amount that you can see in front of you.

Snow and ice

In frosty conditions, you should always assume that ice exists; you should make the same assumption if the road is damp and the temperature below freezing point. Fresh salt or grit on the road usually clears ice, but the converse is true if a freeze follows a thaw, while even salted roads are more slippery than rain covered ones. The most likely trouble spots are deep dips, especially those sheltered by trees, and exposed hill tops. Road repair patches, too, are frequently icy, even when the road itself is ice free.

Snow is simpler to deal with, especially when it is fresh. However, when it becomes impacted by traffic, it is almost as slippery as ice. You should still ride as you would normally, with both of your feet firmly on the foot rest, rather than dangling your legs for extra support. This is because dangling actually destabilizes the machine, while there is always the risk that your legs will catch on a hidden obstruction. In addition, you will be unable to apply the rear brake; the front brake used on its own in such conditions is deadly.

In both cases, it is best to stay clear of the wheel tracks left by other vehicles. Gutters sometimes offer a little extra grip – this is provided by the waste grit that collects in them. Slush is treacherous.

Get into the highest gear you can and ride as slowly as possible, keeping the engine revs low to reduce potential wheel spin. Treat the brakes as your enemy and take added care on bends. Approach down hill slopes with particular caution and do not try to accelerate up hill.

If you encounter black ice, grip the fuel tank with your knees – this will give you a greater sense of stability – and maintain a very light grip on the handlebars. The machine will feel as though it is floating, so do not grab at the brakes, or make sudden throttle adjustments. Keep the machine

Survival on the road/2

upright and reduce speed gently. You will realize things are back to normal as soon as you have cleared the patch because the usual 'feel' of the road surface will be restored.

Approach all hazards cautiously and, when riding in the depths of winter, pay particular attention to weather forecasts. If you are planning a long ride in very cold weather, wear electrically heated gloves and vest – if you can afford them – and make sure that your bike is in tip-top condition.

Summer riding

Summer motor cycling brings its own risks. These are no less dangerous than those of winter riding, although the potential dangers are often less obvious. Many of them spring from rider behaviour, since dry roads and fine, warm weather seem to encourage extremely irresponsible riding behaviour, particular among young riders.

As an example, take a small group of friends on a Friday afternoon, travelling in convoy for a weekend's camping by the coast. Imagine that you are an experienced biker and take a look at their observance of the basic rules of roadcraft. Even a cursory examination will reveal irresponsibility.

Between them, the group has a Honda H100, Kawasaki AE50, Yamaha V80 and a Suzuki A100. The road is crowded with lines of slow-moving vehicles, but the riders are zipping past them, regardless of the road conditions. This on its own makes them a potential traffic hazard.

What else is wrong? In the first place, instead of the slowest bikes leading (the Kawasaki and Yamaha) – thereby ensuring that

a safe overall pace is maintained – the bigger Honda and Suzuki are in the lead. This means that the riders of the other less powerful machines are riding beyond their limits and are inevitably taking risks to keep up with the leaders.

Two of the machines have top-boxes, one of which wobbles constantly. The load is not only too high up for safety, but also bearing on the rear wheel spindle. The unbalanced load means that the front wheel is lightened and so tends to flutter from side to side.

A third machine is carrying a pile of hastily strapped-on luggage, which has moved precariously to one side of the pillion seat. The rider is also wearing a back-pack. This may not be dangerous in itself, but it is tiring. However, two of the bikes have luggage rolls tied to their headlamps. This is potentially dangerous. Either the instruments will be obscured, or tele-fork movement will be restricted. Since any weight forward of the steering axis can affect the steering, this will be affected adversely, too.

As well as riding at an excessive speed, the four riders are all dressed far too casually in sneakers, thin jeans and T-shirts. Two of them have their helmet visors raised, one is wearing a jet-style helmet and no goggles, and none of them are wearing gloves. In summer especially, when the atmosphere is dusty and the roads full of flying grit, eye protection is vital. If the leader of the group – which, remember, is riding in close formation – slows down suddenly because of an injured eye, it is unlikely that the others will be able to avoid him, and the

resulting crash will injure them all.

Summer rules

Having considered this example, think how easy it is not to be thoughtless and to observe a few basic rules. They will not inhibit your riding pleasure – and they may well save your life if an accident occurs.

If you cannot afford proper touring equipment, you should place luggage inside strong carrying bags. These should then be secured firmly – either to the top of the fuel tank, or the pillion seat – using good-quality straps. To balance the load correctly, think of an imaginary triangle, with its apex at the top of the rider's helmet and its base between the two wheel spindles.

In spite of summer temperatures, clothing must provide you with protection in case of an accident. Even in high summer, the rule is to wear strong boots – make sure that these provide you with adequate ankle protection – heavyweight jeans and a thick jacket, a visor or goggles, and leather gloves. If you are riding into the sun, it is a good idea to fix a peak or shade of some sort to the visor to ensure clear vision.

Road sense

On the road, the normal rules apply. Take the same precautions when riding on a wet surface as you would in winter, but, in addition, beware of patches of melted tar. These are extremely slippery.

Riders travelling in groups should overtake one at a time, leaving sufficient clearance between themselves and their companions. The basic rule of thumb is to allow at least the length of the vehicle you are overtaking. Because of the higher speeds and temperatures usually involved in summer riding, you should check your tyre pressures daily, at the same time examining the tyres themselves carefully for foreign bodies and other signs of damage.

It will pay you to study your route carefully in advance on a map and work out a detailed route plan, which can then be secured to the tank or luggage top. This means that you can read it easily, and so avoid erratic riding. If you are carrying a pillion passenger, leave the navigation to him or her. Before you start off, devise a simple code of tapped instructions to indicate changes of direction.

Motorway riding

Motorways are legally out of bounds to learner riders and riders of machines of under 50cc. They also demand special riding skills, which you should be aware of before you venture on to a motorway for the first time.

Remember that high speed motorway riding will put added mechanical strain on your bike, so check that it is in good running condition. A breakdown could cost you dearly if you have to call for assistance, while finding yourself locked into fast moving traffic with a dead engine can be lethal. Also check that you have enough fuel to reach your destination, or a motorway service area.

For safety's sake, your bike should be fitted with at least one rear view mirror. It should also be capable of cruising easily at 50mph (80k/hr) and preferably at the maximum speed limit of 70mph (112k/hr). Top speed

should be considerably more than this to allow a safety margin for accelerating out of trouble.

Read the sections of the Highway Code that cover motorway riding and follow the rules they outline. Also study the motorway signs, so that you know what to expect along the way.

Bear in mind that it is a technical offence to stop on a motorway except in cases of emergency. So, if the weather looks as though it might worsen, you must put your oversuit on before you join the motorway. Wear bright clothing if possible to make yourself more conspicuous to other motorway users. At night, this means wearing a luminous strip, or something similar.

On the motorway

Put your headlight on dipped beam and ride with confidence. Position your machine just left of centre of the lane in which you are travelling. Do not straddle the white lines or studs – other motorway users will be unsure of which lane you are riding in if you do this.

You must command your section of motorway, making full use of indicators when changing lanes. Maintain lane discipline by returning to the slower lane after overtaking.

If you run into trouble – your engine starts to misfire, say, and looks like stalling – signal clearly and move into the slow lane. Be ready to pull on to the hard shoulder, should this prove necessary.

Because motorway traffic travels at constantly high speeds, you must be constantly on your guard. Do not use the motorway if you are feeling under the weather, or are tired. In such

circumstances, it is better – and safer – to use a trunk road, where you can pull over and stop more easily and remain within the law.

Remember to suit your speed to the weather. In heavy rain, for instance, your vision is usually severely impaired by spray thrown up by passing trucks, so a visor, or pair of goggles, is essential – plus some means of wiping them as you ride to keep your line of sight as clear as possible. If the rain is really heavy, it is sensible to avoid motorways completely. When following trucks in dry weather, make sure that the truck driver knows you are behind him by staying back sufficiently for him to be able to see you in his rear view mirror.

As you ride, keep a check on your instrument display, particularly the coolant temperature gauge, the oil temperature and the oil pressure. Engines run hotter when under load and a long motorway ride at speed will soon highlight weaknesses which remain concealed when riding for shorter distances at lower overall speeds.

Be aware of the limitations of your machine. Do not try to overtake unless you are sure that you can pass the vehicle in front of you smartly, with revs to spare, and always allow yourself sufficient braking distance when approaching vehicles in front of you.

Riding at night

For safe night riding, goggles or a visor are essential. Though some riders do not wear any eye protection at night, this is unwise. Though you may be able to get away with this when riding very slowly through a town, the risk of

Survival on the road/3

being hit in the eye by a stone or piece of road grit is simply too great. Your eyes are precious – treat them with respect.

Make sure that visors and goggles are clean and free from cracks and scratches, particularly if you are wearing a plastic visor. Some of these visors scratch easily and so are potentially dangerous, since they impair your vision and cause street lights and oncoming headlights to 'star' across the field of vision.

Never wear a tinted visor at night. These are fine for riding in bright sunlight, but they simply cut out too much light in the dark.

Your clothing should keep you warm – at night, the temperature drops markedly, even during the summer. If you let yourself get cold, your riding will deteriorate, as you become stiff and your reactions slow. Also wear a luminous strip, or something similar, so that car and truck drivers can pick you up easily. This is particularly important if you are riding a low speed bike or moped.

Remember to check that you have sufficient fuel for your journey – all too few garages are open overnight. Double check to see that all your lights are working – in particular indicators and brake light – and that your headlight is clean, with the beam adjusted correctly. If your bike is not fitted with a rear view mirror, you should fit one, so that you are constantly aware of any traffic approaching from behind you. Always be alert and allow yourself longer to reach your destination than you would in daylight hours.

In rain or drizzle, make sure that you have the means to clear your goggles or visor swiftly and

efficiently while you are on the road. You can use a proprietary wiper, which slips over the finger of a glove, or you can simply cut two fingers off a rubber kitchen glove and pull them over the fingers of your riding mitt.

If the night is cold, the obvious risk is that your goggles or visor will mist up. You can use a proprietary spray or solution to prevent this, but the easiest solution is to smear a light coating of washing up liquid on the inside of the lens. This will help to reduce the tendency to mist.

If you prefer a full face crash helmet, you can add a visor with a glass front section and soft plastic backing – this prevents possible splintering. Though the overall field of vision is reduced, such visors provide exceptional optical clarity and so are particularly suited to night riding. The glass visor is designed to fit a standard visor, the centre of which must be cut out in order to take the attachment.

You can also buy a rain dispersant designed to work with this type of visor, though it has virtually no effect on plastic types. When you smear it on to glass, it breaks down the surface tension of the water, causing the rain drops to form beads, which roll off the visor.

Night time riding brings its own pleasures. Because the general hubub of daytime noise is absent, the exhaust note of your bike seems to come alive, while the darkness itself makes you feel even more at one with your machine than usual. If you ensure that your machine and clothing are properly prepared before you set off, such pleasures can only be enhanced.

Irrespective of whether you are

touring at home or abroad, you should plan your tour well ahead of your departure date. Make sure that you have all the necessary documentation, that your bike or scooter is in first class mechanical order and that you can carry everything you will need on your journey packed safely and securely.

Touring at home
For touring at home, you need a minimum of documentation, which usually need extend only to confirmation of camp site or hotel bookings and so on. It is always best to book these in advance. Though many riders prefer to take pot luck, stopping whenever they feel like it, this can be a problem. Some camp site managers and guest house and hotel staff simply will not let accomodation to motor cyclists or scooter riders. Unfair though this is, it is a fact of life.

When planning a route, make sure that you have up-to-date maps and take care not to commit yourself to too many miles a day. If, say, you are sight seeing at a leisurely pace, then 150-200 miles (240-320km) a day is plenty of ground to cover, and may even be excessive if you are riding a small machine.

Touring abroad
For riding abroad, you will need a passport. For the ten-year type, apply at least two months before your departure date. Though you can buy a one-year British Vistors Passport instantly from a main post office, remember to check its validity for all the countries you plan to visit.

For general advice about riding abroad, contact the AA or RAC. Both will be able to tell you whether or not you will need a visa in addition to your passport, whether or not you need to be vaccinated against particular diseases, and will provide you with an International Driving Permit (IDP). This, though not strictly essential in some European countries, is usually a good investment, since it contains translations in various languages.

If you are not a member already, it is well worth joining either organization to get the benefit of the European breakdown service both offer. They also will provide you with specific survival tips, geared to the countries you intend visiting. If, for instance, you plan to tour Spain, they will recommend that you take 'bail bonds' with you. Without these, if you are unlucky enough to be involved in an accident, you could be held in jail while police investigations are carried out. The bonds, however, are accepted by the Spanish police as security, and, in most cases, should be sufficient for you to be allowed to continue on your way.

The AA or RAC will also be able to tell you if you will need petrol coupons – as in Yugoslavia, for instance – and whether or not any currency restrictions are currently in force; in some countries, there is a minimum daily spending requirement. They also will provide you with detailed route plans on request and give you details of major road works or major international events, which may hinder your progress.

Both organizations can book a hovercraft or ferry passage. If you are travelling solo, you will often find it possible to board a European ferry without advance booking, as a solo bike takes up so little space; as hovercraft space is more limited, advance booking is essential. If you are riding a sidecar combination, book in advance in either case.

You will need to work out a budget for your trip. Err on the generous side – being stuck abroad without money is no joke. Take your cheque book and cheque card in case of emergency. Discuss your requirements with your bank well in advance and order traveller's cheques and foreign currency in good time – at least a fortnight before departure.

Traveller's cheques are far safer than cash, though you will need some foreign currency for immediate purchases, such as food and petrol. This is especially the case when travelling at weekends, when banks are not open.

If you intend to camp, you may need a camping carnet – this is particularly the case in France. Though it is not an essential document, it is taken as evidence of responsibility. The AA and RAC will advise you on this and also provide you with lists of recommended camp sites, guest houses and hotels throughout Europe.

Machine readiness
Having completed your personal preparations, you should then turn your attention to your machine. As well as ensuring it is thoroughly serviced before the trip, make sure that the rear tyre has enough tread to get you there and back legally. The rear tyres of big, powerful bikes can wear down to the legal limit in less than 4,000 miles (6,000km), so you are asking for trouble if you set out on a trip of 1,000 miles (1,600km) or more, if the tyre has covered 2,500 miles (4,000km) already.

Assemble all the clothing and luggage you wish to take with you and pack it on to the machine for a 'dry run'. This is particularly important if you have never undertaken a long trip before. Most riders find that they try to pack too much and that the machine's handling is adversely affected as a result. Pack all equipment and clothing neatly and thoughtfully, placing heavy items in the lower parts of panniers.

Keep all items which may be needed in a hurry – official documents and oversuits, for example – close to hand. A tank bag to hold passport and wallet is a useful accessory; this can be unzipped from the machine easily when you stop for a break or for refreshment.

When planning to travel through countries whose language you do not speak, it is well worth finding out their word for 'petrol'. Many riders have mistakenly filled their tanks up with diesel at self-service stations simply because they did not understand the wording. You should also make it your business to find out how to distinguish between the equivalents of our two- and four-star fuel, particularly if you are riding a high performance machine, which requires the premium grade.

Travelling abroad is an adventure. As long as you use your common sense, you will find it extremely enjoyable. You will be surprised how quickly you can learn to ride on the other side of the road, read 'foreign' road signs and cope with strange currencies and different customs and peoples.

Dealing with a garage

Many experienced motor cyclists would argue that the choice of a dealer is as important as the selection of the actual machine.

Much depends on physical proximity. If you live in a large town, with a choice of several dealers within a few minutes' travelling time, then you are spoilt for choice. Whatever make or model of bike you choose, it is almost certain that spares and maintenance back-up will be close at hand. If, however, you live in a remote village, with only one dealer within a reasonable travelling distance, it is simple commonsense to choose a make and model he can not only supply, but service as well.

Choosing your dealer
Theoretically, the ideal dealer is is close at hand, offers a wide range of spares, has a comprehensive workshop and specializes in one make – ideally, that make being the one that interests you. To establish whether or not an actual dealer comes anywhere near this ideal, start by asking around to see whether he has a good reputation for friendly and efficient service.

Striking up a good working relationship depends as much on you as it does on the dealer. Be polite and to the point. A dealer can usually sum up fairly quickly if he is dealing with a customer who is muddled and has no idea of what he wants, or a customer who is genuinely interested in motor cycling, even though his knowledge may be limited. If this is the case, the dealer will normally appear to be willing to help, but it is up to you to assess whether or not the interest is genuine.

Think ahead, especially if you have a choice. Ask yourself which dealer is likely to make the greatest effort to obtain spares quickly for you when your machine breaks down? Though you obviously will not be able to answer this question definitely, having met the dealers, you should be able to make an educated assessment.

Successful dealerships
Successful dealerships are usually run by people with a good business sense. They are also usually motor cycling enthusiasts and care about the products they sell. They communicate well with their customers, making the latter feel welcome and valued.

Often, you will also find that successful dealers have been involved in active competition in motor cycle sport and have progressed from this to put their knowledge to good use in business. Many have distinguished racing careers behind them and many continue their involvement by sponsoring other riders.

For these reasons, you should never underestimate the man behind the counter. He may be able to give you sound advice, which could save you a substantial amount of time and money in the long run.

If you ask for advice and the dealer goes out of his way to provide this, do him the courtesy of listening to what he says. Even if you do not agree with him completely at the time, you may find that, at the end of the day, he was right after all.

Establishing a standard
The smaller the dealership, the more likely it is that you will be able to strike up a personal rapport. Large dealerships, with literally hundreds of customers, are inevitably likely to be more impersonal – but not to the extent that courtesy and those all important personal touches are lost.

Remember, though, that there are no hard and fast rules in the motor cycling world and appearances can be deceptive. Some mechanics, for example, may not look too professional – yet they may love their work and carry out repairs to a very high standard. Even workshops that, on the surface, seem badly equipped and totally lacking in order may be staffed by people who can diagnose a fault in an instant and repair it more quickly than you would have ever thought possible.

In general, however, a tidy, reasonably equipped workshop is a good sign. Ask the dealer if you could have a look at his workshop and speak to the mechanic who will be working on your machine. There will be no problem with this as far as many small dealers are concerned – they tend to send you straight to the workshop to talk the problem over with a mechanic.

Other dealers require you to book the machine in via their office, but still may allow you on to the workshop floor. Others keep all customers firmly away from the mechanics.

In the workshop
If you visit a workshop, do not overstay your welcome. Both dealers and mechanics have their livings to earn; they also have to keep their customers happy by providing speedy service at competitive rates.

Mechanics simply do not have the time for idle chat. Always aim to express your wishes briefly, politely and to the point.

When in the workshop, look out for specialist tools – these should be on boards hanging on the walls. A small workshop should also have a hydraulic or pneumatic bike bench, cleaning tray, bench, vice, drill, compressor, tool chest and adequate storage space. Look out for mechanics' diplomas hanging on the walls of the workshop or showroom as well.

Large workshops, or workshops specializing in high performance machines, may have a device called a rolling road installed. This means that road testing can be simulated to help diagnose faults and to check repairs. The device can be coupled to electronic diagnostic equipment to check ignition performance, carburation, exhaust efficiency and so on.

Spares and servicing

When ordering spares, make sure that you know the engine and frame numbers of your machine, what model it is and the year of its registration. This may sound obvious, but, if you were to stand behind the trade counter in a popular dealership one Saturday afternoon, you would be surprised by the ignorance of many owners.

If you cannot supply these key facts, you are wasting your own time, as well as that of the dealer. You may also delay the repair as well. It is all too easy to order the wrong part without precise identification.

When ordering spares, take along your workshop manual, if possible, so that you can point out the particular component or components you require. All parts have technical names, some of which are confusing. If you can identify the part you need correctly, give the dealer the part number (you need a parts book for this), or take in the broken component, you will get on much better and save yourself time.

When booking your machine in for repairs or service, state the relevant facts clearly and precisely. If, for instance, the bike is misfiring in certain riding conditions but not in others, it will help the mechanic to know what these circumstances are. This may well help him to identify the cause of the problem sooner and ultimately save you expense.

The same thing applies to abnormal engine noises. The mechanic may be able to identify their cause immediately, if the problem is a common one. On the other hand, it may be necessary for him to strip down part of the engine, if the problem is more obscure.

The importance of estimates

Always ask for an estimate for any repairs, but bear in mind that this is simply an estimate. While your machine is in the workshop, other faults may be detected. For safety reasons, these may well have to be remedied to make the machine roadworthy. All estimates should be sub-divided, detailing the parts required, their cost, and labour charges. VAT should be added to the total.

Some mechanics will stop work at this point and contact you to get your agreement to the extra work. For this reason, it is a good idea to leave a telephone number on which you can be contacted should such a problem occur. Often, too, it is a good idea to telephone the dealer a few hours before you are due to collect the machine to make sure that it is ready. This could save you a wasted journey if unforeseen snags and problems have arisen.

Do not be afraid to stick up for yourself if you feel that the dealer has done more work than was necessary simply to charge you more. A written copy of any instructions is valuable evidence should you decide not to pay – though it is rare for a compromise not to be agreed.

Routine servicing

If your machine is in the workshop for a routine service, the task will usually involve changing the oil, adjusting the chain tension, setting the points, checking battery electrolyte level, checking the tyre pressures and adjusting the air filter, brakes and clutch. On a touring, multi-cylinder model, the mechanic also needs to check valve clearances, the carburettor synchronization and cam chain adjustment. If you want additional work carried out – a change of fork oil and a check on the swinging arm pivot bearings, for instance – you should make a specific request for this to be done.

Checking the work

On collection of your machine, try the best you can to assess whether or not the work your dealer has done has been carried out properly. First, check the machine over visually, making sure that all the fluid levels are correct. Then test ride the machine to make sure that any fault or faults have been cured. If not, return to the dealer immediately and complain.

Tools and equipment/1

All motor cycle manufacturers supply a basic tool kit with their new machines, but the number and quality of tools in such kits naturally varies from manufacturer to manufacturer.

Some manufacturers, such as BMW, provide a wide range of top quality tools intended to last for a lifetime and designed to cope with most d-i-y tasks. Others, such as the Japanese, offer the bare minimum in terms of both quality and quantity. In the latter case, you would be unwise to try to carry out regular routine maintenance with the tools that are provided, since you are likely to damage machine fittings and fastenings, such as nuts, bolts and screws. This is because the tools rarely mate with them accurately.

For this reason, you really need two separate tool kits. The first should be an emergency stand by, which you carry on the bike, and the second is your garage, or home, kit. Obviously, there will be some doubling up between the two – indeed, for the sake of economy, this is to be encouraged. Buying identical pliers and screwdrivers, for instance, is pointless.

On-bike tool kits

If the original tool kit is available – this is not necessarily the case with a second hand machine – it should be removed, laid out flat and studied in conjunction with your owner's handbook until you understand what the function is of each and every tool. Some tools are valueless in emergency situations. Carrying around a special valve clearance adjuster, for instance, simply wastes valuable space – it belongs at home in your tool box.

Then, try out the jobs the tools are supposed to tackle. This is not a waste of time, especially with a Japanese-designed machine. You will find that, because such bikes are habitually assembled using machine tools, they are set to defy hand tool unfastening.

It is better to find this out now, rather than in an emergency. It is no good discovering by the roadside one dark, wet night that the cross head screws in the fuse books defy removal, for instance.

Jobs you can tackle

If you have an adequate on-board emergency tool kit, you should be able to tackle all of the following jobs:
*Wheel removal, plus tyre removal if tubed tyres are fitted. ain adjustment, plus spring link replacement if your bike is fitted with a split chain.
*Fuel tank, float chamber, fuel line and fuel tap removal and replacement.
*Battery, fuse and light bulb removal and replacement.
*Electrical terminal and wiring break repairs.
*Contact breaker point adjustment, if contact breakers are fitted.
*High tension lead, plug cap and connection inspection.
*Spark plug removal, cleaning and replacement.
*Control cable removal and replacement.

Though this list may sound daunting, very few of these jobs – with the exception of puncture repair – require more knowledge and skill than an average d-i-y chore, such as changing a tap washer or or wiring a 13amp plug. All of them can be tackled with no more than a handful of tools. In addition, you must obtain the appropriate owner's handbook; if you are without one, you can normally buy one through a specialist dealer or advertise for one in a trade paper.

The tools for the job

As a general guide, your basic emergency tool kit should include the following tools:
*Sufficient large open-ended spanners to tackle wheel nuts and associated nuts and bolts, fuel taps, control cables and chain adjustment. Select spanners without 'spare' ends – in other words, duplicate none.
*An assortment of flat and cross-head screwdrivers to deal with all screws. A professional kit is the best buy.
*A pair of pliers with an integral wire cutter blade.
*A 150mm (6in) adjustable crescent wrench.
*A set of Allen keys.
*A spark plug box spanner with internal rubber grommet, plus a spare plug or plugs.
*A small, sharp knife.
*A length of iron locking wire, lighting flex and a roll of insulating tape.
*Puncture repair outfit, tyre levers and a small pump, if your bike is fitted with tubed tyres. ain spring link.

In addition, there are two tools you should carry in your pocket, not on the bike. You will find a top quality clock type pressure gauge and a small tough torch invaluable. Only buy a pressure gauge marketed by a named tyre manufacturer.

Your workshop tool kit

You will find all the tools listed above useful for home repairs, but you will need extra items as well. As always, it pays to think carefully before you buy.

Though, for instance, sockets are necessary, do not be tempted to buy a comprehensive 13mm (½in) socket based set of tools. As far as motor cycles are concerned, the ideal socket set is the compact, less expensive 11mm (⅜in) variety, the best quality being British, American and German.

Whatever sockets you buy, check that they will actually fit your bike's nuts and bolts. Also make sure that they are thin-walled. If they are not, they will not fit into tight spots.

You will need a top grade ratchet handle; cheap ones are liable to 'let go' under stress, with the consequent risk of injury. You will also require an extension bar and a universal joint for awkward jobs. Other essentials include:
*A set of top quality Allen keys and screwdrivers of all types. Buy the best you can afford; cheap ones fit badly and burr, frequently making extraction almost impossible.
*A Mole, or vice, grip and a bench vice, such as a detachable table-top type.
*Cutting tools, such as a 250mm (10in) hacksaw and an 200mm (8in) medium file.
*A large engineer's hand drill – do not confuse this with a carpenter's brace.
*A wire brush and some fine emery paper.
*Measuring tools, such as a set of feeler gauges and a pair of calipers.
*An electrical mini-tester.
*Taper and centre punches, a small cold chisel and a copper drift.
*A medium hammer and a hard- and soft-faced mallet.
*Blow torch and small soldering iron.

As you progress, you may also want to add certain specialist tools. Good buys here include the commonly used extractors, a torque wrench, stroboscopic timing light, impact driver, dial gauge, micrometer, vacuum gauges and a multi-speed electric drill. Most of these items, however, can be hired cheaply when needed from a motor cycle dealer, or a specialist tool hire store.

In addition to tools, you will need other items of equipment. These are:
*A funnel for pouring oil and fuel, plus a long-spout oil can.
*Silicon oil spray (WD40 grade).
*Modern gasket cement.
*Degreasant, a hardwood, copper or aluminium scraper, a 13mm (½in) stiff brush and a shallow bowl.
*Extension lead and inspection lamp.
*A magnetic nut retriever.
*Large drip and/or washing tray/bowl.
*A good timing disc.
*Clean rags and overalls.
*Antiseptic hand cleanser.

With rare exceptions, cheap tools eventually cause more problems than they solve. So always buy the best you can afford – top quality tools give a lifetime of reliable service. Specialist tool shops will give you good advice on what to choose, but supermarkets, on the whole, will not.

Garage advantages

One of your vital needs is a good garage, or at the least a weatherproof shelter. Remember that it is illegal to 'garage' a motor cycle inside a house; as well as being against the law, you may well invalidate your household insurance if you do so. If there is no alternative to keeping the bike in the open, cover it with a sheet of natural fibre and then a shaped plastic cover to protect the machine against the weather.

Access to a garage means that you can tackle quite complex jobs, which you simply should not attempt at the roadside or in the front garden. The better your working conditions, the more you will reduce the possibility of error, which accounts for 75% of subsequent breakdowns. Remember, too, that it is actually illegal to make any vehicle parked in a public place unroadworthy, which, in itself, limits your capacity to carry out roadside maintenance.

If you do not have a garage, you should move the bike off the road on to private ground to carry out routine maintenance. The jobs you should tackle are limited, so you can concentrate on building up a tool kit containing enough tools to remove all motor cycle parts, with the exception of the engine and the internal components of the transmission. Major repairs should be left to a specialist dealer – this will be cheaper and safer in the long run than doing them yourself, unless you are sure.

Prevention, not cure

One thing you can do easily, whatever your circumstances, is to keep your bike clean. Go over the bodywork weekly with a bucket of soapy water and a 50mm (2in) paintbrush. Used in conjunction, they will prevent more machine problems than anything else. Their use will combat corrosion and reveal mechanical flaws before they turn into expensive repairs. This is no exaggeration.

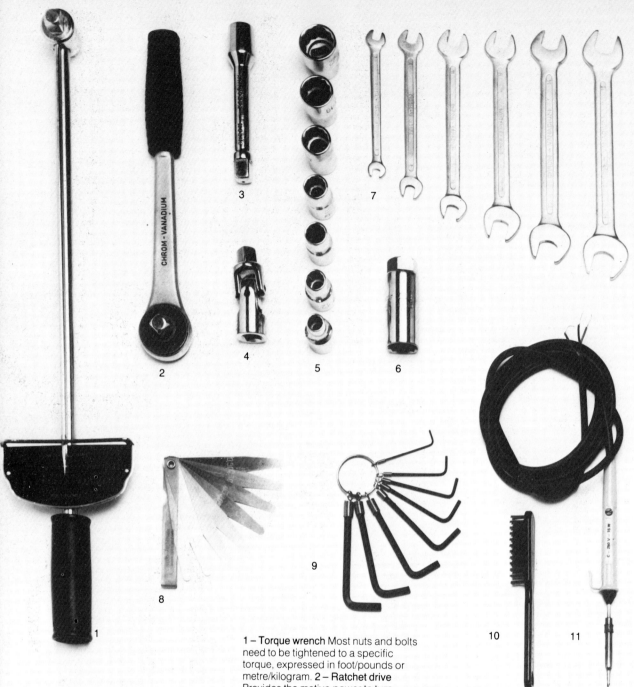

THE GARAGE TOOLKIT

If you decide to carry out any motor cycle maintenance, you will find that a well equipped workshop will make any job you undertake much easier to complete satisfactorily. The tools illustrated here are sufficient to tackle most general maintenance and repair jobs; with the addition of a few specialized tools *(see pp152-153)*, it should be an easy task to keep your motor cycle in good mechanical order.

1 – Torque wrench Most nuts and bolts need to be tightened to a specific torque, expressed in foot/pounds or metre/kilogram. **2 – Ratchet drive** Provides the motive power to turn sockets and can be fitted with an extension bar, **3** or a universal joint, **4**, which allows sockets to be turned from an angle. **5 – Sockets** These are sold in both metric or imperial sizes. Make sure that you buy the type suited to your bike. **6 – Spark plug socket** This socket should be attached to the ratchet drive. It has a cushioned inside to avoid damage to the ceramic insulation of the plug. **7 – Open ended spanners** The essential basis of any tool kit, spanners are available in metric and imperial sizes. Make sure that

you buy the type purpose suited to your motor cycle. **8 – Feeler gauges** Available in metric sizes, expressed as tenths of a millimetre, or imperial, expressed as thousandths of an inch, feeler gauges are used for setting the gap between the contact breaker points and the small gaps necessary between some moving engine components. **9 – Allen keys** As opposed to nuts or bolts, some components are retained with studs with

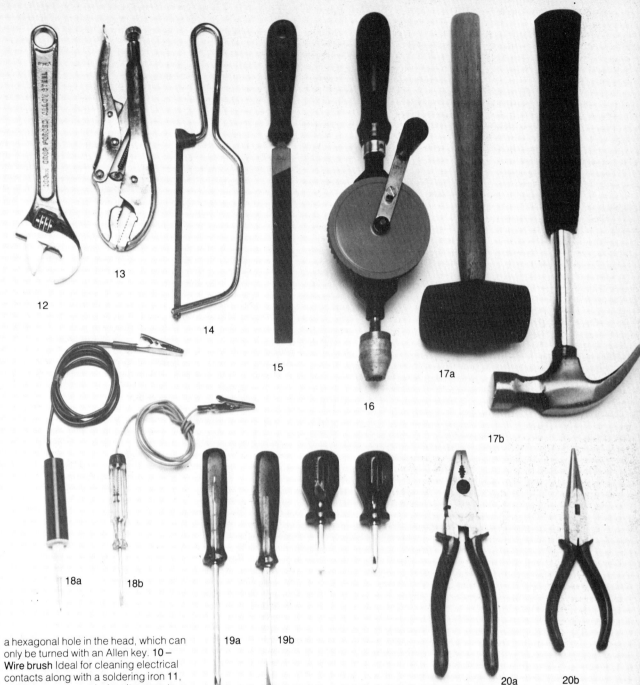

12

13

14

15

16

17a

17b

18a

18b

19a

19b

20a

20b

a hexagonal hole in the head, which can only be turned with an Allen key. **10 – Wire brush** Ideal for cleaning electrical contacts along with a soldering iron **11**, which you may need when it comes to reconnecting them. **12 – Adjustable spanner** Essential for coping with the odd-sized nut or bolt that no ordinary spanner will fit. **13 – Self-locking grips** Often called Mole grips, their jaws can be set to varying widths, so enabling them to be locked solidly on to a nut or component. **14 – Hacksaw** Using a hacksaw is often the only way to remove old cooling pipes and other corroded components. **15 – File** As there are several different shapes of file available, you will probably find you need different

types for various jobs, though a flat bladed file probably will be the most useful. **16 – Hand drill** Particularly when working on aluminium components, a hand drill is much safer than a high speed electric drill. **17 – Hammers** A soft faced hammer, **17a** should be used when dealing with aluminium components, as opposed to the usual steel hammer **17b**. **18 – Circuit testers** If your motor cycle does not have a battery, then you will need a self-

powered circuit tester **18a** to test the ignition and other electrical circuits. An ordinary circuit tester, **18b** can be used if your motor cycle has a battery. **19 – Screwdrivers** Two types are essential – cross head **19a**, and flat-blade **19b**. A set of stubby screwdrivers comes in handy when dealing with awkwardly positioned screws. **20 – Pliers** A pair of bull-nosed pliers, **20a** and thin nosed pliers **20b** should enable you to tackle most jobs.

Tools and equipment/3

Getting down to work

To carry out adequate maintenance, you need a clean robust work bench – either a fixed bench or a portable one – a well-stocked tool box and the appropriate workshop manual. With these to hand, you should assess the tasks the tasks you would like to undertake, both from the point of view of personal confidence and having the right tools to tackle the job.

You can use your bike tool kit for some jobs, for instance, but, rather than use its open-ended spanners, it will pay you to buy and use a set of sockets, since these are easier on the machine's nuts and bolts. You will also need items of extra equipment – other than tools – to tackle some jobs (see p149).

If you are confident, the tasks you can undertake include the removal and replacement of all handlebar and foot controls; the handlebars and foot rests themselves; switch gear; seat; mudguards; wheels; fuel tank; fairing; battery; all electrical ancillaries, including lights and contact breaker points; rear suspension unit(s) and assembly; teleports; chain; outer engine covers; air filter; coolant hoses; and carburettors.

Tool maintenance

If properly used and maintained, tools do not wear out. What damages them is poor maintenance and misuse. The most commonly abused tools are screwdrivers.

Despite appearances, a screwdriver is a precision instrument, its blade form being keyed to fit into specific sizes of screw slot. Once damaged, it usually cannot be repaired. So, do not use a screwdriver as a

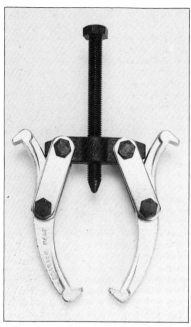

From time to time, you may find a special tool, called a puller, useful. It is most commonly used for taking off the flywheel. Though it is relatively inexpensive to buy, you will probably be able to hire one when you need it.

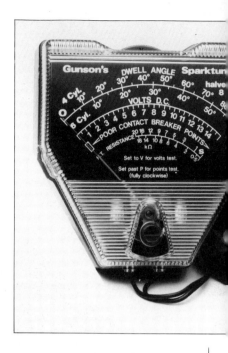

chisel, for instance. If you do, the blade will loose its vital square section and, as a consequence, will slip, burring screw slots, when you try to use it for its intended purpose. Using a screwdriver blade as a lever will curve it and slippage will also result.

The best screwdrivers have cabinet, or round, section handles of unpainted wood. Slim, plastic handled screwdrivers are much less satisfactory.

If damaged, cross headed screws are best replaced with hexagon or slotted screws, though, in an emergency, they can be modified with a few careful hacksaw cuts. All screws come in three sizes – 1 for switchgear, 2 for instrument and ancillary mounting brackets, 3 for engine covers – and you will

need three separate screwdrivers to tackle them all. If you use a screwdriver of the wrong size, the screws will burr and become impossible to extract.

Do not confuse the Phillips cross head screws used on many motor cycles with the household Posi-Drive variety. Attempts to inter-change the two will damage screwdrivers and screws alike.

The best open ended spanners are made of unpolished chrome-vandium and come from America, Britain and Germany. They should fit snugly across the flats of a nut without slipping and feel slim and comfortable in the hand under pressure. When turned under load, the shank should be pointing in the direction of travel, so as not to spring the jaws.

You will need a 11mm (⅜in) drive socket set, plus, as a useful extra, a 13mm (½in) conversion kit in case you ever have to borrow a 13mm (½in) socket.

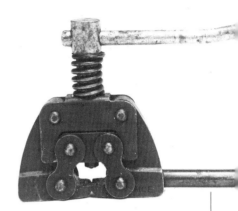

A multimeter *(left)* is a special tool that enables you to set the ignition timing very accurately by measuring the dwell angle. It can also be used for testing electric circuits and measuring voltage. Another aid to setting the timing is the stroboscopic timing light *(below)*. The example here is simple and inexpensive. Some more complex lights can be adjusted with the engine revs. One tool that can be a necessity is the chain splitter *(right)*, which you use to remove a chain lacking a split link.

Keep the set away from other tools, as it is easy to mislay the sockets. Test for quality before you buy. The ratchet handle should turn without slop, but with a quiet, smooth, oily 'buzz', while the sockets should click very positively over the various drive ends – again without slop and without releasing easily from their sprung ball latches. The last should be checked for good working order.

The sockets should be thin wall, made of chrome-vandium for strength and 12 pointed for the sake of operating convenience. Do not buy thick, six pointed sockets, as these are usually made of soft steel. A matt finish is best, since polished chrome tends to slip easily through oily fingers.

Never hammer an undersized socket over an apparently immovable burred nut. If you are faced with this problem, it is better to break the rules and use a six pointed socket, which will not slip, or to split the nut with a hacksaw.

An adjustable spanner – a crescent wrench is best – is an emergency tool, to be used only when no other tool will fit. It makes an excellent stop for a turning bolt head, as the partnering nut is screwed home. Keep the tool's mechanism clean from grit, or the wrench will wear out, become sloppy and not fit tightly.

You will need feeler gauges to check the gap between the contact breaker points, ignition trigger and valve clearance adjustment; more specialised measuring tools, such as micrometers and dial gauges, are best hired, or left to the professionals. Keep feeler gauges clean and lightly oiled to prevent rusting. Dry them off before use.

A small electric test meter – the smallest are little bigger than a pocket calculator and cost about the same – is a useful extra. It can be used for a variety of jobs, including testing switches and circuits, measuring battery voltage, checking static ignition timing and alternator output. The best meters are Japanese.

One final tool to note is an impact driver, which you can use to shift factory tightened, or chemically seized, screws. You should only use a hard faced mallet to strike the driver; a conventional hammer might shoot a metal splinter into your face. This is a common injury.

Treat your tools with respect. Never lend one without noting the name of the borrower – and, equally, never borrow one and fail to return it.

Improving your investment

As any experienced biker will tell you, any standard machine can always stand improvement. No matter whether the bike you own is expensive or inexpensive, there will always be ways in which you can improve it and modify it to suit your own individual requirements. There are also also ways in which you can keep your bike in top condition, so that, when the time comes for you to sell it – or to exchange it for a new model – your bike will be worth more · than its competitors.

Increasing second-hand value

Rather than thinking of your purchase simply as money spent, you should look at it as an investment. You should try to safeguard this as best you can by taking good care of your bike and by making suitable improvements to it.

Remember that second-hand value depends very much on a machine's condition, as well as on its year of registration, as opposed to the car world, where more emphasis is placed on the latter. Thus, if you buy a bike in poor condition, improving it will increase its value.

You must consider carefully how much you would need to spend in order to reach your target second-hand value. A good way of estimating this is to refer to the motor cycling publications specifically intended to provide this type of information.

Pleasure improvements

Basically, however, one of the main reasons for making any improvement or alteration to your machine is to increase your riding enjoyment. The scope is extremely wide – it extends from fitting a screen or fairing to keep the rain off to create a full blown racing replica.

If you are ever stuck for ideas, a visit to a major bike rally or race meeting will usually provide you with more practical inspiration than you ever thought possible. So, too, will going through motor cycle and scooter magazines.

Seeking advice

If you are considering elaborate or adventurous modifications, it is worth asking specialists for advice, especially if you are unsure of exactly what to do. Even the simplest of comments – 'Yes, that can be done', or 'No, that would be dangerous because...' – could save you a lot of time and money.

So the rule is never to be afraid to seek advice, no matter how trivial you may think your questions might appear to an expert. Normally, you will find that experts are flattered by this and only too pleased to help. Occasionally you may come across someone who makes it obvious that he is totally disinterested. Do not be discouraged by this – simply try somewhere else.

Assessing and selecting
When deciding on how best to improve your investment, you should start off by considering your needs. If, for instance, your bike has to get you to work during the week and take you away at week ends, it makes sense to concentrate on practical accessories, such as a screen, fairing, or an extra luggage rack. If, on the other hand, you ride your bike purely for pleasure, then speed will have the greater appeal.

When choosing accessories, remember that, more often than not, the most expensive are the best. In the case of practical accessories, start by looking at how they are constructed and try to assess if they are robust enough for the job.

Check on the manufacturer's reputation, make sure there is an adequate guarantee and that, when applicable, spares are easy to obtain. If possible, talk to someone who has used the goods and so can pinpoint pros and cons.

If you are looking at modifications that are intended to better speed or performance in general, make sure you establish the full story. Modifying the exhaust system, for instance, may also require a carburation change to compensate for it. You must consider ground clearance, access to the oil filter and so on, while, in this case, you must also remember that there are legal noise limits and that you could end up in court if you break them.

Remember, too, that, if possible, you should be able to remove any cosmetic accessories you have fitted when you come to sell your machine.

However, if you have substituted better quality components for certain originals, leave them in place, as they will add to the second-hand value. Such components include tyres, disc pads, brake shoes, a hydraulic brake hose, headlights, engine case screws, and drive chain and suspension units.

The keys to improving your investment are two-fold. You should invest your money wisely, and, at the same time, take pride in your workmanship.

This means that, whatever course you decide to pursue, you should ensure that any modification you make is up to professional standards. Securing a rear rack with odd nuts and bolts, for instance, will look unprofessional and degrade the rest of the machine. A botched paint job will stand out even more for all the wrong reasons.

Painting/1

Though you can transform the look of your bike through the use of paint, remember that any type of painting – from retouching to added decoration – takes skill. If you are impatient or unskilled, the best advice is to leave the original well alone.

If all you want to do is to restore dulled paintwork, you may well find it simpler to use a proprietary restorative, such as T-Cut. This is a liquid, waxy, fine abrasive and a few hours of rubbing with it will soon put back the shine.

Some items of equipment should not be painted under any circumstance. You should never repaint a plastic crash helmet, for instance. If the paint you use contains a solvent, you will weaken the plastic, while, even if you use a water-based paint, it may well effect the helmet's weather-proofing.

If you want to decorate your crash helmet, you must buy a glass fibre brand, as paint or adhesive transfers will not affect the glass fibre.

Spray painting

You can spray paint in many ways. A professional will probably use a full sized, compressor powered spray gun, but it is more likely that a spray kit – such kits come with electric pumps – or an aerosol will be enough to suit your needs. The basic spray kit consists of aerosol sprays for both priming and top coats, thinners, some clean cotton rag, masking tape, clean newspaper, fine wet-and-dry abrasive paper, a bowl of water, a dust-free surface on which to spray, or a hook on which to hang the components you are spraying.

Before you start work, check

the existing surface. All spray paints are based on cellulose, which dries quickly to a hard finish. If you spray this over oil based or plastic enamel, it will lift it. Check by experimenting on a sample spot and, if this is the case, apply a neutralizing undercoat.

Getting down to spraying

Whatever you are spray painting on your bike, the same basic rules apply. The first task is to remove all ancillary parts, such

as fuel taps and badges, and the second is to check the entire surface for blemishes. If any are present, these must be smoothed with wet-and-dry paper. This should be used wet.

Any stains must be washed off the surface you are spraying, which then must be left to dry naturally in a warm atmosphere. Do not wipe dry.

Mask off any areas you do not want the spray to reach with masking tape and newspaper, if necessary. It is particularly

Painting kit
1 Emery cloth and wet and dry paper You will need a coarse emery cloth for the initial preparation, plus medium and fine grade wet and dry paper for smoothing filler and paint. **2 Filler** There are two types of filler, rigid and elastic. Both types come with a tube of hardener and an applicator. If you are repairing a dent in a panel that moves or vibrates, use the elastic filler. **3 Compounding paste** An abrasive paste for getting an initial shine on the paintwork. **4 Cutting fluid** Less abrasive than compounding paste, this will give the paint a high gloss finish. **5 Undercoat** You can use either red oxide or grey undercoat, depending on the colour of the topcoat. **6 Topcoat** There is a large range of colours available, plus some metallic tones. **7 Cloth** A lint free cloth is best for polishing.

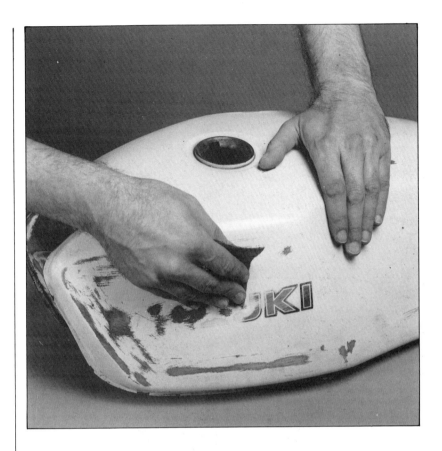

important to protect screw threads – these can easily be gummed up by excess spray.

Remember that, though cellulose feels dry to the touch almost immediately after spraying, it is still soft and may not harden for 12 hours or more. It also needs a warm, dry atmosphere in which to harden. You should not polish it until at least a week after spraying.

Bike decoration
Unless you are a skilled artist, it

Preparation
Whatever you are painting, good and thorough preparation of the area to be painted will pay dividends in the final finish. Rub the whole area down, starting with coarse emery paper to remove any decoration. Take special care over any areas of rust you may find *(right)*. Make sure the area is rubbed down to remove the rust with a surround of clean metal.

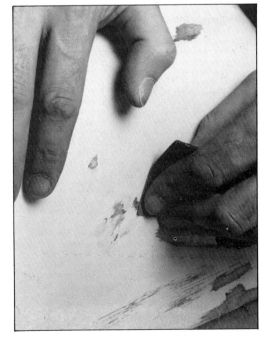

Painting/2

Filler sense

On most dents, you can use a standard filler, but remember that this may crack if subjected to flexing. In such a case, use an elasticated type. Whichever you choose, take care when you add the hardener. If too little is added, the mix may not cure; if too much is added, the mix may cure too quickly and the repair may crack as a result.

Mix on a clean, flat board – cleanliness is vital, because dirt can lead to unsightly scratches showing up on the filled surface – When colour and consistency are both constant, the filler is ready for application.

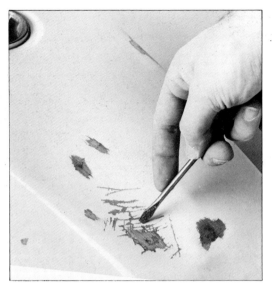

Preparation
Whatever type of filler paste you use, the surface to which it is to be applied to needs to be 'keyed' in order for the filler to grip. The simplest way to do this is to score the surface with an old screwdriver blade *(left)*. If rust is present, rub it down with coarse emery paper.

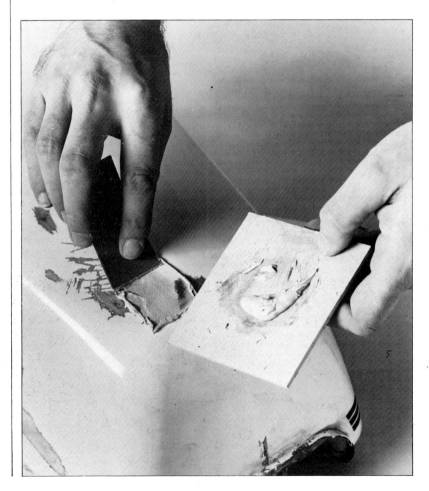

Applying the filler
Mix up sufficient filler to slightly over-fill the dent. Start applying the filler in thick strips *(left)* until the area of the dent has been filled, plus a little of the surrounding area. Carry on adding thinner strips of filler *(below)* in overlapping layers, until the repair stands proud of the surrounding area.

Checking the surface
Once you are sure that the filler is contoured to the surrounding area, lightly run your fingers over the repaired area *(below)* and feel for any ridges or dips. These can be dealt with by rubbing down or by adding a thin layer of filler.

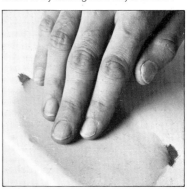

Rubbing down
Leave the filler to harden fully and then rub it down with coarse emery paper until the repaired area is flush with the surrounding surface.

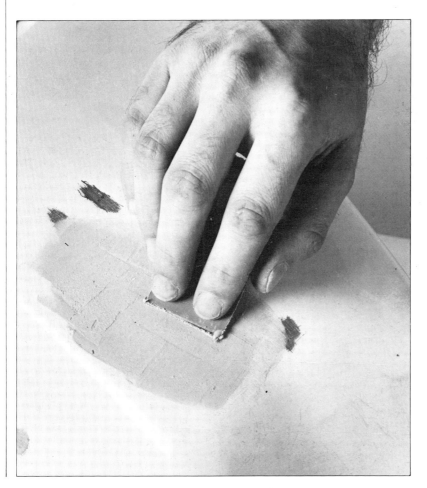

The final layer
A thin layer of filler may be needed to fill in any scratches or pin holes left in the surface *(left)*. When the appearance of the repaired area is totally satisfactory, rub it down with medium grade wet and dry paper and then with fine grade wet and dry paper, used wet *(below)*, making sure that the filler is blended into the surrounding metal. Run your fingers over the area to check for smoothness.

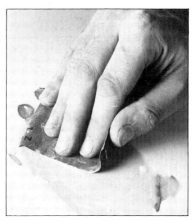

Painting/3

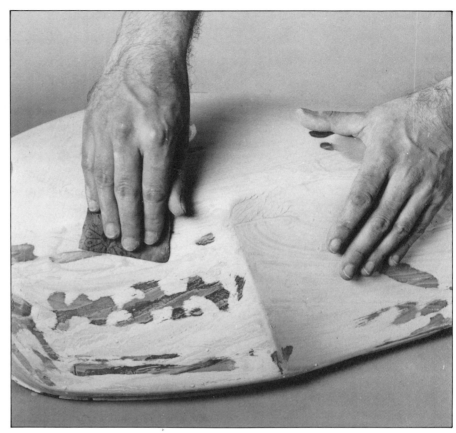

Final preparation

Give the whole area a final rub down with fine grade wet and dry, used wet, to give the first coat of undercoat a 'key' *(right)*. When you are satisfied that all the area has been covered, carefully feel for any ridges or rough spots by running your fingers over the surface *(below)*. If any are located, rub down again.

Masking

Any areas that have to be kept clear of paint must be masked off. In the case of the petrol filler hole, use masking tape to define the edge *(right)*. Carefully position the tape so it matches the masking line. When you have masked the edge, any large areas to be masked can be covered with sheets of newspaper, which you tape to the existing masking tape *(far right)*.

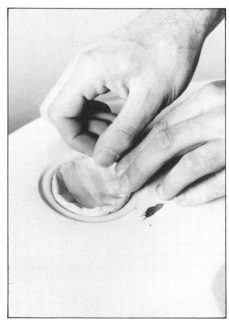

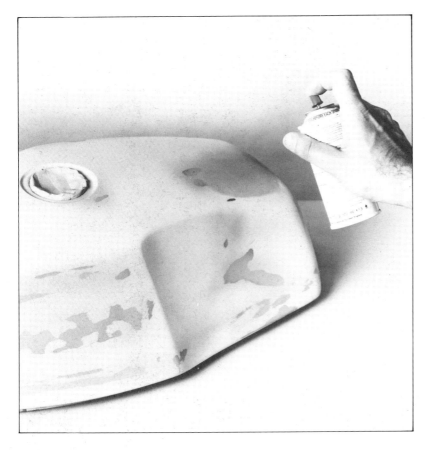

Spraying the undercoat
When you are satisfied with the preparation, you can apply the first coat of undercoat. Shake the can well and test the spray on a piece of scrap paper. Hold the can about 25cm (10in) from the surface and spray in even, horizontal strokes, stopping at the end of each stroke. Spray the whole area, but do not worry about achieving depth of cover at this stage *(left)*. Leave to dry.

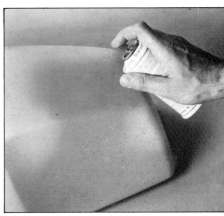

Total coverage
Once the first coat is touch dry, you can build up the undercoat *(above)*. Spray in the same manner as before, taking care not to spray too thickly, as this will make the undercoat run.

Maintaining the surface
Continue applying undercoat until you are satisfied with the covering you have achieved. Allow the paint to harden and then give the area a light rub down with fine wet and dry paper, used wet *(left)*.

Painting/4

Dealing with problems
When the undercoat has hardened, any runs or blemishes can be removed with fine grade wet and dry paper, used wet *(right)*. If there is any pitting in the paint, or further rubbing down causes an indentation, both can be filled with knifing stopper. Apply small quantities of stopper to the area with a spatula and allow it to harden *(far right)*.

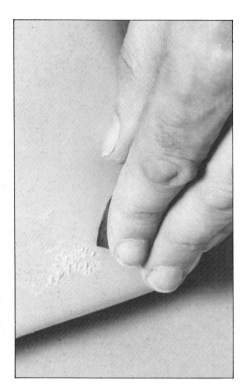
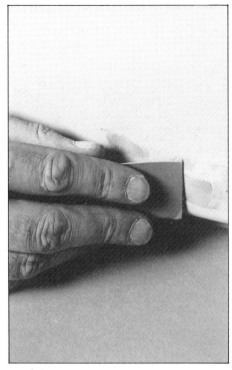

Touching up
Any filling work on the undercoat or rubbing down that has revealed the bare metal will have to be given another spray of undercoat *(right)*. Once again, be careful not to apply the paint too thickly, as this may cause further runs. Apply several coats, continuing until you are satisfied that the area is fully covered and then give it a final rub down with fine grade wet and dry paper.

Applying the top coat

There is a large selection of colours readily available in spray cans for ease of use. Metallic paints are also available, though they tend to be more expensive and it is more difficult to achieve a good finish with them. Make sure the surface is clean and dry before you start spraying. Shake the spray can well and test the paint on a piece of scrap paper. Make sure the paint is coming out evenly and without spatters. Hold the can about 25cm (10in) from the surface and spray in even, horizontal strokes, stopping at the end of each stroke *(right)*.

Paint problems

Various factors can affect the finish you get when spraying. If you hold the spray can too close to the surface, the paint will be too thick and may run. If you hold the spray too far away, the paint will partially dry before it reaches the surface and give a dull, powdery finish. Any grease or polish will cause 'fish eyes', small areas where the paint will not adhere to the surface. Similarly, dirt will make the paint lift from the surface and form a crackle finish. An 'orange peel' finish, where the paint takes on the texture of an orange, is usually caused by the paint being applied too thickly and not being allowed to dry properly between coats. Most of these faults can be cured at the polishing stages.

The final coats

When the first colour coat is dry, check to see if the surface has any blemishes or paint runs. These can be removed with fine grade wet and dry paper, used wet. Do not be afraid of rubbing down to the undercoat; if you uncover the bare metal, however, give the affected area a light spray of undercoat. Carry on applying layers of top coat *(above)*, allowing each coat to dry before spraying the next and checking each one to make sure that the surface is still smooth. Apply coats of colour until you are satisfied with the overall density. It does no harm if you apply extra top coats, as some paint will inevitably be removed during the polishing stages that follow.

Painting/5

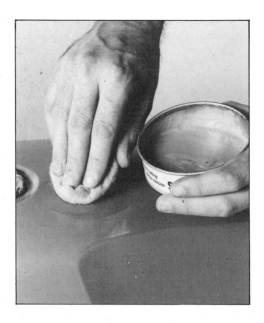

Getting a shine
When the rubbing compound has dried, polish it off with a soft, lint free cloth *(below)*. Look carefully at the finish. It may be necessary to apply further coats of compound if the paint is still dull.

Polishing the surface
When the paint has hardened thoroughly (it is best left for 24 hours), you should polish the surface with rubbing compound *(right)* as the first step in achieving a high gloss finish. The paste is applied with a damp cloth, working in a circular motion, small areas at a time. Try to cover the whole area evenly, taking care not to apply excessive pressure, as you may rub through the paint.

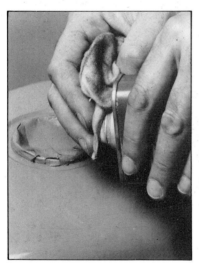

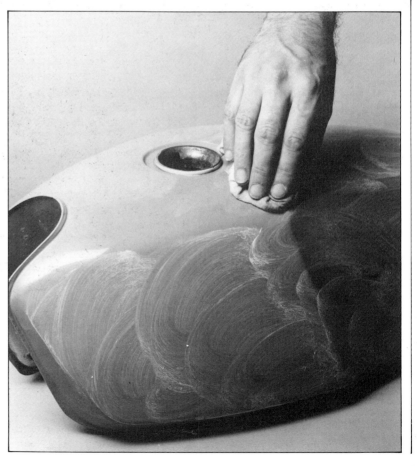

The final touches
While rubbing compound will give the paint surface a basic shine, a high gloss finish can be achieved using a liquid cutting compound *(above)*. This is applied in the same way as the paste and polished off with a clean, lint free cloth. A coat of wax *(right)* will give the paint a degree of protection against the elements and make cleaning and maintaining the shine easier.

is best not to try freehand decoration. However, you can still create striking decorative effects with the aid of masking tape and stencils.

Work out what you want to do in advance. Once the main part of the scheme – the fuel tank, say – has been sprayed, you can easily add coloured panels or pin striping by simply masking off the appropriate areas with masking tape and newspaper.

Do not be tempted to use ordinary sticky tape instead of masking tape. Only masking tape is flexible enough to be contoured, while its adhesive is specially designed not to attack previously sprayed surfaces. When applied, it must be pressed down firmly on the surface – use a hard rubber roller, or ball to help you in this – to ensure that spray cannot penetrate beneath its edges. If this happens, 'feathering' – that is, a ragged edge – will result, which can be removed only by cutting back with wet-and-dry paper.

After spraying, remove the masking tape as soon as possible – certainly before the paint has hardened. This ensures a better, cleaner edge. Never cut the tape while it is still stuck down to the surface, as this will damage the final result.

Stencils and airbrushes

You can cut stencils from clean cartridge, or art, paper. If you are spraying curved surfaces, you will need to practise placing the stencils in position – this is harder than it seems. To simplify the process, tackle small areas at a time and use water based household or office glue to stick the stencil into position. When the spray has dried, wash the stencil and glue off with warm clean water.

Airbrushing enables you to create attractive misty effects. At its simplest, an airbrush is a 'needlepoint' miniature spray gun and can be used to actually draw pictures, usually in combination with stencils. Their use requires practice, however; they should not be used by first-time amateurs.

Brush painting

Incorrectly thought to be second rate, brush painting in fact has many advantages over spraying, while the result looks equally good if the paint is applied correctly. Brush painting needs no special equipment or masking – all you need is a selection of suitable brushes.

If new, such brushes must be 'broken in' by dipping them in old, thin oil or water and brushing with them for around 15 minutes over a brick wall or concrete surface. This will taper the bristles and so help to eliminate brush marks.

Preparation is exactly the same as for spraying, the exception being that each coat of paint you apply must cover the area you are painting completely. The paint must be thick enough not to run – this may mean thinning it slightly. Equally, the paint must not be too thick, as this may cause 'drag', with consequent brush marks.

Each coat of paint must be allowed to dry for 24 hours and then 'flatted' with fine wet-and-dry paper and lots of water before the next one is applied. Usually, you will need to apply two coats of primer and three finishing coats.

The last coat should be 'flatted' lightly with powder grade wet-and-dry paper and soapy water. After a week in a warm, dry atmosphere, it may be cut back with T-Cut. Do not polish the surface for a month after this.

You should start brushing at the top of the area, working downwards with smooth, long evenly applied strokes, never covering the same area twice. Fresh runs can be lifted off with an uncharged brush, while you can deal with tacky runs by rubbing them clear with a finger inside a clean, washed cotton rag. Remove dried runs with a sharp knife and chisel, smooth down the area with wet-and-dry and then repaint.

If you want to brush paint, remember that there are only certain types of paint that are suitable for use. For instance, you cannot use spray paint for brush work, as this dries too quickly; equally, you should not try to modify spray paint to make it suitable for brush painting by This means that the paint will never dry.

Brush paints are enamel or cellulose. The former smells oily and must be thinned with turpentine before use. The latter smells like spray paint.

Paint alternatives

Alternative finish paints, such as metallic, pearl, metal flake, Vreeble, Eirie, Dess and Glowble must all be sprayed. To apply most of them, you will need a special spray gun, while some must be mixed at home together with clear varnishes.

Most custom paint shops, however, can supply a wide range of aerosol versions of various special effect paints. The range is extremely wide, so always read the instructions carefully before you use one.

Accessories/1

Luggage racks and panniers
The most common two wheeler accessory is probably the rear rack. It is a convenience too, since you can strap virtually anything from a pair of lightweight over trousers to a suitcase to it.

Basically, however, a rear rack should be reserved for lightweight items. If you want to carry something as large as a suitcase, lay it flat to keep it stable and do not pack too much into it. If you have too much weight too far back, you will upset the balance of the bike. The front wheel's grip on the road will be reduced as a result – in extreme cases, this can be downright dangerous.

Racks come in various shapes and sizes. No matter what machine you ride, you should be able to find one to fit your steed. Usually, they allow you normal access to all parts of the bike, though in some cases you may find that you cannot lift your hinged seat as far as you could in normal circumstances.

When on the machine, the panniers should be placed over the rider's section of the seat, or over the pillion section, if a pillion passenger is being carried. You can also carry fuel tank panniers, plus a tank bag. Whatever you choose, the aim is to keep the luggage's weight concentrated within the machine's wheelbase.

A tank bag usually comes with a convenient transparent top section. This can be used to hold a road map. The bag's base should be fastened securely to the tank, the bag either being clipped or zipped to the base, so that it can be attached or removed quickly.

For touring – when, in all probability, you will need to carry a fair amount of luggage – soft, throw over panniers are convenient. This type of pannier is usually inexpensive, easily stored when not in use, and convenient to carry. They also allow you to keep the extra weight near the machine's centre of gravity, so preserving handling qualities.

Increasing the load By fitting luggage accessories to your bike, you can increase the load you can carry dramatically. A tank bag *(above left)* with a large map section and side pockets is extremely useful when touring, while rear racks *(right)* provide a convenient platform for carrying everyday and touring luggage.

Safety and style Throwover panniers *(right)* allow you to keep luggage weight within the machine's wheelbase, so assisting stability. Such extras can be more stylish and attractive if they are all of a piece, as in the case of the soft panniers, tank bag and tote bag *(below)*.

Accessories/2

Think before buying Before you buy luggage accessories, think carefully about their suitability. These suitcase style lockable Rickman panniers *(left)* on this 650 Yamaha would make life difficult for a pillion rider. The panniers and top box on this Suzuki *(below left)* are extremely adaptable. A pannier which opens like this allows you to sort out its contents more easily.

Security panniers

If you want to protect your luggage against the risk of theft while you leave your bike unattended, you should consider buying suitcase style panniers, which can be locked to their mounting brackets. Though expensive, this type of pannier has several advantages. They are usually waterproof, and smart in appearance, while most are designed to take a full face helmet. This means you can lock your helmet in a pannier, which, in turn, is locked to your machine.

A refined version of this type of pannier comes with soft cases that slip inside the main fitting. This means that you can pack your clothing in the soft cases indoors and then take them out to the machine. When you reach your destination, you simply take out the soft cases.

Thus, the hard panniers always remain on the machine. It does not matter if they become mud spattered – you always will work into an hotel, say, with clean cases.

Usually, hard panniers designed for specific machines are mounted as far forward as is conveniently possible to prevent poor weight distribution. You should aim for the same goal if you are fitting your own pannier mountings. Also, take note of any maximum weight warnings – these may apply to panniers on certain machines.

Top boxes

Top boxes fitted to rear racks are ideal storage places for crash helmets when the machine is not in use. However, they should not be packed with heavy goods when the machine is being ridden, since they are too high up and too far back on the machine to take the weight without affecting the bike's stability. Experiment to see just how much extra weight can be carried without upsetting your bike's handling.

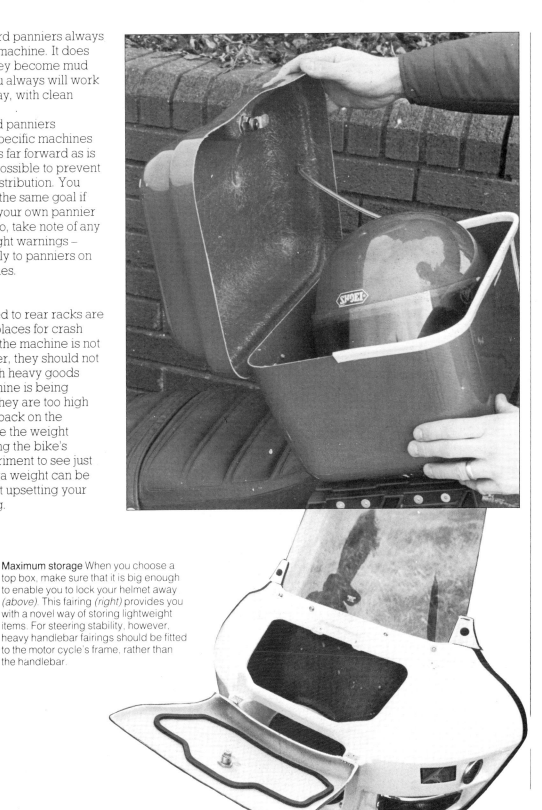

Maximum storage When you choose a top box, make sure that it is big enough to enable you to lock your helmet away *(above)*. This fairing *(right)* provides you with a novel way of storing lightweight items. For steering stability, however, heavy handlebar fairings should be fitted to the motor cycle's frame, rather than the handlebar.

Accessories/3

Winter accessories

Accessories designed to take the sting out of winter riding – or riding in bad weather – are some of the best buys you can make. Humble mudflaps, for instance, will protect you from road spray. Many 'sporty' machines, for instance, have abbreviated front wheel guards. By fitting a small flap at the front of the guard – as well as at the rear – you will stop the spray being thrown up into your face.

Fork gaiters will protect fork stanchions from rust, while a fully enclosed chain case will keep road grime, salt and water off the chain. This will extend chain life and reduce the need for chain adjustment. For extra rider comfort, you can fit heated handlebar grips, or handlebar muffs. Both will help to keep your hands warm.

Winter warmers In winter, the first essentials are warmth and adequate weather protection. Handlebar muffs *(top)* make a world of difference when it comes to keeping your hands warm in freezing weather. The rider of this CD185 Honda *(above)* is completely equipped for winter riding, with, in addition to bar muffs, a two-piece oversuit, an 'apple warmer' to protect the back of the neck against draughts and rubber overboots.

All-round protection Especially in winter, a chain guard *(left)* keeps road grit out and the grease in, so prolonging chain life and reducing maintenance time. Overall protection is equally important; if you cannot keep your bike in a garage or shed, use a cover *(below left)* to keep off the worst of the weather. Even though the integral legshields on this Lambretta provide some weather protection *(below)*, it is still better to wear an oversuit in bad weather.

Accessories/4

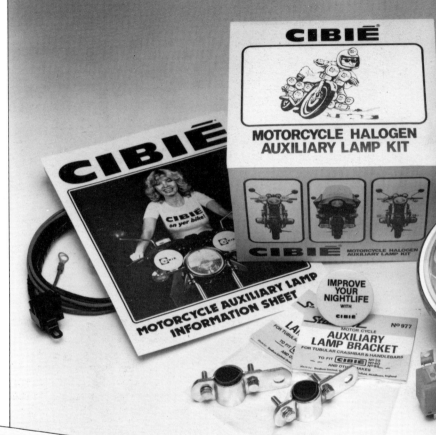

Seeing your way Lucas day riding lamps *(below)* are fitted with 'festoon' bulbs. These diffuse light, rather than concentrate it, so that you can be seen more easily by other road users. Many accessory manufacturers sell a wide range of replacement and auxiliary lights specifically for motor cyclists *(right)*.

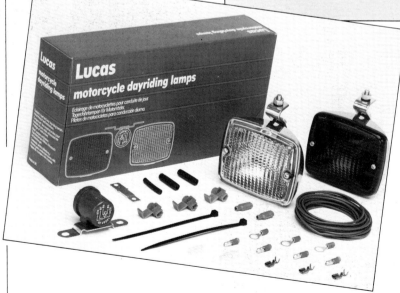

Lighting

Over recent years, two wheeler lighting has been improved substantially; nowadays, even some mopeds feature good quality 12 volt lighting. In most cases, however, even the best standard lighting can be improved, the most popular and straightforward modification being a replacement headlamp.

Obviously you must check first that such a headlamp is available for your machine. In the case of six volt bikes, the replacement will usually be of the tungsten type. You should also check with your dealer to make sure that your generator will produce sufficient output to power such a

lamp – some generators are not up to the added demand.

Headlamp conversions for 12 volt machines normally have quartz bulbs – these are much brighter than the standard fitting. Usually, you will find that your generator can easily cope with the extra load.

You can also fit a fog light, spot light, daytime diffuser riding lamps and rear fog lamp. Whichever you choose, you should again check that your generator will be able to cope with the extra load before you buy and you should also look into the legal requirements. For a start, any lamp fitted to a bike must work!

When fitting any lamp, follow the instructions supplied with it carefully. When you wire it up, do not be tempted to use any odd, spare wire you may have in your tool box. If such wiring is not thick enough to take the current the fitting needs, it may overheat and burn through the insulation.

Improving braking Many late model sports bikes feature a fork brace, such as this bolt-on type *(below)* to reduce fork flex when you brake.

Keeping in touch If you carry a pillion passenger for much of the time, it is well worth investing in a rider-to-passenger intercom *(left)*. This allows you to talk without the risk of turning your head.

Accessories/5

Exhaust improvements Four-into-one exhaust systems *(right)* are extremely popular fittings on four-stroke fours. Replacement pipes are not difficult to find; the sports pipe *(below)* is for a Ducati V-twin. Aftermarket two-stroke expansion chamber *(below right)* are an effective way of increasing engine power, but if you fit one check that you stay within the legal noise limits. Style, too, is important; exhaust pipes with a black chrome finish *(far right)* are currently fashionable. When selecting a non-standard exhaust system for a two-stroke *(far right below)*, it is worth checking to see if the muffler can be repacked with sound absorption material.

Accessories/6

Fairings and windscreens

Fitting a fairing or windscreen to your bike is a good idea for practical as well as cosmetic reasons. Either accessory will help to protect you against the weather and so add to your riding comfort; either will also help you to alter the appearance of your machine, giving it a racing look, for example.

The range of screens and fairings – from the tiniest of flyscreens to the opulence of the Honda Gold Wing Aspencade fairing – is enormous. Have a good look around to see what is on the market and consider carefully what results you want before making your final choice.

The best basic investment is a reasonably sized screen, as this will help keep the wind and rain off you throughout the year. Such screens are reasonably inexpensive and quite straightforward to attach. Most fit to the handlebars.

When fitting such a screen, make sure that you can see comfortably over its top – ideally, you should just be able to see over it when you are settled into your normal riding position. If you have to look through the screen, your vision will be impaired if the screen becomes dirty, while you will find your vision impaired at night.

The next step up is a 'handlebar' fairing. There are two types – frame mounted and handlebar mounted. The former are fairly heavy and so should be mounted to the frame, not the handlebars; the latter are lightweight and so are usually well suited to handlebar mounting.

Fairing drawbacks

Remember that any type of

screen or fairing fitted directly to the handlebars makes the steering heavier and creates wind resistance. However, on most medium speed middleweights and lightweights, the effect on handling is minimal. Though you may loose some top speed potential, the protection the accessory provides will more than compensate for this.

On fast machines, however, frame mounted fairings should be fitted if you intend to ride at high speeds. Because this type of fairing is mounted to the frame and not the handlebars, the steering remains independent and in the main should not be affected.

You must watch your speed, though, because the bike may still break into a weave at high speed. This is because the wind

tends to get under the fairing and lifts the machine slightly.

Machines fitted with large full fairings are also more affected by cross-winds. If you fit such a fairing, you must accept the inevitable compromise between weather protection, comfort and peak performance. Your top speed will be reduced, while handling may also be compromised to some extent.

Fairings and screens also throw engine noise back at the rider, particularly in the case of an air-cooled engine. Water-cooled engines are much quieter.

Experienced long distance riders usually opt for large capacity motor cycles with full fairings. These fairings allow them to take on all weathers, while the size of the engine

Fitting a fairing The handlebar sports fairing fitted to this CZ250 Custom *(top left)* comes as standard equipment. However, fairings come in all shapes and sizes to suit every conceivable taste *(far left)*. The Pantera fairing, for example, houses a radio/cassette, a voltmeter and a clock, as well as providing good weather protection *(left)*; the full fairing on this CB750 Honda *(above)* provides full weather protection.

Accessories/7

Following fashion Endurance fans like the twin headlight look, as employed for this Dyson fairing on a 650 Honda CX V-twin *(above)*.

allows them to keep up a high cruising speed comfortably. Big bikes are also more stable. Thus, a fairing will not affect their handling as much as a fairing fitted to a lighter machine.

Touring fairings often have the added plus of built in storage compartments. These allow you to carry more luggage. Some are also designed to take radio/cassette units.

Fitting a fairing

Though simple enough to fit once you get down to the job, fitting a screen or fairing may take more time than you might bargain for at first. Allow yourself a full day for the task.

Before you start, you should consult your supplier about the compatibility of the type of fairing you are thinking of fitting to your machine. You should bear in mind, for instance, that the wrong choice of fairing may restrict the air flow to the engine. This will effect engine cooling. Your supplier should be able to alert you to such potential problems.

If you intend to fit a full fairing, get a friend to help you – you will need a helper to suppport the fairing on the frame brackets while you belt it up. Always make sure that there is enough clearance to allow you to turn the handlebars from lock to lock without trapping your hands against the fairing. With a road style fairing, it often proves necessary to fit low 'ace' style handlebars, or clip on ones, and either to accept a restricted lock, or to shave away part of the fairing for lock clearance.

Race fairings

If you want the 'road race' look, you should be able to buy a suitably styled fairing from a dealer. Though you can modify a genuine racing fairing to fit your machine, this is often more trouble than it is worth. One major drawback is that there will be no provision for a headlight, while the actual fitting can be time consuming.

If you buy a purpose made race style road fairing, choose the QD (quickly detachable) type if you can – these fairings allow quick and easy access to the engine for repairs and cleaning.

Two piece fairings

If you ride a sports lightweight, such as a Yamaha LC single or twin, you, like many other riders, may well want to fit a two piece fairing. This is a combined handlebar fairing and belly pan. The separate belly section – this is a standard fitting on some machines – is designed to duct air to the radiator. It also gives the body of the bike an integrated look overall.

On the road

Whichever type of fairing you choose, make sure that you can still operate all the controls efficiently. Once you are satisfied that the fairing is fitted correctly, with the headlight wiring routed tidily and so on, go for a steady trial run. When you do, bear in mind that ground clearance may be reduced and handling affected.

The machine will certainly feel different when you ride it. Allow yourself a 'breaking in' period to get used to the engine noise that will be thrown back at you and other unexpected consequences, such as not being able to see the front wheel if you fit a full fairing.

Allowing for comfort The Rickman Harrier fairing *(above)* makes this CB125 Honda look bigger, as well as providing all weather comfort. BMW's RT touring model has this fairing *(right)* as a standard fitting. The screen's rake can be adjusted.

Accessories/8

Cosmetics/conversions

After spending only a few minutes in your local accessory shop, you will realize that you can transform your bike into anything that takes your fancy, progressing from a simple cosmetic tank strip to a total conversion.

Whatever look attracts you – the chopper look, the Formula One look, the café racer look, the drag look, the enduro look and so on – you can create and adapt it to suit pratically any type of machine, from a 50cc model upwards. Much of what can be done depends on what you can afford, but money on its own is no substitute for imagination and ingenuity. The illustrations show you what can be achieved.

Whatever you fancy Dyson Bol D'Or fairings on a brace of four-cylinder Kawasakis *(below)* give the bikes an added touch of style. The 500cc Yamaha single in an alloy monocoque frame *(right)* is a 'Yagon' special.

Faster and faster This Harley-Davidson custom model *(above)* has a chrome engine and 'hard tail' – that is, the rear end is not fitted with rear suspension. The turbocharged GSX1100 Suzuki *(left)* is the fastest bike to be regularly ridden on the roads in Britain. This Norton twin *(below)* is traditionally customized, with a Featherbed frame, race style tank and seat.

Accessories/9

Getting down to business The moto cross XL Honda four stroke single, with lights for enduro riding, is really suitable only for riders with long inside legs *(above)*. The Suzuki-powered 'kneeler' *(right)* is so-called because the rider rides the machine in a kneeling position. The rubber mounted Yamada 250 TD2 road racer frame *(above right)* is combined here with a Triumph Daytona 500 engine to create an unusual and neat café race custom.

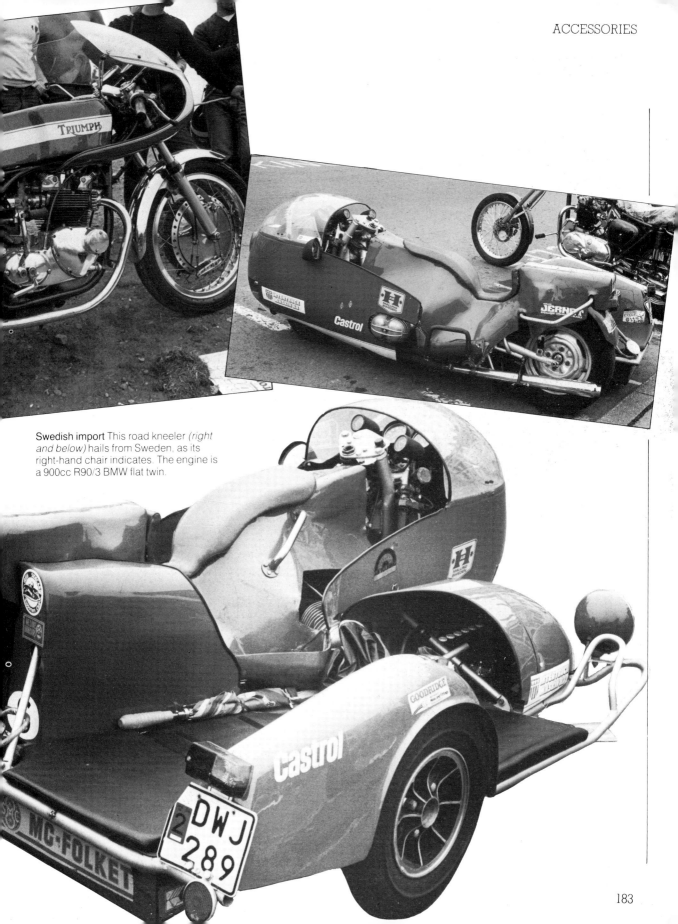

Swedish import This road kneeler *(right and below)* hails from Sweden, as its right-hand chair indicates. The engine is a 900cc R90/3 BMW flat twin.

Accessories/10

The ultimate in bikes The three cylinder Laverda *(above)* is ostentatiously turbocharged. The Volkswagen-powered D.G. Phoenix trike *(below)* comes in kit form, or ready built. You can ride it on a full bike licence – without a crash helmet.

Ready for action The RD400 Yamaha two-stroke twin *(above)* is ready for action, with all its appropriate race custom gear. The two litre eight cylinder special *(top)* is powered by two Hillman Imp car engines.

Fast favourites This RD125LC Yamaha *(above)* was fully customized inside and out by Micron-Alfa in conjunction with 'Performance Bikes' magazine. The Yamaha RD250 watercooled two-stroke twin *(left)* is a modern favourite for race-style modification, as is the same manufacturer's RD350.

Glossary of terms

AC (Alternating Current) An electric current which constantly changes the direction in which it flows.

AF The distance across the 'flats' of a nut or bolt.

Alternator An engine driven electrical generator, which produces an *alternating current*.

Ammeter An instrument for measuring electric current flow.

Amps The term for the rate of flow of an electric current.

BDC (Bottom dead centre) The lowest point in the piston's travel.

Bearing There are two types – plain and roller bearings. Plain bearings are metal shells, forming a ring. Roller bearings consist of two metal rings, one within the other, with either a set of balls or rollers between them, which allow the rings to rotate independently.

Big-end bearing The bearing between the piston *connecting rod* and the *crankshaft*.

Bleeding The term for removing air from a hydraulic system.

Bleed nipple A threaded nut, attached to a hydraulically operated component, that can be loosened to allow air to escape during the *bleeding* process.

Bore The diameter of the cylinder.

Breather A means by which excess pressure can be vented off from the engine.

BSF (British Standard Fine) Thread size of fine pitch.

BSW (British Standard Whitworth) Thread size of coarse pitch.

Bush A sleeve of metal, rubber or plastic fitted as a bearing or spacer between components.

Butterfly A circular plate that rotates to open or close an orifice, used in the *carburettor* for the *choke* or *throttle*.

Caliper The part of a disc brake system that houses the brake pads and hydraulic pistons.

Cam An oval shaped lobe, mounted on a rotating shaft, which bears against a component to push it open as the shaft rotates.

Capacitor A device that can store electricity.

Carburettor The device that mixes fuel and air and feeds the mixture into the cylinder.

Choke A device fitted to the *carburettor* to enrich the *mixture*.

Circlip A sprung metal ring which stops lateral movement in a component.

Clutch A mechanism that can be engaged and disengaged to transmit the drive from engine to gearbox.

Coil An electrical device that converts low voltage current from the battery into the high voltage current required by the ignition.

Compression ratio The ratio between the space within the cylinder when the piston is at the top of its travel and the space when it is at the bottom.

Connecting rod The rod that connects the piston to the crankshaft. It converts up and down movement into rotary motion.

Contact breaker points A pair of electrical contacts within the ignition system that are opened and closed by a cam to switch electric current to the spark plug or plugs.

Crankshaft The shaft driven by the reciprocal motion of the *connecting rod*.

CV carburettor A carburettor in which the fuel flow needle is controlled by air pressure.

CV joint A joint that maintains rotary motion while, at the same time, allowing some lateral motion.

Cylinder head The top part of the engine that contains the spark plug and, on four stroke engines, the inlet and exhaust valves.

Damper Often called a shock absorber, it 'dampens' the oscillations of a spring.

DC (Direct Current) Electric current which flows in one direction only.

Distributor An engine driven device, incorporating the *contact breaker points*, that distributes current to the spark plugs.

DOHC Double Overhead Camshaft.

Dwell The period during which the *contact breaker points* remain closed, expressed as an angle or percentage of the total rotation of the cam that opens the points.

Dynamo An engine driven generator that produces a *direct current*.

Earth The connection from an electrical component to the chassis as part of an electric circuit.

Electrode The key operating parts of a *spark plug*. This has an earth electrode and a positive electrode, separated by a small gap. High voltage current jumps across this to form the spark.

Electrolyte The mixture of sulphuric acid and distilled water within a battery.

Electronic ignition The term given to ignition systems that use an electrically operated device to do the job of the *contact breaker points*.

Feeler gauges A set of thin metal strips of varying thickness used to measure clearance between components.

Final drive The last section of the transmission between the gearbox and rear wheel.

Flat spot A hesitancy of the engine at certain throttle openings.

Forks The term given to the two suspension arms that hold the front wheel.

Four-stroke The operation of an engine in which four up-and-down piston movements are required to complete each cycle.

Friction pads In a disc brake system, the pads that are pressed against the disc.

Gasket Made of paper or heat resistant material, a gasket is fitted between two components to ensure a gas-, air- or fluid-tight seal.

Gear ratio The ratio between the speeds at which two gears of different sizes rotate.

Grommet A rubber or plastic disc that either fills a hole or protects a wire or cable from the rough edges of a hole.

Gudgeon pin A small steel bar that runs through the body of the piston to which the *connecting rod* is attached.

Handling The term describes the steering and road holding characteristics of a motor cycle.

HT (High Tension) High voltage current – often used with HT lead, meaning the lead carrying high voltage current.

Ignition The igniting of the *mixture* within the cylinder. The ignition system consists of the spark plug, contact breaker points, coil and battery or magneto

Ignition advance unit A mechanical device that automatically advances the *ignition timing* as the engine speed increases.

Ignition timing The method by which the *mixture* is ignited at the right moment within the engine's cycle.

Jet A brass tube within the *carburettor* with a tiny hole running through it through which the fuel flows.

Liner A cylindrical sleeve that forms the cylinder, fitted in engines of alloy construction.

Little-end bearing The bearing between the *connecting rod* and the *gudgeon pin*.

LT (Low Tension) The term given to low voltage current, often used with LT lead, a wire carrying such a voltage.

Magneto An engine driven device fitted to batteryless bikes to generate the high voltage current required for ignition.

Main bearings The bearings on which the *crankshaft* revolves.

Main jet A *jet* within the *carburettor* that meters the engine's fuel flow at normal operating speeds.

Mainshaft Shaft in the gearbox that is driven by the engine.

Master cylinder In a hydraulic system, it contains the lever operated piston that applies pressure to a slave cylinder.

Mixture The term used to refer to the combination of fuel and air needed to run the engine.

Ohm Unit of electrical resistance.

O-ring Rubber ring that forms an oil seal between two surfaces.

OHC (Overhead Cam) An engine in which the camshaft is positioned above the *valves*.

OHV (Overhead Valve) An engine in which the camshaft operates the *valves* through *push rods* and *rocker arms*.

Pilot jet A *jet* within the carburettor which meters the fuel flow at low

engine speeds.

Pinking A metallic tinkling noise from the engine caused by the mixture igniting too early.

Piston rings A set of rings around the piston that form a gas tight seal with the cylinder wall.

Pushrod A rod, pushed up by the *cams* on the camshaft, which acts on *rocker arms* to open the inlet and exhaust *valves*.

Rake The angle at which the front *forks* are arranged to the vertical.

Rectifier An electrical device that converts *AC* current to *DC* current.

Rocker arm An arm that is pivoted at its centre and pushed at one end by a *pushrod* to push open a *valve* at the other. It gets its name from its characteristic rocking motion.

Rotor Normally used to describe the rotating part of an *alternator* or *magneto*.

RPM Revolutions per minute.

Running on When the engine continues to run after it has been switched off.

Runout The amount of lateral motion of a rotating component that is out of true.

Shim A thin metal washer used as a spacer.

Shock absorber The common term for a suspension *damper*.

Solenoid An electromagnetic device used as a switch.

Spark plug Device used to ignite the *mixture* in the cylinder.

Spindle A rod or shaft around which a component rotates.

Splined shaft A rod with grooves in it that allow a component to move laterally along a shaft, while the shaft maintains its rotary motion.

Split pin A safety device for locking a nut.

Sprocket A toothed wheel.

Steering damper A device fixed to the front *forks* to reduce steering wobble.

Steering head The assembly that holds the front *forks* and containing the bearing on which they pivot.

Stroboscope A lamp used for checking the ignition timing. When attached to the spark plug's *HT* lead, it flashes each time the *spark plug*

fires, producing a stroboscopic effect that freezes the moving ignition timing marks.

Stroke The distance the piston moves between *TDC* and *BDC*.

Sump The area in the engine under the *crankshaft* that holds the oil.

Swinging arm The part of the rear suspension that holds the wheel laterally and allows vertical movement.

Tachometer The instrument that measures the engine revolutions, popularly termed a rev counter.

Tail pipe The last section of the exhaust system.

Tappet Part of the valve gear on which the *cam* or *rocker arm* bear.

TDC (Top Dead Centre). The uppermost point in the piston's travel.

Throttle. The mechanism that controls the amount of *mixture* entering the cylinder.

Timing chain The chain that drives the *camshaft*.

Torque The amount of turning force produced by a rotating component, usually measured in lb/ft or kg/m.

Total loss Lubrication system in which oil is not recirculated, as in the case of most *two-stroke* engines.

Transfer port The port within a *two-stroke* engine through which the *mixture* passes to reach the cylinder.

Two-stroke Type of engine in which two up and down movements of the piston make up each cycle.

Universal joint A joint within a shaft that maintains rotary motion while allowing the shaft to change direction.

Valve In the engine, valves control the entry of the *mixture* into the cylinder and the expulsion of exhaust gases.

Variable jet A *carburettor* in which the fuel flow needle is controlled by a mechanical linkage.

Venturi The passage within a *carburettor* through which air is drawn to be mixed with the fuel.

Viscosity A liquid's resistance to flow.

Wet sump Name given to the lubrication system in which the oil is contained in a *sump* at the bottom of the engine.

Index

Index

K

kick start, fault finding, 80
knives, 68
knocking noises, 76

L

learner riders, 10
legal aspects, 8
    choosing a machine and, 10
    helmets, 21
    making complaints, 13
    purchaser's rights, 12
life insurance, 18
lights, 172-3
    bulbs, 39
    checking, 14, 39
    day riding lights, 172, 173
    fault finding, 83-4
    fog, 173
    maintenance, 131
    spot, 173
liquid cooling systems, 44-6
loans, 16-17
locks, 26-7
logbooks, 8-9
lubrication
    aerosol, 113
    chains, 112-3
    engine, 34, 35
    gear sets, 43
    oil changes, 91, 124-5
    overheating faults, 81
luggage racks, 166-9

M

magneto ignition, 37, 97, 100
maintenance, 90-131
    air filters, 102-3
    basic essentials, 90
    by garages, 147
    carburettors, 103-7
    chains, 112-15
    checking, 147
    choke cable, 109
    cleaning, 28-9, 149
    clutch, 110-11
    cooling system, 128-9
    electrical system, 130-1
    fuel system, 102-7
    gasket replacement, 126
    ignition system, 96, 101
    importance of, 90-1
    oil changes, 124-5
    punctures, 120-1
    spares, 91
    spark plugs, 94-5
    suspension, 116-19
    throttle cable, 108-9
    tool kit, 90
    tool maintenance, 148-53
    wheels, 122-3
masking, painting, 160, 165
mist, riding in, 141
monoshock system, 57, 58, 59
mopeds
    age restriction, 10
    capacity restrictions, 10
Motor Cycle Association of Great Britain, 13
motorways, 143
mudflaps, 170
muffs, 170
multimeters, 130-1, 153

N

National Rider Training Scheme, 134 138
night riding, 143-4
noises
    cooling system, 83
    drive chain, 79
    engine, 76
    gearbox, 76
    transmission, 78, 79

O

O-ring chains, 113-14
oil
    changing, 91, 124-5
    checking, 124
    cooling with, 47
    gearbox, 43
    levels, 35
    see also lubrication
oil filters, changing, 124-5
overhead cams, 32
overhead valves, 32
overheating, 65
    fault finding, 81-3

P

painting, 156-65
    airbrushes, 165
    alternative finishes, 165
    brushing, 165
    decoration, 157, 165
    final coats, 163
    final touches, 164
    kit for, 157
    masking, 160, 165
    preparation, 157-8
    problems, 163
    shining, 164
    spray, 156, 161-3
    stencils, 165
    touching up, 162
paintwork, cleaning, 29
    restoring, 156
panniers, 166-9
    security, 168
petrol supply, 48
    running out of fuel, 65
    see also fuel system
pinking, 76
piston rings, 34
pistons, 34
    faults, 65-6
pliers, 68-9, 151
points, 37
    checking, 39, 131
    servicing, 96-8
polishing bikes, 28-9
preload adjustment, 59
primary drives, 42
    checking, 43

problem diagnosis, 62-9
    basic diagnosis, 62-3
    breakdowns, 64-9
    consulting professionals, 63
protective clothing, 21-2, 24
provisional licences, 10, 134
punctures, 67, 91
    repair outfit, 69
    repairing, 120-1
push-rods, 32

R

RAC, 62, 144-5
radial tyres, 60
radiators, 45, 46, 47
    caps, 128, 129
    servicing, 128
ratchet drives, 150
reflectors, 39
regulators, 39
repairs, 90-131
    air filters, 102-3
    basic essentials, 90
    by garages, 147
    carburettors, 103-7
    chains, 112-15
    checking, 147
    choke cable, 109
    clutch, 110-11
    cooling system, 128-9
    electrical system, 130-1
    fuel system, 102-7
    gasket replacement, 102-7
    ignition system, 96-101
    importance of maintenance, 90-1
    oil changes, 124-5
    punctures, 120-1
    spares, 91
    spark plugs, 94-5
    suspension, 116-19
    throttle cable, 108-9
    tool kit, 90
    tools, 148-53
    wheels, 122-3
riding, 132-45
    acceleration, 133
    braking, 133
    control, 140
    cornering, 133
    defensive, 132-3
    driving tests, 135-8
    foggy conditions, 141
    golden rules, 140
    icy conditions, 141
    misty conditions, 141
    motorway, 143

Acknowledgements

The editor and publishers would like to acknowledge the invaluable assistance of the following:

Nick Edwards, in charge of Honda Uk's motor cycle training school, for his checking of technical contents, *Dave Minton*, for writing most of the material on rider training, the test, riding techniques, tools and their use, and painting, and *Dave Walker* for writing most of the material in the anatomy section. In addition they would like to thank Honda UK training school and publicity departments for information and photographs, *Performance Bikes* magazine for access to their photographic files and all other companies and individuals who co-operated in the compilation of *You and Your Bike*